Donald L. Tasto, Ph.D., holds a Diplomate in Clinical Psychology from the American Board of Professional Psychology and is a practicing clinical psychologist in Palo Alto, California.

Eric W. Skjei, Ph.D., is a professional writer based in the San Francisco Bay area. He has coauthored numerous nonfiction works on psychological, sociological, and health-related issues, including *Getting Grants, Mastering Pain,* and *Overcoming Writing Blocks.*

SPARE THE COUCH

Self-Change
for Self-Improvement

Donald L. Tasto
Eric W. Skjei

A SPECTRUM BOOK

Prentice-Hall, Inc., Englewood Cliffs, New Jersey 07632

Library of Congress Cataloging in Publication Data

TASTO, DONALD L
   Spare the couch.

   (A Spectrum Book)
   Bibliography: p.
   Includes index.
     1. Success. 2. Personality change.
3. Psychology, Pathological. I. Skjei, Eric W.,
joint author. II. Title.
   BF637.S8T25   158'.1   79-19032
   ISBN 0-13-824466-9
   ISBN 0-13-824458-8 pbk.

Editorial/production supervision
and interior design by Betty Neville
Cover design by Lana Giganti
Manufacturing buyer: Cathie Lenard

© 1979 by Prentice-Hall, Inc., Englewood Cliffs, N.J. 07632

Printed in the United States of America

10 9 8 7 6 5 4 3

Prentice-Hall International, Inc., *London*
Prentice-Hall of Australia Pty. Limited, *Sydney*
Prentice-Hall of Canada, Ltd., *Toronto*
Prentice-Hall of India Private Limited, *New Delhi*
Prentice-Hall of Japan, Inc., *Tokyo*
Prentice-Hall of Southeast Asia Pte. Ltd., *Singapore*
Whitehall Books Limited, *Wellington, New Zealand*

Contents

Preface

Spare the couch?

Sure. Why not? Do you really feel you need expensive professional help to straighten your life out? Why not do it yourself? Take charge of your own problems and your own designs for changing yourself. You know what's good about you and what's wrong with you as well as, if not far better than, a professional therapist—someone who's probably never seen you before, has no idea what your life is really like, and who will need first to spend quite some time just trying to reach a basic understanding of your complaint before being able actually to offer you any help. Why subject yourself to a prolonged and often inaccurate labeling process if it really isn't necessary?

Most of the information that a psychologist or a psychiatrist would use to try to help you isn't at all mysterious or difficult to understand. Quite the opposite. It's profoundly simple, something that nearly all of us can grasp with ease and can often apply entirely on our own.

But, you may be saying to yourself, *I don't know what's wrong with me. That's my trouble. I know I'm never content—I'm always dissatisfied. It's driving me crazy. But I haven't got the faintest idea why I feel this way, so how can I possibly change it all by myself?*

The answer is, you don't need to know *why* you feel dissatisfied in order to change or to feel better about yourself. You may *want* to know why you do what you do, especially why you do the things that make you unhappy, but it's something of an unnecessary luxury—and possibly even a hindrance—to real change. You don't have to know the emotional reasons for your behavior before you can change it. The point of this entire book is that changing the way you act, not analyzing *why* you act the way you do, is the most practical and efficient path to acquiring a greater sense of control over your life and a sense of real satisfaction with yourself and your achievements. In fact, an obsessive interest in figuring out why you do what you do is often a technique for clinging to thought instead of action, for holding out, for refusing to make decisions about how you're going to run your life, what you're going to accomplish, and when you're going to get down to the business of really living it.

Actions cause feelings as much as, if not more than, feelings determine actions. And actions are far more accessible to strategies for change. You can't always get at your emotions, to hold them up to the light, to tinker with them and redesign them so that they suit you better. But actions, by definition, are always easy to observe. So the best way to go about changing your life, including your moods, is to work on your behavior first and use it as a tool to mold your attitudes and feelings into more rewarding patterns.

Let's go back for a moment to the complaint above, that you don't really even know what's wrong with you. Nonsense. You may not know what psychiatrists or psychologists would call what's wrong with you, but you know that you don't feel right. You know you're not happy, don't you? And you know that you want to feel good about yourself. Why do you need to know more than that? If you think that knowing more about why you act the way you do leads inevitably to changing the way you act, let us disillusion you. As generations of patients who have spent years analyzing their emotions can assure you, there's no automatic connection between conscious, rational, intellectual understanding of yourself and the process of change, of actually becoming a different human being. Instead of pondering possible explanations for your unhappiness, you need to get out and do something about it.

This simple exercise should make this point even clearer to you. As soon as we ask you the questions in the next paragraph, write down whatever comes into your mind. Don't hesitate or think about it; just write down whatever first comes to you. (Be sure you have a pen or a pencil ready before you begin.)

Ready? OK, here's the first question: What one *specific* thing that you consistently do, say, or think would you most like to stop doing?

_____

_____

And here's the second: What one *specific* thing that you *don't* do, say, or think now would you most like to do more often?

_____

_____

Notice that we do not want you to write down an abstract, general goal or objective, like "Be rich and famous" or "Find my niche in life." For the purposes of change, these abstractions are so universal and general as to be quite meaningless. You must be able to define *specific* facets of your life first before you can begin trying to change them. So we asked what specific behavior you would most like to change. Would you like to be able to handle disappointment better? Would you like to feel more comfortable at parties? Would you like to spend more time with your children?

Be as specific as possible, even if it initially seems to narrow your wishes down to something trivial, like "Stop biting fingernails." Under even the smallest change wish lies an entire iceberg of interconnected problem areas, all represented in capsulized form in your automatic response. "Stop biting fingernails" can also mean "Get rid of anxiety and compulsiveness." Or "Learn to cope with stress at work." The point is, if you can learn to stop biting your fingernails, we guarantee that you'll feel better about yourself, as well as less anxious and harassed. Changing a specific problem behavior leads to a generalized change in your feelings about yourself. The feeling that you've managed to control a difficult area of your life inevitably brings with it a surge of renewed self-esteem.

None of this means that feelings are unimportant or irrelevant—not at all. They're an invaluably precious element in our experiences. But the same qualities that make them so essential—their fluidity, their complexity, their elusiveness—are those that make them hard to manage directly by trying first to understand them before you let yourself do anything about them. Trying first to understand precisely and completely *why* you feel anxious is like trying to understand why you think, or why you feel charmed by rainbows and small children, or why you felt sorry when your grandmother died. It's undeniably fascinating to try to puzzle out what makes you what you are emotionally, but the way to change, to cope with life, to master yourself, is to *act*, and to act so that you thoughtfully and systematically achieve the changes in your life that you want.

Take money, for example. That we live in an acquisitive, materialistic age has come to be a truism, one that few people would disagree with. Most of us would agree that we'd like to

be rich; some of us make pursuit of wealth the entire purpose of our lives.

But if you dig a little deeper and ask what having money
would mean to most people, nine times out of ten, it turns
out that they're not really sure. They have a vague idea that it
would let them "do what they wanted"—to travel, to visit
anyone they wished whenever they wanted, to be safe, to be
generous, to do nothing, to buy whatever they felt like own-
ing. What they seem to mean is that they would feel free,
spontaneous, and impulsive. In short, that they would be
able to *act* differently, to behave without the constraints that
they now face.

But you don't really need fabulous wealth in order to
become more impulsive and more spontaneous, to enjoy life
more fully. Not having endless wealth is one of many excuses
that we use to explain our nagging lack of gratification in life,
gratification that is, in fact, entirely within our reach and that
really depends on nothing more complicated than
courage—the strength that is needed to confront ourselves,
admit our defects, and then do something about them. You
don't need money to be more impulsive.

We're also not trying to imply that this book will give you
All The Answers. We can't solve all your problems. No one
can. As long as you're vertical and breathing, you'll have
problems. Having money won't free you from the limitations
of being a mortal, biological organism. What we *can* do for
you is to put powerful tools in your hands, tools that you can
use to achieve whatever ends you desire, to take yourself in
any direction you care to go, simply to expand your ability to
change.

Put it to a pragmatic test: try it out and see if it works. Do
what we say, the way we tell you to, and see if it makes a
difference in the way you feel. If it doesn't, *then* look for a
therapist.

Acknowledgments

The quote by F. Scott Fitzgerald from *The Crack-Up*, edited by Edmund Wilson, is reprinted by permission of New Directions and The Bodley Head. Copyright 1945 by New Directions Publishing Corporation.

The lines from "If" by Rudyard Kipling from *Rudyard Kipling's Verse: Definitive Edition* are reprinted by permission of The Executors of the Estate of Mrs. George Bambridge, Doubleday & Company, Inc., and The National Trust of Great Britain. Copyright 1910 by Rudyard Kipling.

The quote by Sigmund Freud from *Totem and Tatoo* is used by permission of Routledge & Kegan Paul Ltd. and W. W. Norton & Company, Inc.

The excerpts from *Type A Behavior and Your Heart*, by Meyer

Friedman, M. D. and Ray Rosenman, M. D., are reprinted by permission of Alfred A. Knopf, Inc. and Wildwood House Limited.

The quote from the poem "Two Songs," by Adrienne Rich from her book *Necessities of Life*, is used by permission of W. W. Norton & Company, Inc.

The quotation from Bertrand Russell's *Marriage and Morals* (London: George Allen & Unwin Ltd., 1930) is used by permission of George Allen & Unwin (Publishers) Ltd. and Liveright Publishing Corporation.

one

Introduction

Nothing is so constant as change. Like every other living thing, we are born, we grow, we reach maturity, we flourish, we age, and eventually we die. At every stage of this process, during every single instant of our existence, we are faced with the need to adapt, to be flexible, to learn, to change. From figuring out how to tie our shoes, to writing out twenty-six funny symbols on paper, to pulling together a term paper, to closing a deal, to living with another person and perhaps raising children together, we constantly confront hurdles in life—obstacles that can be insurmountable if we don't know how to go about adjusting to them. Even on the minutest physical level, our molecules themselves are part of an endless cycle of creation and destruction that goes on continuously as our cells themselves divide, feed, grow, age, and die.

Unlike most other living things, however, human beings have a powerful advantage in life. We can exert control over our experiences. A plant can't learn how to design, build, and drive a car; but we can, and we can also learn how to *re*design that same car to meet new demands, to make it lighter, safer, more efficient, and even cleaner if we choose. Above all, we are an *adaptable* species.

The same is true of our personal emotional lives. We have the ability to learn to modify our actions, thoughts, feelings, and surroundings so that we can meet new demands successfully. We have the ability to take basic raw materials—our intelligence, our experience, and our skills—and forge them into something better, into ways of acting and thinking that make us more productive, more alive, and proud of ourselves as well as influencing others so that they respond to us with greater appreciation for what we are and what we have to offer.

Unfortunately, we are also our own worst enemies.

Take smoking, for example. Most people who smoke know that it isn't healthy, and they will quickly admit that they would like very much to stop. But they can't. No one forces them to continue steadily to subtract minutes from their probable life span, and no one rewards them for taking this losing gamble, but they continue to risk it.

In this and many other ways, we allow ourselves to feel more helpless than we really are. We may recognize useless fears that we know are unfounded and unreasonable, but we feel that they are not under our control. We'd like to do something about the sweating palms and the choked feeling in the throat that we get every time we have to stand up and speak before a large group of strangers, but this panicky distress just doesn't seem to go away, no matter how often in the past we have tried to talk ourselves out of what we know is an irrational anxiety.

The results of feeling chronically helpless are frustration, defeat, and bitterness. We know we can do better, but we don't seem to be able to put that conviction into practice. We begin to believe that our plans for change are doomed to failure. Something about the process of setting up a program for change and then sticking to it seems to defeat us every time. We begin to feel like failures.

If the anger and the frustration at our inability to control our responses get strong enough, they can become problems in themselves, and the feeling of helplessness that we experience when we can't seem to manage our lives very well can be extremely destructive. Chronic alcoholism, for example, can destroy families, careers, and personal health and well-being, all because of an overpowering wish to escape from the painful sense of personal futility and uselessness.

For other people, feelings of helplessness provoke a desire—essentially a very healthy one—to seek help rather than to escape.

The kinds of problems we discuss in this book—depression, anxiety, submissiveness, passivity, obsessiveness, compulsivity, stress, poor relationships, and sexual dysfunction—are so common that nearly all of us succumb to one or another of them to a greater or lesser degree at some point in our lives.

Most readers of *Spare the Couch* consider their personal problems to be significant but not overwhelming. They feel that they generally manage their lives well, and that they are usually successful in what they set out to accomplish, but that there are one or two definite areas that need work. They know that their careers are progressing nicely, that their family lives are basically sound, and that they never become profoundly depressed or fearful. But they also realize that they are not able, for example, to communicate effectively with a supervisor at work, or that mild insomnia has been interrupting their sleep more and more regularly.

Occasionally a reader does find that his or her problem has become too serious or too large to handle alone. If this is happening to you, you shouldn't feel any hesitation at all about admitting to yourself that you really don't feel like trying to cope with your problems on your own. Seek the assistance of a trained therapist. For many kinds of personal distress, the relationship that may develop between you and the therapist can provide the best possible setting for resolving your conflicts and freeing your emotional energy for more satisfying pursuits. Local hospitals, churches, and mental health organizations can help you find reputable and experienced assistance.

Learning how to change is an art, the most subtle art of all. As with any art, the first steps are taken to learn its techniques. At first, these can seem clumsy, mechanical, and somewhat artificial. And unless they eventually do take on a life of their own and acquire personal meaning for you, they remain clumsy, mechanical, and artificial.

So it is with the methods in this book. They will at first seem unnatural to you, and you will probably feel a little self-conscious and uncomfortable as you begin to practice them. Change means behaving differently, and it is normal to be quite aware of these differences at the outset of any change program. But with time, they become so familiar as to be virtually automatic. At that point, the change you once only imagined will have been totally incorporated in your life.

Don't let these first uncomfortable feelings that you're "manipulating" your emotions dissuade you from sticking to your decision to do something about whatever it is that troubles you. Too many of us have adopted a romantic allegiance to the notion that emotions simply well up unbidden from inside us and that we can only passively experience them, that we have no choice but to comply reverently with them, and that they are basically forces beyond our control.

Our emotions are not beyond management, and there is no hypocrisy, deception, or sacrilege about trying to change them. You're not indulging in some monstrous brainwashing technique; if anything you're cultivating greater respect for the breadth and depth of your powers of self-control.

Learning to change is like learning to drive a car, or bake a quiche, or create a sculpture. As you first fumble through the motions of a strange new process, it always seems unfamiliar and awkward. The car seems large and ponderous, and it's hard to remember what to do with your feet and hands as you try to remember to watch out for the other drivers on the road. But you also, from the outset, feel a great sense of excitement at the new adventure you've embarked upon.

Then, as you get more and more accustomed to any learning process, it takes on an easy, smooth fluidity of its own, and pretty soon you're sweeping along in the fast lane, automatically judging the speeds and directions of other cars, perhaps anticipating what they're about to do before they do it, and punching the buttons on the radio at the same time.

Change is educational. It offers us discoveries about ourselves, discoveries that are important because they can become those rare occasions when we gain insight into ourselves and greater understanding of what the fabric of the life we're so busy living is all about.

Change can give us a sense of power. Nothing is more important than knowing that we do have the skills needed to determine the course and significance of our own lives.

And change is inevitable. Every moment, we are faced with a choice: we can choose to look back nostalgically at the past, or we can look forward confidently to the future. The past is important—it's the record of how we got to where we are now—but dwelling on it to the point of obsessiveness, struggling to unravel its mysteries, to make sense of it somehow through intense retrospection, can—to paraphrase James Joyce—become a nightmare that we are unable to wake up from.

Facing the future means learning how to take risks.

Since none of us can know in advance what our choices will bring, anything we do involves some risk. Thinking about change, wanting to change, planning a change can go on for just so long; at some point, the decision to act must be made. We just have to close our eyes, take a deep breath, and step out into the unknown. If we don't, if we try to keep from acting until we think we know enough to make the safe decision, life will make our decisions for us, will carry us along like a twig in the stream, whether we like it or not.

This doesn't mean that risks should be taken rashly or impulsively. Indulging in careless impulsiveness is not the same as risk taking; if anything, it's escape, a flight into childish fantasies, a testing to find the limits to your security. The right way to take risks is reasonably, carefully, and methodically, with constant attention to what can be learned in the process, to the effect that each successive step you take has on your surroundings.

You don't take on Everest in your Adidas and tennis shorts; you climb it by moving from crevice to crevice, one step at a time. Like everything else in life, it's a balancing act: you have to judge when to wait and when to go, how much to prepare and how much to leave to the inspiration of the moment. It's a demanding process, and it takes work— patient, committed, diligent work.

Spare the Couch is about learning constructive ways to change. It's about the challenge of confronting the most difficult obstacles in life, those that we impose on ourselves. It's also about unlearning—unlearning patterns of weakness and fear, so that we can take the risks that will allow us to leave behind the unhappy patterns in our lives that often seem to be so far beyond our control.

The single most important principle underlying the methods of change that we describe is that the connection between your inner self and the world around you is a two-way street. Not only does your mood influence the people and events around you, but the opposite is also true: what happens in your immediate environment can have a profound effect on your emotions. For instance, when you feel depressed, the world around you seems dull, bleak, forbidding. But you've probably had the experience of finding that when a friend smiles, asks how you're doing, and seems genuinely interested in you, the depression vanishes. It may return, of course, within minutes, but for that short period of time when someone familiar is responding to you, things don't seem quite so bad.

The second most important principle of this book is that we consider most of our habits, thoughts, and actions to be learned, not instinctive. We know, for example, that a person who grows up with a fear of heights can learn to stand on the edge of the twenty-seventh floor of an office building without a shiver. We're not born with fear. Anxiety is not an innate drive. This means that the potential for change is always present: anything that has been learned can be unlearned. No pattern of thought or action is so basic to human life that it cannot be altered, eliminated, created, or enhanced as desired.

Third, as we stated earlier, we do *not* feel that you must first know *why* you act the way you do before you can start working to change yourself.

Traditionally, there has been a great emphasis in the healing arts on asking *why* as the first step in any search for self-understanding and improvement. For example, a woman who is afraid to ride in elevators would first seek help from a therapist who would normally go about trying to help her rid herself of this fear by asking her how she felt about elevators, about what went through her mind when she approached them, and about what images and thoughts were associated with elevators for her. In this way, the therapist would hope to uncover a previously hidden level of meaning to her apparently irrational fear—a new *why* that hadn't been recognized before. For instance, this woman might recall a long-forgotten experience of having been trapped in a refrigerator as a child and nearly suffocating. The important assumption in this process is, of course, that knowing why—that getting at a deeper understanding of the "true" reason for the unreasonable fear—will cause it to go away.

We would approach this type of problem in quite a different fashion. We agree that greater insight into the reasons for fear like that described above would be interesting, but we also consider it irrelevant to the process of helping this woman and others like her learn to overcome their fear. Instead, we assume that she already knows enough about it to know that she wants to get rid of it, and that we can be of even greater assistance to her if we can help her determine *how* best to go about making that change happen. To do this, we would first ask her to describe her goals in specific detail, to define very clearly the changes in her behavior that she wishes to undertake and deadlines for accomplishing them. We would then outline a detailed series of steps that she should take, one by one, so that she could *gradually* and *methodically* overcome her fear; and we might also help her set up a system that encouraged her to move on to each successive step by connecting it to a reward for its completion, or perhaps to a penalty for failing to complete it.

Stated as simply as possible, our approach is a highly pragmatic one. It focuses on *what works*. It also focuses attention on *how* best to bring a desired change about, not *why* the problem exists, and it assumes, as a bonus, that the changed pattern of behavior will probably *cause* changes in mood, thought, and feeling. Once our client can ride in elevators, she will feel great. She may even spontaneously recall the same suffocation memory that was the object of the traditional introspective approach.

Furthermore, our techniques can be understood by anyone. As we said earlier in this chapter, they may work best for you if they're first presented to you by a therapist; some people respond best to the setting and the power of suggestion that a therapist can offer, in order to start processes of

self-change. But there's nothing about the techniques themselves that is so intrinsically complex or esoteric that they
can't successfully be put to use by practically anyone.

Here's just one small example of what we mean. Many of
these change methods are based on the fact that it is virtually
impossible to feel two opposite moods—tense and relaxed,
afraid and confident, nervous and calm—at the same time.
In short, there are incompatible emotional and physical
states, conditions that just don't mix, like oil and water. If
you're having trouble with anxiety, you can learn to substitute relaxation for it, and the anxiety will gradually come
under your control.

If the woman in the foregoing example, the one with the
phobia of elevators, can train herself to become physically
relaxed and to *stay* relaxed as she approaches elevators, it will
be impossible for her also to become tense and anxious. This
new experience, of remaining calm while approaching something of which she has always felt a terrible fear, will in turn
have a calming effect on her overall emotional and mental
state. Experiencing the unfamiliar sensation of relaxation in
a situation that has always made her tense in the past will
cause her also to feel a new sense of self-confidence. Greater
self-confidence will boost her overall self-esteem. Thus, she
will learn that emotional responses are not fixed in permanent, preestablished patterns but that they are instead
relative—and even arbitrary. She may go on to find that she
is also able to relax in other situations that she once found
threatening. She may, for example, find that confrontation
with an angry person, which would once have made her automatically tense and hostile, now leaves her quite unruffled.
She will have made the invaluable discovery, through her
own experiences, that control over external events and control over internal emotions go hand in hand. Control over
one's inner self comes from learning control over specific
actions and thoughts.

A second method that we use to promote change is

based on the view, equally self-evident, that we are inclined to do something more often if we are rewarded for it, or if we feel good about ourselves once it's been accomplished, and conversely, that we tend to do something less if we are punished for it.

Our friend with the elevator phobia will find that a system of gradually bringing herself into greater and greater contact with elevators can be made substantially more attractive to her if she indulges herself in a reward as she succeeds in moving up to levels of greater contact. It's the same method used, very successfully, by generations of parents who give their kids a small gratuity for better grades or who turn off the television when the grades start to slip.

Human beings enjoy feeling that their lives are under their own control. We fear the experience of helplessness, whether it's due to physical circumstances or to our own inner turmoil. And rightly so. It is essential to our continued survival and prosperity to know that we exert an influence on the world around us and that the world's effect on us, no matter what life may bring, is something we can handle. This confidence is impossible to achieve if we aren't able to learn to manage our inner selves.

HOW TO USE THIS BOOK

In the next two chapters of *Spare the Couch,* Chapters 2 and 3, we give you brief, clear descriptions of basic tools for change. Read these two chapters carefully before going on to subsequent sections of the book. Pay special attention to the relaxation instructions set forth in Chapter 2; at various points in later chapters, we refer back to these instructions and urge you to use them to become adept at the PMR method.

The remaining eight chapters, with the exception of the concluding one, apply the tools and techniques of Chapters 2 and 3 to specific problem areas. We cover depression (Chapter 4), phobic anxiety (Chapter 5), assertiveness (Chapter 6), obsession and compulsion (Chapter 7), stress (Chapter 8), relationships (Chapter 9), and sexual dysfunction (Chapter 10). You can read these chapters at random or in succession.

The final chapter (Chapter 11) is very important. Change is not easy. You can't expect to resolve overnight problems that you may have been living with for years. It takes practice, practice, and more practice. It takes perseverance. But it can be done and is being done, right now. All you need to do is start, and then stick to it.

Good luck!

two

Relaxation
One Important
Change Technique

Learning to relax quickly and completely is an essential first step in most self-change programs. Once you've mastered your relaxation to the point that just thinking about relaxing automatically cues the response, you can learn in later chapters how to integrate relaxation with other self-modification procedures.

Why is relaxation so important?

There are three parts in the answer to that question. First, there is the basic fact that many conditions of emotional arousal, such as anger, hostility, and anxiety, are characterized by excessive levels of muscle tension. For example, when you get mad, your jaw muscles may tighten, your fists may clench, and your entire body may shake because your muscle system is spasmodically agitated by chemical changes caused by your emotional changes. Thousands of years ago, this heightened level of tension and arousal probably served a useful purpose by preparing us in dangerous situations either to fight a threat or flee from it. Tension in and of itself is not necessarily bad—small levels of it are probably good for you—but an exaggerated level of tension, especially if it becomes a *constantly* exaggerated level, is a signal that your nervous system is overreacting to your environment. This is one major contributor to conditions like peptic ulcer, headache, and heart disease.

Second, if we realize that our troubles are making us tense, we usually begin intuitively to long for some peace and quiet, some kind of escape from the pressure. But we usually also assume that the process of shifting from arousal to calm isn't something we can just will ourselves to do. After all, we didn't *choose* to become tense in the first place, so we don't usually see how our conscious volitional powers can help us reverse the arousal process. We may also assume that relaxation only comes about passively, as a by-product of an intermediate stage, perhaps an adjustment in our attitudes about life or some other internal reorientation that will better equip us to respond in a less urgent way to the demands in our lives. We usually implicitly reject the thought that we can just will ourselves to relax, because it seems so paradoxical. There is something contradictory about *trying* to relax. It's like saying: "Gee, I'd give my right arm to be ambidextrous."

But—and this is the third part of the answer—remember our statement in Chapter 1 that it is as natural for external events and changes to cause internal, emotional transformations as it is for change to come about in the opposite way. The same holds for relaxation: conscious, methodical, external manipulation of our bodies can bring about corresponding changes in our moods and attitudes. Focusing on relaxing away the tension in the muscles will work its way back into the mind and will help induce positive, calm, and self-confident attitudes.

So, one way to manage turbulent and uncomfortable tensions of any kind is to work deliberately to dampen down the physical arousal that they cause. And this dampening process, achieved through a systematic relaxation technique, can in turn circle back and help cool out the intensity of the distressing emotion.

There's a physiological basis for this cycle. Until the last decade or so, Western medicine held that certain areas of the human nervous system, particularly those responsible for the processes of the body that function continuously (such as respiration and the circulation of blood), were virtually automatic. This system has long been called the *autonomic* nervous system, since it was thought to function autonomously, without our conscious attention.

Research over the last decade has increasingly shown that it is quite possible for us to learn to exert voluntary control over those physiological processes that were once thought to operate independent of our conscious wishes. Such functions as heart rate, blood pressure, the rate at which saliva and urine are produced, and the motions of the gastrointestinal tract have all been shown to be responsive to some degree to intentional efforts to slow them down or speed them up.

What this means is that many of our bodily processes— and thus our emotional states—are subject to greater conscious control than we once believed possible.

But you're wondering, what is the connection, really, between our circulatory system and our mood? Well, the "autonomic" nervous system is divided into two different subsystems: a *sympathetic* and a *parasympathetic* division. The sympathetic division is responsible for increasing our pulse rate, our blood pressure, and our general levels of tension and physiological arousal. It brings blood to the center of the body and reduces its flow to the body's peripheral areas, so that if that saber-toothed tiger takes a chunk out of your hand, you aren't likely to bleed to death quite so quickly. It's a survival mechanism.

The sympathetic division comes into play when we are hostile or anxious, when we are struggling, when we are fighting, or when we are ready to flee. In short, whenever we find ourselves in a highly charged emotional state of any sort, then we know that the sympathetic division of the autonomic nervous system is in dominance.

As you might have guessed, the parasympathetic division is connected with just the opposite kind of internal conditions. Whenever we feel calm, tranquil, peaceful, and contented—especially if our muscles are relaxed—we know that the parasympathetic division is in dominance. (This may help account for the recent surge in the popularity of sports and exercise; we are intuitively rediscovering that relaxing our muscles through physical exertion can act as a healthy antidote to the stress and tension of modern life.)

Dr. Herbert Benson, author of *The Relaxation Response*, has uncovered a number of specific physiological indications that relaxation is conducive to physical and mental well-being. Benson's research has shown, for example, that relaxation reduces oxygen consumption, thus lowering our rate of metabolism. It can also increase alpha brain waves, which are thought to be associated with feelings of calm and contentment. High levels of blood lactates, which have been linked to anxiety, are lowered by relaxation exercises.

> Learning to relax your muscles can reduce sympathetic division activity and increase parasympathetic activity, thus making you feel more calm.

This simple fact makes relaxation an ideal tool for use in self-treatment programs. Anyone can teach him- or herself to relax. Once learned, muscle relaxation becomes an adjunct in the management of many common types of psychological distress, such as phobias, anxiety, tension, hostility, and aggression, as well as such somatic disturbances as insomnia, muscle tension headaches, migraines, ulcers, colitis, chronic pain, and dysmenorrhea, or menstrual cramps.[1]

More recently, it has also become increasingly clear that learning greater control over emotional arousal and the sympathetic division can help decrease the risk of coronary heart disease and heart attack. At this writing, Dr. Tasto is engaged in a major research project that has been undertaken to determine if modification of the overly tense, driven, aggressive life-style that is characteristic of many heart attack victims can reduce their risk of suffering additional coronaries once they've recovered from the first one.

Relaxation procedures are also being used now quite successfully to help individuals learn to improve their performances in a wide variety of sports.

Coauthor Tasto has also shown, in research performed with Margaret Chesney, that one type of menstrual pain can be quite successfully treated using an approach that depends heavily on learning a standard muscle relaxation procedure. In collaboration with James E. Shoemaker, Dr. Tasto has demonstrated that blood pressure levels of essential hypertensives can be significantly reduced by the muscle relaxation process presented here.

The process of learning to relax is incomplete until you are able to master the relaxation response, and also to evoke it systematically as needed and to apply it in precisely those situations that cause you the most tension and distress. Most people have no difficulty working through the relaxation program we describe below, and they invariably find that doing so leaves them feeling more relaxed than ever before, but they have trouble learning to cue this response into disturbing situations. If you have, for example, a severe dog phobia, all the relaxation practice in the world is of very little

[1]The extremely broad potential for a systematic relaxation training program was first recognized by Edmund Jacobson, who published the prototypical work in this area in 1929. Most of the progressive muscle relaxation procedures in use today are indirectly derived from Jacobson's pioneering studies.

use when you're suddenly confronted by a snarling Doberman unless you have *also* worked very methodically on techniques for inducing relaxation in these circumstances.

Furthermore, relaxation is best used as a preventive technique. Once you become very tense, it's usually too late to do anything to forestall extreme emotional arousal and anxiety. Relaxation must be practiced in advance, in a highly systematic way. So, as you begin actually to apply relaxation to phobias, social anxieties, uncomfortable states of arousal, muscle tension while driving, and so on, do not wait until you're already tense. Try to anticipate the tension. Learn to identify the settings and events that bring it on. Make a conscious effort to prepare for these situations in advance, so that you can relax yourself and control tension and sympathetic arousal before they develop. Once they are in full force, there's not much you can do to reverse their effects until you eventually leave the stressful setting.

You will find that you must keep practicing. When you first begin to apply relaxation in real-life circumstances, you will experience a lot of failures. It won't always work. But you *must not* give up. You have to keep at it and keep at it . . . relentlessly. Eventually you'll start to notice small changes . . . consider these to be your first successes, early signs that a major change is beginning to take place. Only by keeping at it, by continuing to whittle away at your problems gradually, will you begin to feel better.

THE PROGRESSIVE MUSCLE
RELAXATION (PMR) METHOD

Relaxation as a basis for a self-change program has a number of advantages over other techniques. For one thing, it's entirely portable. You can relax anywhere. At first, it's best to learn the relaxation method in a quiet, familiar, semidark environment, but you will quickly learn to relax in the office, in cars or on planes, in social settings, even at parties and in restaurants or other public occasions.

The proper circumstances for starting to learn this method are: (1) a quiet environment, (2) a comfortable physical position, and (3) a passive but alert mental attitude. Let distracting thoughts slip away from your conscious attention. Focus it, instead, as completely as possible on the procedures themselves.

- The best place to begin relaxation practice is in a recliner adjusted to its most extended position, or while actually lying on your back with a couple of pillows to support your head. Be sure your neck and head are well supported.

- Set aside a time of day for practicing relaxation when you will be free from distraction, since uninterrupted concentration is essential for the success of this process.

- Remove your shoes and wear loose clothing, so that your breathing will not be constricted.

- If you have a choice, try to practice before you eat a meal, or wait at least two hours after eating.

- Since the first few times you go through the procedure you will have to be reading the directions from this book, you should probably sit in a comfortable chair rather than lying down, so that reading will cause less tension in your arms. During the first few sessions, just concentrate on learning the mechanics of the procedure.

- You will probably not be able to achieve a thorough state of relaxation at first, but each time you practice you will become more and more relaxed. As you work through The Relaxation Script, you will gradually become more aware than ever before of the excess tension in your body's muscle groups. You will learn to make finer and finer distinctions between tense and relaxed muscles in each group, and with repeated practice, you will be able to focus your attention on those that are most tense. You will also learn to become progressively more relaxed each time you practice the relaxation exercise, and you will learn to do so more and more efficiently. Eventually, you will be able to allow all your muscles to become quite relaxed using only very brief intervals of concentration and self-suggestion techniques.

THE RELAXATION SCRIPT

Begin with your hands, then your arms, then move to your face, neck, chest, stomach, and finish with your legs and feet. For each muscle group, you are to experience a feeling of complete, total relaxation. As each muscle group is relaxed, you will maintain its relaxation while moving on to the next group. In this way, you will arrive at a final state of deep and complete relaxation in all muscle groups. As we proceed, follow the instructions as accurately and easily as you can without thinking about them as you do so.

Do not fall asleep. Just focus all your attention on each muscle group as you tense, hold, then relax the muscles, so that you relax all tension and achieve complete relaxation. You will notice, after you have gone through the process of tensing a muscle, holding it, and then letting it relax, that it becomes more relaxed than it was before you tensed it. As you learn to become more and more deeply relaxed, you will probably experience pleasant sensations of warmth and heaviness flowing through your limbs.

Begin now with your right hand and arm. With your right hand resting on the arm of the chair, make a tight fist and hold it. Tense the muscles of this hand and forearm as tightly as you can. Hold them. Notice how the muscles pull across the top of the hand, in the fingers, and in the upper and lower part of the forearm.

Now relax, let this arm and hand drop and go completely limp. Pay close attention to the feeling of relaxation in these muscles. Notice how their tension gives way to greater relaxation than before. Focus all your attention on helping the relaxation become as complete as possible.

Now once again, with this same hand, make a tight fist

and hold it. Again notice how the muscles tense and pull in your arm and forearm. Now relax it. Feel how the relaxation flows throughout the hand and arm. Your hand and arm will become more and more relaxed, more deeply relaxed than ever before.

Now, without lifting or moving your right arm, tense your right biceps muscle and hold it tight. Hold it. Hold it. Notice how the muscle pulls on top and underneath the arm. Now relax. Let the relaxation flow down your arm. Let your entire arm become more and more relaxed. Focus on this feeling of relaxation, and go on relaxing. Allow your entire right arm and hand to become deeply and totally relaxed.

With your right arm remaining completely relaxed, turn your attention to your left hand. Make a fist of it. Clench it tightly, so you can feel the muscles pull across the fingers and in the upper and lower parts of the forearm. Hold it, tightly. Now relax it. Release the muscles and let the relaxation flow. Pay close attention to this feeling of complete relaxation as your arm and hand become more and more relaxed.

Once again, make a tight fist with your left hand, and hold it. Feel the tightness and pulling sensation in the fingers and forearm. Now relax. Observe the feeling as you let these muscles go completely slack. Permit this arm and hand to continue relaxing until they are as totally relaxed as your other arm and hand—deeply and completely relaxed.

Now without lifting or tensing your left forearm, tense your left biceps muscle and hold it tight. Hold it. Hold it. Feel the sensation of the pull of the muscle on top and under the arm. Now relax it. Let the relaxation spread throughout your arm and hand. Enjoy the relief and freedom from effort as you continue to let both arms and hands become more and more relaxed. Retain this state of relaxation for the next few moments.

Now imagine two strings coming down from the ceiling above you, each one connected to one of your shoulders so that your shoulders could be lifted by them. With your arms still limp and relaxed, raise both your shoulders as if pulled up by these two imaginary strings. Lift them as high as you can. Hold it, and feel the pull of the large muscles across the shoulders. Now relax. Drop your shoulders as if the strings had been cut. Allow them to sag down as far as they will go. Let all your shoulder muscles go slack. Experience the effortless, pleasant relaxation. Notice how the feelings of relaxation start to spread throughout the rest of your body.

Begin to relax the muscles in your scalp now. Smooth out your forehead. Relax your eyes, your eyelids, and all your facial muscles. Let your jaw sag comfortably.

Now tighten the muscles in your forehead and scalp by wrinkling up your forehead and raising your eyebrows at the same time. (Avoid the natural tendency to also tense up other parts of your body in sympathy with the facial muscles.) Hold it. Now relax. Let your brows smooth out and completely relax. Let your scalp and facial muscles go slack and heavy.

Now pull your forehead down. Again notice the feeling of tightness and tension. Bring your eyebrows together tightly. Now relax. Let your forehead and eyebrows smooth out again, smoother and smoother. Observe how the tension vanishes from your forehead and scalp. Let it become more and more relaxed.

Now squint your eyes tightly and wrinkle up your nose. Tighter, tighter. Notice the tension around your eyes and nose. Now relax them. Let all the muscles around your eyes and nose completely relax. Let the relaxation spread out over your entire face. Notice the feeling of complete relaxation intensify as you let your muscles become more deeply and totally relaxed. Keep your eyelids half-closed, and go on relaxing.

Now, with your mouth closed, pull back the corners of your mouth as tight as you can pull them. Feel the tension in the cheek and jaw muscles as you pull the corners back farther and farther. Now relax. You may notice a sensation of warmth around your mouth as the blood flow to these muscles increases as they become more relaxed.

As you practice the tensing and relaxing of each muscle

group, be sure the rest of the body remains entirely comfortable and totally relaxed.

Now tense your jaw muscles by biting your teeth together. Bite hard. Notice the feeling of tightness in your jaw muscles, particularly in the muscle that runs down your cheek in front of your ears. Now relax. Let your jaws go completely limp. Let your mouth hang slightly open. Feel the surge of relief as relaxation flows in.

Now push the tip of your tongue against the roof of your mouth, so you can feel tightness in the muscles under your chin and in front of your throat. Push hard. Hold it. Hold it. Now relax. Feel the sensation of relaxation stream down the sides of your face, under your chin, and into your throat, as your whole body becomes more and more totally relaxed. Retain this state of relaxation for the next few moments.

Again relax all the muscles in your forehead. Make sure there is no tension around your eyes or nose. Let your face become relaxed and expressionless as you allow all the muscles in your cheeks and jaws to loosen up. Let your whole face become as totally relaxed as your arms and shoulders are, thoroughly and deeply relaxed.

Now push your head back as far as it will go. Hold it. Observe the pressure in the back of your neck. Now relax. Let your head return to its normal position.

Now bend your head forward, touching your chin to your chest. Feel the tightness in the back of your neck. Now relax. Return your head to its normal, comfortable position. Once again, go on relaxing calmly and peacefully.

Now take a deep breath. Fill your lungs and hold your breath. Hold it. Notice how the muscles pull across the chest. Now exhale. Relax. Relax. Breathe out and feel the sensation of pleasurable relief throughout your chest. Continue breathing normally now, in and out, regularly and easily. Allow the rest of your body to be as relaxed as possible, but fill your lungs once again. Take a deep breath and hold it.

Hold it. Again notice the increased tension. Now relax. Just breathe normally, easily, freely, completely relaxed.

Both hands, both arms, both shoulders, your face, your neck, your chest are all completely relaxed now.

Now, making sure that your other muscles stay relaxed, tighten your stomach muscles. Make them hard, as if someone is about to push against your stomach and you're preparing to resist the pressure. Hold it tight. Hold it. Now relax. Focus on the surge of relief and the complete comfort of relaxation. Once again, tighten your stomach muscles. Hold it. Hold it. Now relax. Let your muscles become completely relaxed. Notice the general sense of well-being that comes with relaxing your stomach muscles.

Continue relaxing for a while, enjoying the calm, pleasant sensations of deep, total relaxation. Your hands and arms are limp. Your shoulders are resting naturally, your face muscles relaxed and serene. Your breathing should be easy and rhythmical, in and out, in and out. No effort should be required as you completely relax in the chair. Retain this state of relaxation for the next few seconds.

Now take a deep breath. Fill your lungs and hold your breath. Hold it. Notice how the muscles pull across your chest. Now exhale. Relax. Breathe out and feel the pleasurable relief throughout your chest area. Continue breathing normally now, in and out, regularly and easily. Allow the rest of your body to stay as relaxed as possible, but fill your lungs once again. Take a deep breath and hold it. Hold it. Again notice the increased tension. Now relax. Just breathe right out, relaxing and enjoying the soothing relief. Notice how all the muscles of your body tend to become more relaxed when you exhale. Go on breathing normally, easily, freely, completely relaxed. Both hands, both arms, both shoulders, your face, your neck, and your chest are still completely relaxed.

Now tighten only the muscles in the upper thigh of each leg. Observe how it feels when you tighten both the top and the bottom muscles of both thighs. Now relax. Completely relax all your muscles in your thighs, your stomach, your chest, your face, your arms, and your hands. Once again tighten the upper thigh muscles in both legs. Hold it. Now relax. Feel the surge of relief as the relaxation flows back in. You may even observe pleasant sensations of warmth as these muscles become more and more relaxed.

Now raise both your legs up, so that only your toes are touching the floor. Notice the tightness form in the calves of your legs. Now relax. Just drop your feet flat to the floor, and relax all the muscles of your legs and feet. Once more raise both legs up on tiptoe. Pull them as tight as you can. Hold it. Now relax. Drop your feet flat to the floor, and notice the relief of relaxation. Allow all your muscles throughout your entire body to become more and more relaxed.

Finally, push down with your toes, and arch up both feet. Feel the pressure as if something were pushing up under each arch. Hold it. Now relax. Let your arches fall, and enjoy the release and freedom from effort. Go on relaxing. Make quite sure there is no tightness anywhere in your body. Just let your body totally, completely relax. Enjoy the feeling of deep, complete, pleasant relaxation. Relax more and more.

Now, slowly, over the next few moments, allow yourself to return to a normal state of waking tension. This doesn't mean that you'll be nearly as tense as when you started relaxing, but you will be just alert enough to go about the rest of the day's activities without any trouble. Do it gradually, counting from 1 to 4. On the count of 1, move your feet and legs slightly. On the count of 2, move your hands and your arms. On the count of 3, sit up in the chair, and on the count of 4, open your eyes. When you do this, you'll feel very refreshed and relaxed, much as you would feel if you had just awakened from an afternoon nap.

O.K. .... 1, move your feet and your legs ... 2, move

your hands and arms . . . 3, slowly sit up in the chair . . . just stay as comfortable as possible . . . and 4, open your eyes.

- The lighting should be just bright enough so that you can read this book without straining. Later, when you're familiar with the process, dim the light further.
- If your neck and head are not comfortably supported by your chair, put a pillow behind your neck. As little muscle tension as possible should be required to maintain your sitting position. Just relax and let the chair completely support your body.
- At this point, you would ordinarily close your eyes. They would remain closed throughout the practice so that you wouldn't be distracted by light or motion around you.
- Be sure not to rush through the PMR program. Move through it at a slow, even pace. Take your time tensing and relaxing each muscle group. Pause for a minute or two after working on a particular muscle group before going on to the next one in the sequence.
- If you find that you're having trouble concentrating as you work through the relaxation procedure, try one of these strategies: First try reading the instructions onto a tape, which you can then play back to yourself. If this doesn't work, have someone you know record them, slowly, so that the voice giving you directions and setting a pace for you will be a different one than your own.[2]

To really get this procedure down pat, to acquire the relaxation response as a virtual reflex, you must practice it repeatedly. Work through it three to five times in the first week, at least twice each time, until you've actually gone through the entire process, slowly and methodically, about ten times. By that point, you should know it thoroughly.

Each time you go through the PMR process, pay special

[2]The authors of *Spare the Couch* can also make a tape of the relaxation instructions available to you. Write to: Donald L. Tasto, Ph.D., P. O. Box 5507, Redwood City, CA 74062. Enclose $6.50 and we will send you a copy.

attention to the muscles that are the most tense. By doing this, you will begin to make finer and finer distinctions between tense and relaxed muscles, and you will refine your ability to focus the PMR technique on the areas of your body that need it most. If you do this, you will find that you do not need to tense and relax every muscle each time you go through the procedure. Instead, you can focus your attention on those that will give the greatest results when tensed and then relaxed.

Once you've become quite familiar with the PMR process, expand your versatility with it by applying it in real-life settings. For example, the next time that you're driving your car, try and sense your overall level of muscle tension. Slowly, not rapidly, *slowly* begin to ease up on the tension in your hands, arms, shoulders, the rest of your upper body, and your legs. Gradually lower the tension in these areas until you're maintaining just enough muscle tension to continue to drive competently. This exercise should vividly demonstrate to you just how much excessive muscle tension you normally tolerate before relaxing. It is invariably a far higher level than you need to function effectively.

One last comment. Many people first beginning relaxation training unconsciously worry that being more relaxed somehow also means being less mentally alert. Because they tend mistakenly to equate alertness with a high level of general muscle tension in the body, they assume that relaxing their muscles will dull their cognitive processes and that they will lose a measure of their ability to analyze and interact with their surroundings.

If you think you may share this worry, you must consciously learn to separate the sensation of muscle tension from your thought processes. Try this exercise. The next time you're seated at a desk, writing or performing any other task that involves a static posture and active mental processes, briefly interrupt what you're doing, and try deliberately to reduce your level of muscle tension slowly; yet maintain the same level of cognitive functioning. Take a few minutes to relax; then go back to work. We're certain that if you will compare your work before and after you relax yourself, you will find that you are in fact *better* able to engage in complex cognitive and intellectual tasks when you're physically relaxed. Rather than being an obstacle to alertness, relaxation is much more conducive to creative mental processes than tension is.

Remember, learning this process of relaxation is the first step in treating many of the problems in this book. It is not the only step, but it is an important one. Learn it thoroughly before proceeding with the other steps in your program.

three

Additional Tools for Change

Throughout the chapters following this one, we describe change techniques that have been developed and refined over at least half a century of research into human psychology and learning processes and that are already in widespread use by thousands of counselors, therapists, physicians, ministers, and teachers throughout the world. This chapter is intended as a brief glossary of the well-established labels for these techniques, which you should read to be sure that you understand the concepts involved. None of them is especially complex. In fact, most are purely a matter of common sense, and like the character in the Moliere play, *Le Bourgeois Gentilhomme*, who found that all his life he had been speaking "prose" without knowing that that was what it was called, you will probably find that many of these techniques are simply old friends with new labels.

Relaxation, as we explained in the previous chapter, is the first step to take in treating most of the problems described in this book. It serves frequently to set the psychophysiological stage for application of the more specialized techniques described in Chapters 4 through 10.

Reinforcement is also an important concept in these change procedures. To define it simply, change is made easier if it is hooked up with a system of rewards and/or penalties. *Positive reinforcement* means that you reward yourself when you do something you want to do more of. For example, if you're trying to learn to express your feelings more effectively, to become more assertive, you may reward yourself for speaking up when a clerk in a store ignores you and waits on a latecomer. *Penalties*, of course, are the opposite of positive reinforcement. Using penalties means that you punish yourself when you do something that you want to stop doing. People who want to eat less may, for example, prevent themselves from watching a favorite television program on days when they overindulge. As you might expect, positive reinforcement tends to be more useful than penalization for bringing about most kinds of change; we're all more likely to respond to praise than to blame, for instance.

Reinforcement is a term that formally describes the way most of us typically behave under normal circumstances in our lives. It's entirely natural for us, after a hard day's work, to look forward to various types of rewards. It may be nothing more unusual than a book, a warm shower, and a dry martini, and we may not usually call it a "reward"; but nevertheless, nearly all of us look for a little gratification here and there at regular intervals to keep us going. And by the same token, we're usually willing to penalize ourselves for infractions of the standards we set for ourselves.

When to reinforce yourself can become quite a complicated issue. If you're always rewarded for an action, a kind of boredom can develop that makes the reinforcement gradually become uninteresting unless it's an especially attractive one. Similarly, if you're never rewarded, you will tend to give up, to quit making further efforts. This is called *extinction*. As a very general rule, the best kind of reinforcement is positive and intermittent, so that it isn't available constantly but it isn't always withheld from you either.

The concept of *contingencies* is closely related to reinforcement. "Contingent" literally means that one thing is *dependent* on another. The essential condition of a reward, of course, is that it is available *only if* something else has first been accomplished. You don't get this until you do that. For rewards and punishments to be effective, they must be made contingent upon accomplishing a step in the process of working toward the desired change.

One way that programs for change can make very powerful use of contingencies is to identify an action that you enjoy doing frequently, like looking in the mirror, and then to make it dependent on first doing something else, like completing twenty sit-ups. By connecting an action that you perform often with one that you would like to do more, you employ the built-in power of your desire to look in the mirror to encourage an increase in your exercise activity and thus a decrease in your waistline.

Picking contingencies and knowing what to make dependent on what else is more difficult than it may sound at first. If the contingency is readily available to you, you may have trouble indulging in it only when you have first completed the action that you want to encourage. It's hard to stop looking in the mirror when you're so used to doing so and to reserve this activity for the occasions when you've finished your sit-ups. By the same token, it's not very effective to pick a contingency that is completely out of reach, like taking a cruise around the world. Throughout the following chapters, we suggest a number of contingencies that should give you a sense of the most appropriate ways to reinforce your change program.

Contracting is another concept that is also closely related to the ideas of reinforcement and contingencies. Contracts are explicit agreements, often in writing, made either by you alone or between you and someone else, that describe what the desired change is, how much of it is to be accomplished and when, and what kind of reward (or penalty) will be associated with it. One example of a contract is shown in Figure 3.1.

Overall Goal: To get along better with others, thus improving my social support system, as part of my self-help program for depression.

Immediate Objective: To become more socially assertive.

Contract: If I can begin initiating progressively more involved contacts with others, I will allow myself the reward of watching Walter Cronkite every evening. The process of making these contacts will follow the steps outlined below:

Baseline: Few if any efforts to make new acqaintances.

Level 1: Say hello to someone I know but don't usually speak to (first week).

Level 2: Say hello to someone new (second week).

Level 3: Hold a short conversation with a new acquaintance (third week).

Level 4: Call a new aquaintance at home to talk (fourth week).

Level 5: Call an acquaintance to make plans to get together (fifth week).

Penalty: Every time I fail to keep this contract, I will not only prevent myself from watching Walter Cronkite, but I will also put a quarter in the garbage and leave it there.

Figure 3.1 A Sample Contract

Desensitization is a method first developed by Joseph Wolpe[1] that has been successfully used to eradicate many kinds of fears and anxieties. Basically, desensitization is a process of learning to stay completely relaxed while you

[1]Joseph Wolpe, *The Practice of Behavior Therapy* (New York: Pergamon Press, Inc., 1973).

gradually expose yourself to slowly increasing doses of whatever it is that you fear. The contact is made in very carefully
structured stages, called *hierarchies*, and may be done either
in the imagination or in real-life settings (*in vivo*).

Flooding is derived from desensitization. As part of the
desensitization process, you build a step-by-step hierarchy of
scenes that make you anxious, each one a little more frightening than the last. Under normal desensitizing conditions,
you progress up the hierarchy only as far as you can while
remaining relaxed, and you move back down the hierarchy if
you become too tense.

Under flooding, however, once you've constructed the
scene at the very top of the hierarchy—that which you identify as the most terrifying for you—the next step is to relax
and then, in your imagination, immerse yourself in that
scene. There's no gradual progression up the hierarchy at all
in flooding—just sudden, complete confrontation with the
feared object or situation. *It is critically important, however, that
you remain in the flooding scene until you begin to feel yourself relax.*
That is the whole point of the exercise: bringing together in
your imagination your worst possible fears *and* your relaxation responses. Otherwise, if all you do is thoroughly upset
yourself without experiencing the decreased arousal of relaxation, flooding is pointless.

This technique has been used most successfully to treat
obsessive fears of dirt, disease, and other kinds of contamination (Chapter 7).

Positive scanning simply means systematically training
yourself to interpret events in as positive a manner as possible. Both positive and negative thought processes and internal monologues have a strong self-fulfilling potential. If you
expect the worst from your surroundings, chances are good
that your attitudes will deteriorate; this will affect your mood
and other behavior, and sure enough, you will be miserable.
The best defense against bringing yourself down like this is
to teach yourself to focus on the pluses rather than the
minuses in a given situation.

A close counterpart to positive scanning is *thoughtstop-ping*, an extremely simple but effective technique that can be used to interrupt sharply a train of negative thought patterns, so that you can then deliberately apply positive scanning or other cognitive techniques to revise the overtones of your internal monologues. Thoughtstopping works like this: as soon as you notice yourself starting out on a negative, overly critical, or particularly derogatory or self-demeaning train of thought, instantly imagine the word *STOP*, shouted out inside your head as loud as you can make it. As simple as this may sound, it works. It disrupts the negative thoughts long enough to give you time to reorient yourself and to begin thinking about something positive.

Modeling. It often helps, when you're trying to begin a self-change program, to get someone else to run through the desired pattern of behavior for you, to show you how it's done, particularly with the treatment of phobia and with strategies designed to increase your assertiveness. Saying no to unwanted invitations is a good example. It can be awfully hard to do in some situations, but having a friend demonstrate how he or she manages the same difficulty can make it infinitely easier.

Modeling can also be practiced somewhat less deliberately, by simply placing yourself in a setting where others are likely to be doing whatever it is that you wish you were able to do yourself. (The classic example of this is the use of silverware at elaborate dinners. Most of us as children were advised, if we weren't sure which implement to use, simply to watch what everyone else did and then follow suit.) Observe the details of their actions, and note what emotions are allowed and expressed by others in these settings. Then begin to practice it on your own.

Television commercials use modeling techniques pervasively to sell products. The next time you're watching TV and you find yourself suddenly confronted with an athlete exclaiming about rental car services or breakfast cereals, pay less attention to the verbal message than to the emotional one. The upshot of it is that you're supposed to want to emulate these individuals, and the manufacturer hopes you will associate eating its cereal or driving its cars with the kind of physical performances these individuals are known for. On a less blatant level, you will also see modeling used to sell household products, especially those that are traditionally purchased by women, such as laundry soap and coffee. This type of commercial often works by presenting a very subtle conflict, perhaps a tactless husband who won't drink his wife's coffee but loves the coffee her neighbor serves. Aside from all the dialogue spoken by the actors in these contemporary morality plays, the ultimate message is that you should imitate the people in the commercial—your models—if you want to manage your personal relationships effectively.

Paradoxical procedures. Some of the methods that we describe in the following chapters work by first making the problem worse. For example, one treatment for insomnia is to try to stay awake for as long as possible. This approach is not always appropriate for every problem area. When it is, we describe it in detail.

Cues. Changes in your mood, such as those brought on by depression and anxiety, may seem capricious and arbitrary to you, but close evaluation of the events and people around you when you first feel them coming on will often reveal a close relationship between some specific aspect of your environment and the appearance of a distressing emotion. These environmental triggers are known as *cues*, and identifying them plays a very important role in learning to manage emotional states.

four

Depression
and Feelings
of Worthlessness

In a real dark night of the soul, it is always three o'clock in the
morning, day after day.

—F. SCOTT FITZGERALD

When you're depressed, you feel worthless. You feel that you
have no purpose, that you're of no use to the world. You fear
that the people around you are indifferent to you. They may
behave pleasantly toward you, but you sense that underneath
a polite veneer, they really find you dull, boring, and insignificant. You find yourself constantly dissatisfied with all
your relationships, from the deepest to the most superficial.
It seems to you that something intangible is missing, some
element of interest and concern that would bring rapport
and meaning into all these routine, mechanical, painful interactions with others.

You have the constant feeling that your life is an unfair,
bleak, and bitter struggle, and you secretly feel outraged that
such a cruel hoax was ever perpetrated on you. You wish
you'd never been born.

It's not my fault, you protest. *I didn't ask for this. I can't help it if no one cares about me/if I'm stuck in this crummy job/if I've given up all chance for a career of my own just to play servant for these demanding brats while he goes off and hides in the office all day.*

The truly sad part of this litany of despair is that all your depressive fears are probably true. Depressed people *do* tend to alienate others. No one likes to be around a negative, unhappy person. And because you're depressed, you're not getting out and doing things, so you really are less productive, less useful, and less interesting than people who, because they aren't depressed, are actively living life. Life *is* harder for you and much less rewarding than it is for other people.

The way to change, in a nutshell, is to pull yourself together, get out, and start acting in ways that will bring you the kind of responses from your surroundings that you want and need. In the following pages, we give you step-by-step instructions on how to do just that. First, though, let's gain a clearer idea of what depression is and how severe a problem it is in the United States.

Some depression is a natural part of life. Serious personal loss of any kind, whether of a loved one, a job, status, money, or health, can bring on depression. Paradoxically, even success can cause depression, since one can lose the need to strive for it any longer. This type of natural depression, called reactive depression, is entirely normal; in fact, not to feel grief, sorrow, or possibly even anger under such circumstances is highly abnormal. As long as a reactive depression doesn't persist beyond an appropriate length of time, there's no reason to worry about it, and there's really nothing to do. This type of depression is cathartic. Once you've worked your way completely through a reactive depression, it's gone for good.

Depression is one of the two or three most prevalent kinds of psychological disturbances in the United States today. Federal sources estimate that at any given moment, between 8 and 18 million Americans need professional care for depression. Depression costs us from $1 to $4 billion each year in lost work hours and in the price of treating its victims. Few of us will escape some measure of depression in our lives. Some of us will never know a day without it.

A small percentage of depression may be caused by biochemical imbalances in the body, but the research to date in this area is inconclusive. We know, for example, that norepinephrine (or noradrenaline, as it's sometimes called) plays an important role in the biochemistry of depressive reactions and states, but we don't know whether it actually helps *cause* depression or is only one of the many *effects* of a depressive episode.

Even in those few cases where it seems that a depressive state might be the result of organic imbalances in the body's physiological makeup, the best treatment procedure is to go ahead and try to change your patterns of behavior in the ways we describe in this chapter. Acting and thinking differently can exert a powerful beneficial influence on your body, even to the point of recomposing its chemical processes.

Give our recommendations a diligent try. If, after repeated efforts, you can't seem to make them work for you, consider seeking professional help, particularly from someone who is familiar with depression and who will help you investigate the available pharmacological treatments.

Most depressions, however, do not stem from biochemical causes. Instead, most result from an inability to obtain the positive and rewarding kinds of responses from one's social environment, particularly from other people, that one wants and needs.

Martin Seligman[1] calls this condition "learned helplessness." In a series of sobering experiments, Seligman has shown that animals who are taught that their exertions are useless tend to quit, to give up much sooner than others. For example, a dog that is immobilized in a harness and then

---

[1]Martin Seligman, *Helplessness: On Depression, Development and Death* (San Francisco: W. H. Freeman, 1975).

painfully shocked while it can't escape will learn helplessness and won't try to avoid a later series of shocks, even when it is free to do so. Instead of jumping a barrier to escape, it will shiver and whimper and lie down, trembling. Similarly, laboratory rats that are first held in the hand until they learn they can't escape quit struggling and drown much sooner when placed in a tank of water than do rats who are not first subjected to this experience of helplessness. College students who are first exposed to a loud, blaring, uncontrollable noise do worse on a series of tests than those who are not thus confronted with helplessness.

The important lesson here is that if helplessness is learned, it may also be possible to unlearn it. People who become depressed are often those who, when faced with a frustrating situation, tend to respond by giving up and becoming despondent. Others have different reactions—anger, or fear—but depressed people just quit trying. Depression that stems from a feeling that your actions are useless can be alleviated by teaching yourself ways to make your responses more effective, to improve your ability to get what you want from friends, family, and work.

DIAGNOSING DEPRESSION

Most of us are painfully familiar with our depressive moments. We know all too well the feeling of oppressive dullness and apathy that weighs like a stone on our spirits. We know how everything in life seems hollow and empty to us, and how unbearable it can be to do anything more than simply try to endure the passing hours. It's the psychic equivalent of climbing a foggy mountain. All you can do is concentrate on putting one foot doggedly in front of the other as you plod steadily on, hoping to break through the mists eventually into clear skies and sunshine again.

It's possible to be mildly and chronically depressed without really being aware of it. This state is a far cry from the total immobilization of severe, acute depression, but it can be just as debilitating over the long run. Living for years with the faint impression that your senses and mental faculties aren't quite as sharp as they used to be, or that the small pleasures in life aren't quite as gratifying as they once were is the emotional equivalent of driving around with one foot on the brake. You just don't function quite so well if you're slightly depressed all the time.

Take Test 4.1, and see where you stand. If you have a considerable number of items checked in the two columns on the right, you're probably experiencing depression.

Test 4.1 How Depressed Are You?

	Never	Rarely	Some-times	Usually
I feel sad.				
I get bored very easily.				
I feel despondent.				
I feel that life is meaningless.				
I feel that life is filled with suffering.				
I feel that I am insignificant.				
I'm losing my interest in sex.				
I don't have enough pep.				
I feel constantly exhausted.				
I don't feel like I recover from stress the way I used to.				
I feel that I'm becoming unattractive.				

	Never	Rarely	Some-times	Usually
I can't seem to make my mind up about anything.				
I feel that I work much harder at relationships than others do.				
I feel that nothing amuses me anymore.				
I feel worthless.				
I wish someone would tell me what to do with my life.				
I find that I'm not very deeply interested in my friends or family.				
I feel guilty about my detachment from others.				
I feel that I'm very different from everyone else.				
I've lost all interest in sex.				
I feel like crying.				
I notice that I don't seem to be interested in anything anymore.				
I wish I could start my life over.				
Other people seem to have more energy than I do.				
I wish I could go somewhere else.				
Other people seem to enjoy life more than I do.				
I don't have much of an appetite anymore.				
I feel that life isn't as good as it used to be.				

	Never	Rarely	Some- times	Usually
I tend to lose weight.				
I'm lonely.				
I can't seem to get enough sleep.				
I feel that I've never succeeded at anything.				
I feel like crawling into bed and ignoring my responsibilities.				
Nothing satisfies me.				
I think about aging and death a lot.				
I feel suicidal.				
I don't seem to be able to get any rest.				
I feel irritable all the time.				
I believe everyone is really alone in life.				
I'm disappointed in people.				
I don't feel that I can trust anyone.				
I think enthusiastic people are foolish.				

Depression symptoms can range from mild feelings of irritation or apathy to stupefying despair. Severely depressed individuals often contemplate or attempt suicide.

Depressed people quite commonly feel that they are socially inadequate, that they are not effective in groups. And, because this conviction tends to make them withdraw, to say very little, to wait until someone else speaks first before saying anything, their fears are often justified. They tend to pick one or two people to talk to and to exclude others. They are often thought to be shy, aloof, or arrogant. If they encounter criticism or hostility in a group, they tend to take it very personally and are quite hurt by it.

And, in fact, depressed people *are* socially inadequate. Whether it's because they overtly behave in a way that other people don't like or because they passively fail to act in a responsive way toward others, they alienate people. Instead of wondering why others in a group do not respond to them in ways they would like, depressed people must learn to redirect their attention to evaluation of their own actions, to see what they can do differenly so as to generate better interaction with others.

Although depression is often first triggered by a specific type of circumstance, setting, or personal interaction in one's life, it usually tends to mushroom, to spread like an infection until one's entire environment has been blighted. At that stage, every thought, feeling, or action only contributes to more powerful downward spirals. And the further down one goes, the harder it is to climb back up ... that's why it's very important to learn to catch depressions early, to stop them before they have a chance to become severe problems.

WHAT TO DO ABOUT YOUR DEPRESSION: THE TREATMENT PACKAGE

The great majority of all depressions, regardless of severity, duration, or symptoms, happen because the people who suffer them are not taking systematic steps to change the way they act, so as to bring forth from their surroundings the degree and type of positive, pleasant responses that they need and desire.

We all know people like this. In fact, it's a trait of human nature that we can more easily recognize ineffective patterns of behavior in others than in ourselves. For example, there is the young man of our acquaintance, quite successful in his profession, who is nevertheless very depressed about his inadequate sex life; but he isn't doing a thing to meet eligible women.

Or there's the proprietress of a small, new, interior decorating business who has just lost her largest account. Instead of getting out and meeting prospective clients, she's in bed, watching television and feeling very sorry for herself.

Another close friend, a highly qualified and dynamic humanities instructor at a small private college, routinely suffers a week or so of devastating depression each year, just before the beginning of the fall semester. He feels that he is overworked, underpaid, and underemployed, but he won't lift a finger to look for a better job.

Each of these people knows from bitter experience that the road back from a depression involves time and some very hard work. Each would agree that it's easier to avoid becoming depressed in the first place. And the way to do that is to follow this sequence of treatment steps:

1. *Rewrite your internal monologues.*
2. *Diagnose your depression cues.*
3. *Learn to apply relaxation.*
4. *Modify your unrealistic standards.*
5. *Develop positive fantasies.*
6. *Develop positive scanning skills.*
7. *Create a better social support system for yourself (the most important step).*

Now we'll take each of these steps and examine it in more detail.

1. Rewriting Your Internal Monologues

We all talk to ourselves constantly. There's a little voice, like that of an especially well informed sports announcer, who gives a running commentary on our habits, our thoughts, our fantasies, our weaknesses, our stupidities, our aspirations, and our fears, to name only a few topics. Most of us keep an intuitive balance in these internal diatribes: we talk a lot to ourselves about our problems, our weaknesses, and our failings, but we also periodically give ourselves great big pats on the back for doing the right thing. When we know we've done well, we tell ourselves about it—unless we happen to be depressed.

Depressed people tend to ruminate exclusively and obsessively over past failures and mistakes. They dwell at length on only the negative experiences of their lives, almost as though they felt compelled to punish themselves, to drive themselves deeper and deeper into moods of despair and futility. The first step in managing depression is to change the way you talk to yourself.

You may not realize that the constant internal monologues that you and yourself carry on with one another have a profound effect on your attitudes and actions. Unfortunately, negative thoughts tend to beget negative thoughts. You've heard of "psyching yourself up"? Well, it's just as easy, though far less desirable, to "psych yourself down," and depressed people tend to do it all the time. Once a chain reaction of internal gloom and doom gets started, it is very hard to disrupt. If you insist on berating yourself, on telling yourself that you're worthless, you will begin to *feel* worthless, you will begin to *act* as though you were worthless, and people—sensing your emotional signals about yourself—will begin to *treat you* as if you were, in fact, worthless. It's the old self-fulfilling prophecy at work, in one of its more vicious forms.

There is even a certain amount of concrete evidence

now to show that what you think and tell yourself about a situation has far more influence over your emotional response to it than does any objective assessment you might make. And these same experiments show that if you can alter what you tell yourself about a situation, your response to it will probably change. It may be difficult to do this at first, and the recommended techniques may seem awkward and clumsy; but they work, and they get easier to use the more you work with them.

And what is it that depressed people tend to ruminate about most? Well, nearly any topic or event can provide grist for the pessimism mill, but if asked, most report that their most potently depressing monologues tend to be about the past, specifically about past failures.

If you're going to stop depressing yourself, the first thing you're going to have to do is to set your past failures aside. There is absolutely nothing at all that can be done to change them now. Adopt the point of view expressed in the adage, "Today is the first day of the rest of your life," and mean it. Or, to quote Satchel Paige's immortal words, "Don't look back. Something may be gaining on you."

Occasionally, we hear people respond to our admonitions about their internal monologues by insisting that they dwell on the negative aspects of their past only because they don't have much choice: not much has happened to them that has been positive, they claim. Nonsense. Everyone has had so many experiences of both kinds, positive as well as negative, in their lives that we could all stop right now, this very minute, and sit back and do nothing but contemplate the unqualified pleasures of our past lives for as long as we liked.

The second most common complaint we hear from depressed people, who often admit that focusing on negative memories may be contributing to their despondency, is that they can't do anything about it, that they don't seem to have any control over the ruminations.

There are techniques for controlling this problem. For

example, if you find that negative thoughts tend chronically to preoccupy you, try this: the next time you notice yourself slipping into a mood of critical self-absorption, stop what you're doing, sit down, and record every last element, in vivid detail, of the entire invective that you're berating yourself with. Get it all down on paper or on tape. Put intensity and feeling into it. Really lambaste yourself. Then listen to it. We can assure you that the experience of hearing you tell yourself how worthless and incompetent you are will prove highly enlightening. Some people find the exaggerated intensity of the emotion in these recordings disgusting and outrageous. Others find it amusing. Still others find it slightly frightening. Nearly all find it quite therapeutic.

If you don't have a tape recorder available, writing your self-criticisms down and then asking a friend to read them aloud to you has much the same effect.

A second highly effective technique for blocking negative thoughts and memories is called _thoughtstopping_. It works like this. The next time you notice that you're beginning to feel that familiar jaundiced and bitter mood steal over you, immediately stop what you're doing, relax, and imagine yourself screaming STOP at the top of your lungs. Go ahead and do this out loud if it's appropriate for the setting; the shock of the noise alone will make you temporarily lose track of your train of thought.

Then immediately begin to supply another kind of thinking to replace the negative train of thought that you've just brought to an abrupt end. Tell yourself positive things about you.[2] Do this out loud, also, if it's appropriate. At first, you may not feel like it. This procedure may feel awkward, clumsy, artificial to you. But do it anyway. Try it, and see what happens. Start right away, as soon as you've blocked the negative chain reaction. It's critical that you first catch negative thought processes as soon as they begin, stop them, and replace them with positive thought processes. You can turn

[2]This second step, called positive scanning, is discussed later in detail in step 6.

your emotional state around *if you catch it early enough.* Otherwise, it just won't happen.

It's important not only to break up negative rumination about yourself but also then to build positive anticipation about your future. If necessary, *force* yourself to envision with pleasure a positive event that you know will soon be taking place in your life.

Here's an example of how thoughtstopping works. We know a lawyer who has to commute quite a long distance to get to and from work every day. He knew he was somewhat prone to depression, and he found that as soon as he got into his car and began his commute every day, the content and pattern of his thoughts would begin to become quite negative. (Many people who are prone to depression do find that in situations where their minds are somewhat idle, their thoughts seem to gravitate almost automatically to negative topics.) So he began to tell himself negative things about himself, without really realizing what he was doing, and by the time he got to work in the morning or home in the evening, he would be feeling extremely discouraged.

Once it was pointed out to him what he was doing, he tried the thoughtstopping technique. As soon as traffic would bog down, which was when the negative thought patterns would really take off, he would relax, sit back, and bellow STOP to himself. Then he would immediately begin to repeat positive things to himself, like: "I am a successful and respected attorney"; "I have a lovely wife, a beautiful family, and good health"; and so on. He would describe to himself events and experiences that he was looking forward to in the future.

He tells us now that he doesn't always feel like talking to himself in this situation, but as soon as he turns the internal monologue around and begins concentrating on these positive thought processes, he invariably gets quite wrapped up in them. "I seduce myself into feeling good," he says. He becomes completely oblivious to the things that seemed like insurmountable problems only minutes earlier, and he arrives at his destination in a much better frame of mind.

2. Diagnosing Your Depression Cues

Even if you know all too well what your depressions feel like, you may not know just what triggers them. Chronic, repetitive cycles of depression are frequently cued by a specific category of event, a particular aspect of your environment that has the power to instigate repeatedly a depressive reaction in you. To defend yourself against depression, you need to identify carefully the special circumstances, events, settings, or interpersonal interactions that serve to evoke your depression. You don't need to know *why* these cues provoke depression in you, just that they do. Anything can act as a depression cue. You may find that phone calls from a relative, demands from a colleague at work, and the lack of praise from your spouse are the most potent antecedents of depression for you. Some people get mildly depressed just before they go on vacation. Remember, though, that the main point is not to analyze the reasons for the connection between these cues and your depression, but just to identify the link, to realize that the first usually leads to the second.

A very important point needs to be clearly understood here. You will probably find that it isn't what happens in your environment that depresses you, it's what *doesn't* happen. Depression is far more often due to a *lack* in one's life, an absence of something good, rather than an event that *does* take place. You will probably find that you're getting depressed because something is missing, *not* because something else is present.

What's missing in nearly every depressed person's life is

a sense of satisfaction with the kinds of responses they are attracting from other people. The painful lack is one of personal reinforcement, of praise, of attention, of interest in them expressed by the other people around them.

Sometimes these people are just lonely. For one reason or another, they've become physically or socially isolated, and the sheer absence of human contact is depressing them. But it's usually not this simple. More often, we find that depression is a function of the quality, not the quantity, of personal interactions in the depressed individual's life. He or she may have what appears to be a surfeit of engagements, appointments, meetings, dates, and so on, but upon close inspection, all these encounters turn out to be characterized by a common, terrible emptiness, a superficiality that is directly responsible for the ensuing depressions. Hyperactivity is not a substitute for, first, knowing and, second, getting precisely what you most intensely need and want from personal interactions.

Now, when you're trying to analyze your own depression cues, it's obviously quite a bit harder to put your finger on something that is absent from your life than on something that is present in it. One valuable technique that can help you in this process is simply to keep a detailed list of all your activities for a week or two. You might use a chart like that shown in Figure 4.1. Simply record what you're *doing* during each of your waking hours in the boxes on the chart. They should contain everything from "showering" to "working" to "brooding," if that's what you're doing.

Keeping this list will serve three purposes. First, it will set up a basic yardstick of your overall level of activity. One prominent symptom of depression is reduced activity levels. As your depression disappears, you'll find that your level of physical activity rises, and this increase will be reflected in your activity chart.

Second, and perhaps most important, the list will help you: (1) identify precisely what it is in your environment that precipitates your depression, and (2) crystallize these things into a general class of events that serve as depression cues for you. You may find, for example, that being criticized is for you a powerful depression precursor.

	MON.	TUES.	WED.	THURS.	FRI.	SAT.	SUN.
7–8 A.M.	asleep	asleep					
8–9	asleep	asleep					
9–10	asleep	asleep					
10–11	asleep	10:30 ; up's coffee ; potty					
11–12	drinking coffee, smoking						
12–1 P.M.	visit by cop re court date						
1–2	bathing, getting dr'n, getting his clothes;						
2–3	cleaning house; coke break						
3–4	cleaning house ; cook break						
4–5	at church phone calls						
5–6	on way to kids						
6–7	visit w/ kids						
7–8	back to church						
8–9	at church w/d i h						
9–10	"						
10–11	"						
11–12	"						
12–1 A.M.	home; "supper"						

Figure 4.1 Activity List

Third, and also quite important, is the likelihood that keeping the activity list will help you define more clearly the type of response that you're seeking from your environment, the kinds of interactions that would prevent depresssion from developing in the first place.

Once you've maintained this list for one to two weeks, take it a step further. Include not only your activities, but also the moods that are associated with them. This second list, which should follow naturally from the attention paid to your activities alone, will further define what it is that brings on your depressions and what it is that forestalls them. A chart for keeping a record of moods and activities is shown in Figure 4.2.

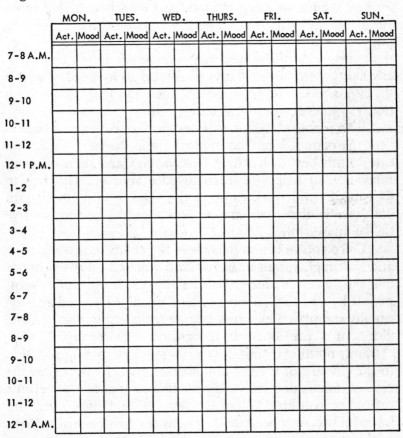

	MON.		TUES.		WED.		THURS.		FRI.		SAT.		SUN.	
	Act.	Mood	Act.	Mood	Act.	Mood	Act.	Mood	Act.	Mood	Act.	Mood	Act.	Mood
7-8 A.M.														
8-9														
9-10														
10-11														
11-12														
12-1 P.M.														
1-2														
2-3														
3-4														
4-5														
5-6														
6-7														
7-8														
8-9														
9-10														
10-11														
11-12														
12-1 A.M.														

Figure 4.2 Mood and Activity List

3. Learning and Applying Relaxation

This step is an easy and pleasant one. As we explained in Chapter 2, relaxation is fundamental to most of the change methods described in this book. It is of particular value for treating one kind of depression, that which follows a manic episode. For many people, the effort to get reinforcement from their environment goes in cycles. One part of the cycle is the frantically hyperactive manic phase, in which they rush around madly, working far too hard on schemes that often verge on the grandiose. Then, when their energy bubble pops, as it always does, they sink back down into a despondent torpor until the next surge of manic intensity strikes. It's like an engine that revs wildly up to a speed where it threatens to tear itself to pieces, then suddenly drops back down to a level where it is barely idling.

The way to break up this destructive sequence is to prevent the manic stage from happening in the first place. You can do this best by learning first to relax and then by using relaxation to help you learn to pace yourself. Go back to Chapter 2, and work through the relaxation method until you have it under command. This should take four or five half-hour sessions.

Once you've begun to achieve the ability to relax quickly and thoroughly, wait until you find yourself on the verge of embarking on a manic episode. This stage is signaled in most people by a sudden, almost ecstatic burst of frenzied activity, usually stimulated by a new plan, a fresh inspiration, a novel vision of a previously unrecognized opportunity. There's certainly nothing intrinsically wrong with diligent application to the pursuit of a risky but realistic goal. However, in the case of manic-depressive cycles, there's typically a definite refusal to consider potential obstacles, and such states are harmful precisely because they deny the existence of realistic problems, which inevitably tend to make themselves known.

Catch yourself as quickly as you can when this mood begins, because once it's in full force, you won't be able to slow yourself down again. Instead of maintaining level flight, you'll burn out and crash.

As you apply the relaxation technique, tell yourself that you do not need to put forth the burst of energy as you're inclined to, and that you can enjoy yourself and feel just as fulfilled by throttling back, slowing down, and generally keeping yourself in check, rather than expending yourself in a furious blaze of energy until it's utterly dissipated and you're exhausted and depressed again. Also, tell yourself that letting the sympathetic nervous system get overly aroused is very definitely hard on your health; it will deplete your nervous system of many biochemical elements, and this depletion will in turn make you more susceptible to depression.

Become much more deliberate and far less impulsive about what you do. Plan your activities for the day, the week, the month, and as you do so, give yourself less to do than you would normally undertake. Limit the number of tasks that you try to accomplish. Pace yourself.

4. Modifying Unrealistic Standards

Closely related to an ability to live, work, and play at a steady, relaxed pace is the problem of setting unrealistically demanding, perfectionistic standards.

Depression-prone people tend to expect the impossible of themselves. When they fall short of their absurdly high expectations, they become depressed. We venture to predict that analysis of your depression cues in step 2 will show you that you often tend to get depressed following specific disappointments, which themselves stem directly from the exaggeratedly high demands that you impose on yourself and others. If you couple this trait with the fact that, like most depressed people, you also have an abnormally low tolerance for stress, failure, mistakes, and the unpredictable, it's easy to see that you're putting yourself in a very precarious position: you expect too much, and you tolerate too little. The entire sequence of attitudes looks like this:

> perfectionistic standards + low tolerance for error →
> inevitable failure → disappointment → frustration →
> negative internal monolgue → sense of helplessness →
> depression

The process wouldn't constitute quite such a difficult bind if the depressive's unrealistic expectations were focused primarily on the self. After all, most of us are predictable enough that we have some idea of our strengths and weaknesses, and though we may be discouraged when we fail, we're usually not terribly surprised. Quite the opposite: we may even become overly resigned to our own patterns of failure. But unfortunately, depressed people are as likely to set exaggerated standards for others as for themselves; and since other people—even those who are very close to us—can never be as predictable as we are, this adds shock and surprise to the depressive cycle, and we tend to feel excessively wounded when others also fall short of our inhuman performance expectations.

To free yourself from this pattern of behavior, start by admitting that you're expecting too much from yourself and others, that you're looking for perfection in an imperfect world. As you do this, continue to apply systematically the relaxation procedures of step 3 to counter the automatic urge to demand too much of yourself, as we described earlier.

Also, as you begin to follow the planning process we recommended at the end of step 3, review your agenda and pick three tasks that strike you as involving unrealistic expectations. Examine these expectations carefully, and find ways in which they can be modified. Tell yourself that you don't need to perform these tasks quite so perfectly as you had planned. Tell yourself that your expectations can be reduced without jeopardizing your sense of self-esteem, and begin to determine in concrete ways just how they can be reduced.

One of the most common occasions on which we invariably tend to expect too much of ourselves is when we meet new people, especially if they're in a position of some authority. The job interview is a classic example of this type of situation. Here we're confronted with a person we don't know, one who will be evaluating us throughout the interview, and whose estimation of our value can play an important role in determining our future economic security. It's entirely understandable and even reasonable to feel somewhat uncomfortable in this setting—unless you're a perfectionist, in which case you expect the impossible: never to say anything that the other individual will disagree with; to be friendly, relaxed, and alert throughout the entire meeting; and to be instantly liked and appreciated in a wholly unqualified way.

5. Developing Positive Moods: The Give-Yourself-Some-Credit Card and the Perfect Week Exercise

There are also two sound procedures that can be used to fight depression by working methodically to create more positive attitudes and moods in oneself. The first is extremely simple; the second takes a little more effort but can be a lot of fun.

The first technique involves nothing more complicated than writing down ten positive things about yourself. Give yourself a pat on the back. Select anything you want ... whatever you feel are genuine accomplishments, whatever things make you feel particularly proud of yourself when you bring them to mind. They can be related to your family, your career, your education; special talents and skills that you possess; unusual experiences that you've undergone; or remarkable and significant moments out of your past—occasions when you feel you accomplished something that was especially remarkable.

Then write these down on a card that you can carry in a wallet or purse, and keep it with you. That's all there is to it. This is the Give-Yourself-Some-Credit Card, shown in Figure 4.3. Whenever you start to feel the first symptoms of the onset of depression, get the card out, read the list to yourself, and spend a little time just reflecting on your special attributes or achievements. The little shot of self-esteem that you will feel can be just the right antidote to the negative thought that often signals the first stage of depression.

The second technique is called the Perfect Week Exercise, and it involves slightly more effort and a lot of imagination. The first step is to develop a list of ten pleasant events, things that you know you enjoy beyond a shadow of a doubt. They can be anything from a walk in the park to reading the latest whodunit, but they should be unequivocally rewarding experiences for you, and they should be realistically accessible to you. (It's not much use fantasizing about a flight to Tahiti with a new lover if you have neither the money to get to Tahiti nor anyone to go there with.)

Refer to the mood and activity list that you began keeping earlier in step 2; reviewing it should help you identify events in your immediate surroundings that are associated with positive moods for you.

Another source of pleasant events is your memory. Lie down, relax yourself, and simply let your mind take itself back to occasions in the past when you felt very good. This exercise can not only provide you with suggestions for your pleasant events list but can also, in and of itself, help relax you and elevate your mood.

```
┌─────────────────────────────────────────────────────────────┐
│               The Give-Yourself-Some-Credit Card             │
│                                                               │
│  1.  2 years of college          6.  no weight gain since high school │
│                                                               │
│  2.  part-time job as docent     7.  Jim                      │
│                                                               │
│  3.  compliments on my cooking   8.  Jilly's scholarship      │
│                                                               │
│  4.  taught Tim to swim          9.  organized women's group  │
│                                                               │
│  5.  tuned up the car           10.  book project             │
└─────────────────────────────────────────────────────────────┘
```

```
┌─────────────────────────────────────────────────────────────┐
│               The Give-Yourself-Some-Credit Card             │
│                                                               │
│  1. _____        6. _____         │
│                                                               │
│  2. _____        7. _____         │
│                                                               │
│  3. _____        8. _____         │
│                                                               │
│  4. _____        9. _____         │
│                                                               │
│  5. _____       10. _____         │
└─────────────────────────────────────────────────────────────┘
```

Figure 4.3 *Top*, An Example; *Bottom*, A Blank for You to Use

An example of one person's pleasant events list is shown below.

A PLEASANT EVENTS LIST

- Wearing very formal attire for an evening out.
- Contributing time to a charitable or volunteer organization.
- Getting a large check in the mail.
- Stopping at a flea market.
- Taking my kids to a park.
- Writing a letter to a close friend.
- Sleeping late in the morning.
- Making love well.
- People watching over a glass of wine in an outdoor cafe.
- Reading the paper in the morning over a cup of excellent coffee.
- Being the center of attention at a party.
- Winning awards and recognition for professional or artistic achievement.
- Giving my wife a massage.
- Meditating.
- Getting a sound night's sleep.
- Enjoying a delicious meal at a fine restaurant.
- Being right about something.
- Getting into a bed with clean, sun-dried sheets on it.
- Walking on the beach at low tide.
- Going disco dancing.
- Lying in the sun and reading a good novel.
- Playing classical guitar.
- Taking a sauna and massage.
- Buying a surprise for my wife.
- Jogging five miles.
- Watching "60 Minutes" on Sunday evenings.
- Refinishing furniture.
- Soaring/skiing.
- Going on a vacation to fish in the mountains.
- Telling a good joke well.
- Winning at blackjack.

Once you have a list together, lie down, close your eyes, relax yourself, and project yourself into the future. Hour by hour, day by day, compose a perfect week for yourself, one in which every moment is filled with positive and rewarding experiences. Take your time, and work through the procedure slowly and deliberately, so that the mental images are as vivid and detailed as possible. If you find you have trouble concentrating, focus for a moment on your state of physical relaxation. You will find that the more you practice the muscle relaxation process described in Chapter 2, the easier it is to become deeply absorbed in the Perfect Week fantasy.

Try not to let your suspicion that there is something unreal, or childish, or selfish about this kind of fantasizing inhibit you. Human beings fantasize constantly, in both negative and positive ways. All you're doing is mobilizing the fantasies, so that they help introduce and support positive rather than negative moods in you.

Portray to yourself the fullest and richest week you can imagine. Don't deny yourself anything that is realistically available. Everyone has a universe of potentially rewarding experiences at hand. Imagine yourself behaving in an animated, active mood. If you're overweight, picture yourself as being thin. That's realistic and it's possible. If you're currently involved in an unhappy relationship, imagine yourself sharing your perfect week with someone—even a fantasy person—whom you love and who you know loves you.

In short, let yourself daydream. Plan it and structure it so that it is as fulfilling and plausible as possible. Work at making it persuasive. Imagine what you'll say, how you'll look. Imagine what people will say to you, how they will respond to you.

Remember to stay relaxed. The obstacles, for many people, to actually realizing more gratifying experiences are self-imposed. If you can learn to shed your tension and your anxiety while vividly anticipating rich pleasures, you will be able to respond to those pleasures in reality much more fully and effectively, and you will be much more likely actually to seek them out, to make your fantasies become real experiences.

Here's an example of how a similar technique was applied in an actual therapy session:

> It is almost 3:15 P.M. on Wednesday, April 14, 1965. (This was the date of the actual consultation.) Apart from sleeping, eating, etc., how could you have occupied these 24 hr? You could have gone horse-riding for a change, or taken your guitar out of mothballs ... (5-sec pause) ... Let's push time forward another 24 hr. You are now 48 hr. ahead in time. Enough time has elapsed to have started a painting and done some sculpting. You may even have enjoyed a ride in the country and attended a concert. Think about these activities; picture them in your mind; let them bring a good feeling of pleasant associations, of good times... (5-sec pause) ... Let's advance even further in time. A whole week has gone by, and another, and yet another. Now these past three weeks into which you have advanced have been busy and active. Reflect back for a moment on three weeks of enjoyable activity ... (10-sec pause) ... Now you move further forward in time. Days are flying past; time advances; days become weeks; time passes; weeks become months. It is now 6 months later. It's the 14th of October, 1965. Look back on the past 6 months, from April to October. Think about the months that separate April from October. What have you done during May, June, July, August, and September? (Pause of 5 sec) ... Now six months ago, going back to April, you were very upset. In retrospect, how do you feel? Think back; reflect over an incident now more than 6 months old.[3]

When you've made this projection of your fantasy into a more complete and rewarding future, lie back and consider all that you were able to do and enjoy in this completely possible week. Appreciate the fact that you have launched

---

[3]Arnold A. Lazarus, "Learning Theory and the Treatment of Depression," *Behavioral Research and Therapy*, 6 (1968), 87.

yourself on the path to a higher level of satisfaction with yourself and your life, and that you are at this moment pursuing it. Give yourself some credit about this, too.

Write down all the details of this perfect week, or better yet, tape it while you fantasize aloud. Use these notes, or the tape, to prompt the pleasant associations of this exercise any time you feel that you may be on the verge of slipping into a discouraged mood.

6. Developing Positive Scanning Skills

Have you ever noticed that some people seem to have a consistently positive approach to life? They aren't by any means Pollyannas—they don't insist that *everything is always perfect*—but they do emphasize the positive rather than the negative side of any experience, and the result is that they in turn become more vibrant, more dynamic, and more satisfied with themselves.

People who are prone to depression behave in just the opposite way. As they begin to get involved in any typical situation, such as a social encounter with someone they don't know well, they become *negative scanners*—they compulsively look for the minor flaws and defects in the situation. As comedian Mort Sahl once put it, these are the people who chronically "look at the rose through world-colored glasses."

You can always find something wrong with a person, an event, or a setting if you look for it. And it rarely stops with one criticism: the first negative thought leads to another and another, and soon you're experiencing an entire chain reaction of negativity. When you leave the situation, you look back on it as having been a very negative experience. But it isn't apparent to you that the negativity came from you.

By the same token, you can always find something positive in your surroundings if you look for it. Positive people are those who automatically focus on the pluses in their environment; they are *positive scanners*. It isn't that positive scanners have a greater storehouse of positive experiences to draw from. Not at all—each of us possesses a virtually inexhaustible supply of both positive and negative experiences to draw from. The essential trick is to learn how to focus on one type, not the other, to keep yourself from becoming depressed.

First and foremost, you must learn to break up the chain of negativity before you really start feeling down and out. Remember, what we tell ourselves at a subvocal, subconscious level has an enormous impact on our emotional state.

To become a positive scanner, we recommend this: the next time you find yourself in an environment in which you typically start thinking one negative thought, then a second, and another and another, bring that chain of mental events to an immediate halt by using the thoughtstopping procedure that we described earlier, in step 1 of this chapter. Imagine yourself shouting STOP! to yourself. This will momentarily interrupt the negative cycle. Then pause for a moment. Make yourself look around. Make yourself notice and start thinking about something pleasant in your immediate environment. No matter what your surroundings are, there is always something positive in them to focus your attention on. Do this.

Then begin to talk to yourself about it—it may be something as simple as a picture on the wall, or the features of one of the people you're with, or the scenery around you. As you talk to yourself, you'll find that your mind soon becomes quite taken up with what you're saying. If you also check the effect that the process of positive scanning has on your emotional state, you'll find that it can completely reverse your moods and attitudes. And it can thus dramatically affect the way you interact with others, which will in turn change the way they respond to you.

It is particularly common for people who are prone to

depression to have trouble with groups of people they don't know well. In these situations, depressives tend to impart very negative attributes to strangers automatically. The negativity in these situations is largely projected into them by the depressed person, because he or she invariably begins to react critically long before new acquaintances have had a chance to show what kind of people they are.

Even in groups of people the depressive person knows well, negative trains of thought and mood can be set off by the kinds of extended, extremely pessimistic conversations that often develop in large social groups. These are treacherous situations for the depressive, because they are very hard to avoid and depressives seem to be fatally attracted to them. But, as seductive as they are, they are potent depression triggers for susceptible people.

The next time you find yourself in either of these situations, remember what you've read here about positive scanning, and tell yourself that it's completely possible to reverse the tone of the group. Pick something positive, something humorous perhaps, and inject it into the conversation. You'll find that this can have a remarkable effect on the people you're with. *But also, remember that the responsibility for initiating this move is on your shoulders. You can't afford just to sit and wait passively for someone else to take this step for you.*

People frequently report to us that they have tried deliberately applying the positive scanning technique in a situation that looked as though it was going to turn out very badly and that it has worked surprisingly well. So well, in fact, that they sometimes confess that they feel a little guilty about "manipulating" the others in the group. They looked for something positive in the people around them, they began talking to themselves about it, they infused it into the general conversation, and they managed to avert an emotional catastrophe. Many of these people also report that positive scanning can even change the tone of one's voice—they actually began to sound much more pleasant, they tell us, and people around them then began to interact with them in a much more positive way.

For example, one man we know had been feeling very negative about an impending father–daughter dance that his daughter's school was sponsoring. He knew that it was inevitable, that he had no choice but to attend it with his daughter, but he also couldn't help dreading it. However, recalling our descriptions of the way positive scanning works, he decided to try it out, so he began to force himself to change his expectations from negative to positive. As he puts it, "I honestly didn't feel like doing it, but I made myself start to think about the evening and the people I knew I would meet there, focusing intentionally on only the most positive aspects of my mental images, and after a while I started really getting into it. Before long, the big day came, we went to the dance, I found myself feeling very alert and excited, I started talking to people I hardly knew and initiating myself into their conversations, and it turned out that we had a genuinely *great* time." He knows, he adds, that if he'd continued his usual routine of negative scanning, the evening would have been boring at best, a disaster at worst.

As we mentioned earlier in this chapter, people who are prone to depression often find themselves falling into negative thought patterns when they're doing something that doesn't require a lot of mental activity. Driving the car is an excellent example. These people find that when the mind is left to itself, it seems to gravitate naturally toward very negative thoughts, and they begin ruminating obsessively about what went wrong today, yesterday, three years ago, as well as what's about to go wrong tomorrow.

If you find that this is happening to you, then driving is also a good time for you to practice both relaxation and positive scanning. Work through the PMR muscle groups, become as relaxed as is reasonable and safe while driving, then begin to think about an event in your life—something very positive—that could or will take place in the near future.

Let yourself imagine it in vivid detail. Dwell on it. Relish every aspect of it. See if this exercise doesn't improve your mood.

The critical step is to intervene in the negative sequence before it becomes too entrenched and powerful to reverse.

The first few times you try to use the positive scanning technique, it will feel strange to you. It's going to feel clumsy and awkward to tell yourself deliberately, "I've got to find something positive here. I've got to find something good about this situation." But if you simply persist, you will also find that it works. Something positive will appear, you will become absorbed in it, and you will suddenly find that you really are feeling much more comfortable and relaxed.

7. Creating a Better Social Support System for Yourself

An essential part of depression is the nagging feeling that something is missing in your life. And it is this sense of an important absence, of a lack, that makes you feel dejected and despondent and that in turn enmeshes you in negative patterns of thought, attitude, and conversation.

The lack that you feel so keenly is usually one of positive reinforcement from your environment. When you're depressed, you're not being given enough evidence from the world around you that you're valuable, lovable, significant, important, or useful. And the most persuasive source for this kind of reinforcement is other people; if you're depressed, you're simply not managing to elicit enough positive responses from those around you. And the reason you're not getting these responses is that you're not doing whatever needs to be done to encourage them.

Most people who are inclined to become depressed have

to learn to build better social support systems for themselves. This is probably the single most important step anyone can take to avoid repeated depressive episodes. It can also be astonishingly difficult, when you're feeling grumpy, dissatisfied, and more than a little sorry for yourself, to take the responsibility for creating more rewarding interactions with others, but you *must* make the effort.

When they examine their patterns of personal and social relationships carefully, depression-prone individuals usually find that they do not enjoy the best social support systems they could, because they are themselves behaving in ways that tend to make other people lose interest in them. This can happen for a wide variety of reasons—for example, it may simply be that they are not reciprocating adequately, that they're not extending invitations to people who have previously asked them out—but what it usually boils down to is that they are failing to think through their words and actions, to anticipate what effect behaving in a certain way will have on others. Often, they tend to act impulsively—even childishly—on their immediate emotions, which are often negative. And because most people do not normally like to be with someone who is consistently negative, they alienate others.

If you do not have a positive social network working for you, it's probably because you have either overtly sabotaged it by acting in an excessively aggressive, sarcastic, flippant, or discouraged manner, or it's because you've behaved passively, always waiting for someone else to make the first move. To change this situation, you must first learn to hold back on your negative emotions, and then to begin actively working to generate more positive responses from the people around you. It's entirely up to you to reverse the trend toward isolation and depression that your negative patterns of behavior have fostered.

Start on a simple level. Be pleasant to the waitress in the coffee shop. Offer a smile to a stranger on the street, to see what effect it will have. Usually, they will respond to you in a positive, pleasant way, and you will automatically feel a little bit better about yourself.

You cannot afford to wait until you *"feel"* like being pleasant to start this process. It doesn't work that way. You first have to start *acting* in a pleasant way. This will in turn bring forth positive reactions to you from others, and *these* responses are what will make you feel happier. What you're doing is like casting a pebble into a pond. The reverberations you set up will eventually ripple back in your direction. If you give off positive emanations, you will eventually get positive responses back.

It has been convincingly demonstrated that individuals who have developed a solid system of relationships with others do not have as much fluctuation in the activity levels of the sympathetic and parasympathetic divisions of the autonomic nervous system. As we discussed in Chapter 2, the sympathetic division is associated with states of high emotional arousal, such as intense fear or anger, whereas the parasympathetic division is associated with lowered physiological arousal and inactivity. Excessive fluctuations between the antagonistic activities of the sympathetic and parasympathetic divisions may play a role in the maintenance and exacerbation of depression.

In short, social support systems help smooth out our common tendency to overreact to the stresses and strains of life. For example, other experiments have shown that if you paralyze a dog with curare (that is, you temporarily paralyze it) and then frighten it, the sympathetic division of its nervous system will instantly show a high level of response. This is natural. It is the response we would expect in ourselves under the same conditions. But if a person walks into the same room the dog is in, the mere presence alone of that person—who may not even be close to the dog—will have a definite calming effect on its high levels of sympathetic activity.

People with good social support systems are thereby better equipped to deal with stressful jobs and other tense life situations and crises than people without this support. This may be why married men live longer than single men. Coronary patients show a better chance of surviving their heart attacks if they have learned how to get along well with other people and to generate positive responses from them. Having available the social support that this ability leads to will give you a different perspective on life and will help protect you from feelings of worthlessness and depression.

People who are not used to the idea of working to encourage better responses from others often feel that to do so would be giving in, letting others have their way, or somehow acting hypocritically—being "nice" even when they don't feel like it. They tend to ask, "But what should I do when I get mad? Should I hold my feelings in and let them simmer inside me until I get ulcers and who knows what else, or should I just go ahead and explode and get it out of my system? I can't be friendly *all* the time!"

These aren't the only two alternatives. There's a third, in which you go ahead and say what you have to say, you tell others how you feel about the way they behave or what they say, but you do so in a relaxed, pleasant, confident manner. You stay calm and cool. You don't let your emotions get totally out of control. You don't let yourself get hostile and aggressive, because as soon as you do, that is exactly the response you will produce in the other person.

The PMR method of dampening down the sympathetic nervous system is of great value in this process. Practiced regularly, it will allow you to *learn* how to substitute deep relaxation and mental calm for fury and anger.

Remember: people respond much more intensely to your emotional state than to the content of what you have to say. You can tell people to go straight to hell, and if you do so in a relaxed and pleasant manner, you won't alienate them half so much as if you compliment them but radiate tense, hostile, aggressive feelings as you do so. It isn't *what* you say so much as *how you feel as you say it* that has an impact on other people. And you *do* have control over what you will allow yourself to feel.

This process takes systematic practice. Be sure to follow the relaxation procedures in Chapter 2 as you go about improving your social support system. Also, Chapter 6 discusses additional ways to become more effective in personal interactions.

So, whether you feel like it or not, step up the number of pleasant things that you say to the people around you. Write down a list of five very simple ways to encourage positive responses, ways that do not take a great deal of effort, and carry it with you. Here's an example:

- Say good morning to people you wouldn't normally greet.
- Smile at people on the street.
- Tell your boss you like his tie.
- Chat with a clerk in a store.
- Call someone you haven't talked to in a while just to say hello.

Sometimes, particularly when you first start this process or when you're facing an interaction that you know will be negative, it can seem impossible to stay calm, collected, and yet effective. You'll feel that trying to be nice under these conditions will drive you right up the wall. And there will be times when you will fail. Many times. Don't let this discourage you. If you can get through it the first time, the second time will be easier, the third will be easier still, and pretty soon the process will become second nature.

If you feel certain that the circumstances are such that the other person is likely to get upset, prepare yourself for the interaction. *Plan* on encountering hostility, and plan also on remaining relaxed and pleasant in spite of it. If you can stay calm and communicative, you'll notice that rather than losing control, you may gain the upper hand. *You* begin to call the shots. *You* get what *you* want out of the interaction. And the other person will simmer down a lot quicker than if you let yourself also get angry and aggressive. Try to learn to view as a challenge situations where you may be called upon to try to confront and transform negative emotional states in others, to create a positive social environment where there probably wouldn't have been one before.

Remember, how other people treat you is very much up to you.

Here's an example of how one woman found that being pleasant was a much more effective way to get what she wanted out of a relationship that was very important to her:

Joan originally came into treatment because she recognized that she was alienating everyone around her, including her husband, who was on the verge of leaving her. She had an impulsive, hostile manner of interacting with those around her and evidently had little experience with the need to empathize with other people, to put herself in their place and try to figure out what effect her harsh, abrasive manner would have on them.

Her typical mode of interaction with her husband was simply to bark out commands to him, without consideration for his feelings or prior obligations. His reaction, understandably, was anger, resentment, and resistance to complying with her orders.

However, as her treatment progressed, she began to explore alternative ways of eliciting his cooperation, some of which were so successful that Joan at one point confessed that she actually felt mildly guilty because it was turning out to be so easy for her to get her husband to do what she wanted.

On one occasion, a Saturday, she found herself with a number of errands to run, some important business engagements, and a party to prepare for that evening. She urgently wanted her husband's help, specifically with washing the dog. Instead of just saying to him, "Well I've got a million things to do today, so you wash the dog," she sat down where he was eating breakfast at the kitchen table and began simply to describe her agenda, in a pleasant and positive tone of voice. "Well, I have to get bids on the carpet, then see Jim, then go to the cleaners and the laundry, go by the delicatessen and the liquor store, then maybe I'll be able to get to wash Toby before the party." His response was, "Let me help you. I'll wash Toby."

There is one kind of interaction with others that you should simply avoid if you feel that you're becoming overly depressed. We strongly recommend that you *not* discuss what it is that's depressing you. Other people may at first seem sympathetic, but the simple fact is that most people do not like to hear other people talk about negative things, and they do not like to subject themselves to exposure to negative emotional states in others. They will not, therefore, continue to give you substantial positive feedback if you persist in dwelling on your despondent condition.

As difficult as it may seem to get your mind off your problems, try instead to find some positive, interesting, amusing topic of conversation, and then make yourself talk about it. This will have a much more positive effect on the other person, which is in turn much more likely to produce the kind of response that you need.

ONE LAST COMMENT

Give these procedures a systematic, determined trial to see if they can help alleviate your depressions. Write down the steps and some notes on the methods in each one, then use this list to cue yourself into different patterns of behavior when you feel your mood beginning to slide.[4] Once you've worked your way through one depression on your own, the rest tend to become progressively easier to cope with.

However, if your depressions persist, and you've given the techniques in this chapter a thorough try, but you just can't make yourself feel better, get some help ... from a friend, a psychologist, a physician, a minister, a relative ... from someone.

[4]The initial synopsis of the depression treatment package that we gave on page 43 provides a convenient summary that you may want to carry with you.

five

Phobias
Managing Fears and Anxieties

How much pain have cost us the evils which have never happened.
—THOMAS JEFFERSON

Darkness . . . heights . . . open spaces . . . public speaking . . . closed places . . . sudden, loud noises . . . elevators . . . blood . . . street curbs . . . crowds . . . strangers . . . fire . . . flying . . . deep water . . . small, furry animals . . . birds . . . snakes . . . thunder and lightning . . . surgery . . . contamination . . . needles . . . insects . . . germs . . . being left alone.

An evocative list, one that seems to conjure up vestigial memories of a primordial past, a common human heritage as vulnerable creatures, and a time when survival was constantly threatened by wild animals and the caprices of nature. And yet common, ordinary, everyday things, but every one of them holds the power to cause overwhelming panic to certain individuals, those we call *phobic.*

Most of us can appreciate the faint latent threat that these phobic objects and situations evoke, though we also normally consider such a threat to be quite improbable. After all, we tell ourselves, some planes *do* explode or crash. Some snakes *are* venomous. And thunder and lightning, an impressive spectacle on any occasion, now and then *do* cause destruction and fatalities.

But even the most phobic individual also recognizes that these threats are very remote, and that the feared events and things are—for all reasonable and practical purposes—harmless, and that even those that might be potentially dangerous do not under most circumstances pose any serious threat to one's well-being. All of us, even those with flight phobias, know that flying is statistically safer than driving our car down the freeway to get to work in the morning. And we know that elevators are carefully and regularly inspected, that they are equipped with safety devices, and that it is extremely unlikely that they will suddenly plummet to the basement. In short, we know quite well, even if we ourselves are phobic, that our fears are irrational.

Phobias are a highly exaggerated fear of a very specific external object or situation that is considered harmless by most people. The number of items and situations that can conceivably cause phobic panic is extensive (see the partial list which follows); those already cited are among the most common.

COMMON PHOBIC OBJECTS OR SITUATIONS

1. Noise of vacuum cleaners
2. Open wounds
3. Being alone
4. Loud voices
5. Dead people
6. Speaking in public
7. Crossing streets
8. People who seem insane
9. Being in a strange place
10. Falling
11. Automobiles
12. Being teased

COMMON PHOBIC OBJECTS
OR SITUATIONS (continued)

13. Dentists
14. Thunder
15. Sirens
16. Failure
17. Entering a room where other people are already seated
18. High places on land
19. Looking down from high buildings
20. Worms
21. Imaginary creatures
22. Receiving injections
23. Strangers
24. Bats
25. Journeys by train
26. Feeling angry
27. People in authority
28. Flying insects
29. Seeing other people injected
30. Sudden noises
31. Journeys by car
32. Dull weather
33. Crowds
34. Cats
35. One person bullying another
36. Tough-looking people
37. Birds
38. Sight of deep water
39. Being watched working
40. Dead animals
41. Weapons
42. Dirt
43. Journeys by bus
44. Crawling insects
45. Seeing a fight
46. Ugly people
47. Fire
48. Sick people
49. Being criticized
50. Strange shapes
51. Being touched by others
52. Being in an elevator
53. Witnessing surgical operations
54. Angry people
55. Mice or rats
56. Human blood
57. Animal blood
58. Parting from friends
59. Enclosed places
60. Prospect of a surgical operation
61. Feeling rejected by others

62. Journeys by airplane
63. Medical odors
64. Feeling disapproved of
65. Harmless snakes
66. Cemeteries
67. Being ignored
68. Darkness
69. Premature heartbeats (missing a beat)
70. Nude men
71. Nude women
72. Lightning
73. Doctors
74. Crippled or deformed people
75. Making mistakes
76. Looking foolish
77. Losing control
78. Fainting
79. Becoming nauseous
80. Feeling different from others
81. Harmless spiders
82. Being in charge or responsible for decisions
83. Sight of knives or sharp objects
84. Thought of being mentally ill
85. Taking written tests
86. Being a member of the opposite sex
87. Large open spaces
88. Dogs
89. Germs
90. Being seen unclothed
91. Drugs
92. Giving off an offensive odor
93. Being ugly
94. Becoming sexually aroused
95. Being punished by God
96. Homosexual thoughts
97. Being dominated by others
98. Loss of loved ones
99. Being dressed unsuitably (wearing the wrong clothes)
100. Ministers or priests
101. Hurting others
102. Leaving outside doors unlocked
103. Kissing
104. Being X-rayed
105. Laughing or crying uncontrollably
106. Undertakers
107. Leaving the gas on

COMMON PHOBIC OBJECTS
OR SITUATIONS *(continued)*

108. Sexual inadequacy (impotence or frigidity)
109. Open doors or windows
110. Pregnancy
111. Police
112. Fish
113. Thoughts of being sexually assaulted
114. Buildings where someone has died
115. Masturbation
116. Leaving home
117. Physical examination
118. Thoughts of suicide
119. Thought of having a defective child
120. Going alone into a dark theater
121. Marriage
122. Insecticides

Phobias are usually intense enough to interfere seriously with normal activities. A man who can't bear to ride in elevators but who works on the thirty-sixth floor of an office building is in for some strenuous stair-climbing exercise and unnecessary embarrassment at least twice a day, five days a week. A woman who can't leave her house because she's afraid she'll faint in the parking lot of the local supermarket is virtually a prisoner in her own home.

We all experience trivial, irrational fears throughout our lives, but they rarely evolve to the point where they dominate us so completely that we can no longer pursue normal and necessary activities. We usually find it possible to ignore them, to put them out of mind, and to continue functioning without difficulty or harm. Occasionally we may go so far as to make minor adjustments in our lives to avoid encountering whatever it is that we fear—for example, there are plenty of mild hematophobics about, those who fear the sight of blood and who will never see the inside of a blood donor clinic because of this phobia—but this accommodation to their fear won't ever cause much disruption of their life-style or even loss of self-esteem. However, if the hematophobe happens to be a nurse or a premed student, the potential price of adjusting to the phobia, of giving in to it, becomes much higher.

Severe phobic reactions are not manageable, and they cause intense disruption to normal routines. These reactions can include headaches, stomach pains, diarrhea, nausea, dizzy spells, shortness of breath, heavy perspiration, heart palpitations, and even loss of consciousness. Probably the best description of a phobic response is that it is like a very bad nightmare.

The underlying impulse in every phobia is avoidance, an overwhelming desire to escape, coupled with overwhelming fear and panicky expectations of imminent disaster.

Phobias are characteristically directed at very specific objects or situations. The trigger for the fear and avoidance response is easily identifiable and is readily acknowledged by the phobic person.[1]

In short, if you suffer from a phobia, you're already painfully aware of it. You may not know exactly *why* you're afraid of sudden, loud noises or insecticides, but you're very much aware that they scare you to death. Your phobic conflict is something you must confront often, and it's something that other people encounter with little or no fear at all, which only adds to your sense of shame and discomfort.

What causes phobias? No one knows for sure. One view tends to regard them as symbolic substitutes for other, less acceptable types of fears, especially those involving sexual fantasies or highly aggressive urges. The classic examples cited by proponents of this point of view are the man who developed a morbid fear of lakes and other large bodies of water because, as it later turned out, he unconsciously wanted to drown his wife; or the woman who feared sharp objects, especially knives, because she secretly felt like slashing her husband's throat. Fear of flying, according to this

---

[1]We discuss a treatment program for more generalized anxiety states at the end of this chapter.

school of thought, may represent a more acceptable version of a fear of losing control over powerful but socially circumscribed emotions, like anger or sexual arousal.

The underlying theory here is that because certain kinds of fears and impulses are too threatening to one's self-esteem to be acknowledged consciously, a substitute is found that may not appear to make much rational sense on the surface, but that has a symbolic value in helping the phobic individual maintain control over his or her real impulses.

Others have pointed out that in some cases, phobic behavior may actually provide indirect benefits to its victims and that this may contribute to their development and continuation. A woman who can't leave the house isn't obliged to go shopping or run errands. A boy who won't go outside because he has developed a phobic fear of dogs may, as a consequence, get much more attention from his parents than ever before.

Though these speculations are intriguing, they are also largely irrelevant to the method of eradicating a phobia that we describe here. Phobias are especially recalcitrant to management through understanding alone. It's not at all uncommon to find that a phobic individual possesses detailed insight into his or her problem but feels helpless to actually do anything about changing it. The approach taken in this book, however, which depends on learning to replace anxiety with relaxation systematically, has been used successfully for some years now to help phobic individuals learn to master their panic, regardless of whether or not they understand its underlying causes.

Phobias are in our opinion *learned* responses. They are incorrect but powerful associations of intrinsically harmless aspects of our environment with highly distressing emotional reactions. For example, a mother who happens to be consistently angry and upset when she bathes her child may inadvertently teach that child to hate and fear water, or soap, or women.

But for the same reason, precisely *because* phobic responses are *learned* responses, they can also be unlearned. When these responses are altered through a system of gradual, step-by-step reexposure to the feared object while, at the same time, a condition of relaxation is maintained, the fear and anxiety as well as the panicky thoughts can be dissipated and brought under control. The harmless object or event then loses its ability to provoke pathological fear.

WHAT TO DO ABOUT YOUR PHOBIA:
THE TREATMENT PACKAGE

The process of treating a phobia is known as *systematic desensitization*, developed as an experimental technique in the late 1940s by a psychiatrist, Joseph Wolpe.[2] The steps in our adaptation of this process are set forth and are discussed in more detail in the following pages.

1. Make a phobic event list.

2. Form a phobic hierarchy.

3. Induce self-relaxation.

4. Work through the hierarchy in your imagination.

5. Work through the hierarchy in real life.

6. Monitor your progress.

7. Repeat prolonged exposure to the most frightening scene in the imagined hierarchy.

The process is easy to describe, but it requires commitment and motivation to work effectively.

Basically, the treatment amounts to a slow and steadily increasing exposure to greater and greater contact with the

[2]Joseph Wolpe, *The Practice of Behavior Therapy* (New York: Pergamon Press, Inc., 1973).

phobic object. This reexposure is first achieved in the mind using imaginary scenes in which you approach closer and closer to the object of your phobia, while at the same time being very careful to keep yourself in a thoroughly relaxed state. Thus you provide yourself with an opportunity to relearn what it feels like to remain calm in a situation that has gained an irrational power to make you feel very panicky.

One reason this process works is that in real life, you rarely have the option of choosing to encounter a phobic object *gradually*. It's just not typical or natural. You're either suddenly confronted with it, or, because you've learned that you fear it intensely, you avoid it and are *never* confronted with it. Setting up a hierarchy of small steps that take you into closer and closer contact with the phobic object allows you literally to desensitize yourself to it.

The imaginal process is entirely under your control, and it allows you to teach yourself a more workable way to encounter phobic situations and objects in real-life settings. Once you have been able to experience the displacement of anxiety by feelings of calm relaxation, you are then better equipped to transfer this newly learned response into real life, where you then repeat the same procedure: a gradual, carefully structured reapproach to things that can make you pathologically tense and upset.

Contrary to what you might at first expect, the control you learn through imaginal desensitization *does* transfer quite well to real life. You must also practice real-life desensitization as well, but the imaginal stage does effectively prepare you to remain relaxed as you do so.

Systematic desensitization has worked well for many people as a technique for learning to manage phobia. Under both experimental and real-life conditions, they have consistently been able to learn to replace a frightened response with a confident, calm, normal one. You can, too. But it is important that you follow each step just as we have it set forth here. And that you do so at the right pace. If you move through these steps in some other sequence or try to rush through them too quickly, you'll simply be wasting your time. This method won't work if you don't use it correctly.

1. Composing the Phobic Event List

We assume that anyone with a phobia is already well aware of it. Rarely is it necessary to help the phobic individual acknowledge and identify the phobic object, since it invariably is perfectly well known to him or her. However, it is sometimes necessary to analyze carefully exactly what element of the phobic setting is most feared by the phobic person. This is not always as simple as it might at first seem. Take flying, for example. Many people have mild anxieties about flying—these are not actually full-blown phobic reactions. But even among those with only mild anxieties of flying, the reason for the anxiety can vary quite a lot from person to person. Some people are afraid that the plane will crash and that they will be severely injured or killed. Others fear that the fuselage will be punctured, the air will rush out, and they will suffocate. Still others fear being in close proximity to a large number of strangers for a long period of time; usually this fear specifically focuses on the possibility that someone in the plane will begin to act irrationally or aggressively.

To make as clear as possible exactly what it is about the phobic setting that you fear, begin by preparing a phobic event list. On a piece of paper, write down from eight to twelve different scenes of exposure to the phobic object, ranging from the least threatening to the most. One of these should pose no threat at all, and one should pose the most extreme threat you can imagine. For example, if you have a snake phobia, your last scene might be of a large boa constrictor wrapped tightly around your body. An example of dog phobia follows.

A SAMPLE PHOBIC EVENT LIST:
DOG PHOBIA

- *A large dog running toward me.*
- *A dog sitting and watching me at some distance.*
- *A tiny dog so far away I can just barely see it.*
- *A tiny dog, so far away I can just barely see it, locked in a cage.*
- *A huge vicious dog, a Doberman, leaping at me, snarling and snapping.*
- *A large dog running up behind me without warning.*
- *A dog nearby, barking as I walk by, behind a fence.*
- *A large dog running at me, barking.*
- *A small dog running at me, barking.*

Don't worry about putting the scenes of exposure to the phobic object in any particular order, just get them down on paper. Try to make them detailed and specific, but keep them within the limits of a sentence or two. This first step will serve two purposes: (1) It will help you clarify precisely what it is about the phobic stimulus you fear most, and (2) it will provide material for the hierarchy that you will construct in step 2.

When you're doing this, it helps actually to imagine yourself in various stages of the phobic situation. Describe it to yourself as vividly as possible, including all the typical thoughts, emotions, gestures, and physiological responses that you can remember. Ask yourself what things seem to make it worse. What makes it better? What do you usually say to yourself in this situation? What do you do immediately afterward? How do you feel?

2. Forming the Fear Hierarchy

Now arrange the events you listed in step 1 in order, according to the degree of fear they can cause in you. Put the least frightening at the bottom of the hierarchy, and the most frightening at the top. The highest items can be exaggerated beyond realistic limits, so that during imaginal desensitization, you can become accustomed to a phobic scene that overshoots any you are likely actually to encounter in a real-life setting. (Few people, for example, are likely ever actually to experience a large boa constrictor entwined around them.) This is your fear hierarchy. Example hierarchies for a number of common phobias, shown here and on the next few pages, can be used as models to help you construct your own hierarchy.

A FEAR HIERARCHY: DOG PHOBIA

1. *A huge, vicious dog, a Doberman, leaping at me, snarling and snapping.*
2. *A large dog running up behind me without warning.*
3. *A large dog running toward me, barking.*
4. *A large dog running toward me.*
5. *A dog sitting and watching me at some distance.*
6. *A dog nearby, barking as I walk by, behind a fence.*
7. *A small dog running at me barking.*
8. *A tiny dog, so far away I can barely see it.*
9. *A tiny dog, so far away I can just barely see it, locked in a cage.*

A FEAR HIERARCHY: SNAKE PHOBIA

1. *Letting a large snake, a boa constrictor, wrap itself around my arms, shoulders, and neck.*

2. *Holding a large boa constrictor in my hands.*

3. *Holding a small garter snake.*

4. *Seeing a boa constrictor, loose in the same room with me, crawling toward me.*

5. *Seeing a boa constrictor, loose in the same room with me, but not moving.*

6. *Seeing a small garter snake, loose in the same room with me, but not moving.*

7. *A large boa constrictor, not too far away, in a glass case, coiled and looking at me.*

8. *A small garter snake, locked in a glass case not too far away.*

9. *A small garter snake, locked in a glass case so far away I can hardly see it.*

A FEAR HIERARCHY: HEIGHTS (ACROPHOBIA)

1. *Finding myself standing on a cable slung between the tops of the two tallest buildings in the city, holding my arms out from my sides and looking straight down.*

2. *Going to the top floor of the tallest building in the city, standing right at the edge of a room and looking down to the streets below.*

3. *Going to the top of the same building and looking out horizontally through the window from ten feet away.*

4. *Going to the twentieth floor, midway up the building, and walking to within a yard of an outside window.*

5. *Going to the twentieth floor and walking into a room with a window to the outside.*

6. *Going to the tenth floor and getting close enough to a window to look down at the street.*

7. *Getting close enough to a fifth floor window to look down at the street.*

8. *Climbing the stairs to the fifth floor and looking out the window from across the room.*

9. *Climbing the stairs to the first floor and looking out the window.*

10. *Climbing to the top of a stepladder.*

11. *Standing outside the ground floor of a tall building and looking up at it.*

A FEAR HIERARCHY: OPEN SPACES (AGORAPHOBIA)

1. *Leaving the house, driving some distance to a large shopping center, getting out of the car in the middle of a large, empty parking lot, walking to a large, busy department store, going inside, and walking around.*

2. *Leaving the house, driving to the shopping center, and getting out of the car.*

3. *Leaving the house, walking to a nearby grocery store, and going inside.*

4. *Walking to the grocery store without going inside.*

5. *Walking to the end of the block.*

6. *Walking to the steet in front of the house.*

7. *Walking ten feet away from the front door.*

8. *Stepping outside the front door.*

9. *Going to my front door and opening it.*

10. *Looking out the window of my house.*

A FEAR HIERARCHY: FLYING

1. *Flying in a plane as it suddenly jolts and drops in a steep dive toward the ground.*

2. *Sitting in a plane as it flies high above the ground, looking out the window, and hearing the captain announce how high we are and how fast we're flying.*

3. *Sitting in a plane next to the window as it takes off.*

4. *Sitting in a plane as it taxis rapidly down the runway for takeoff.*

5. *Sitting in a plane as it is slowly towed to the runway.*

6. *Sitting inside a plane that is sitting on the ground with its engines turned off.*

7. *Walking up next to a plane.*

8. *Watching planes take off and land from an airport observation deck.*

9. *Watching a plane take off some miles away.*

10. *Seeing a plane fly past high overhead.*

11. *Hearing the sound of a plane passing by overhead.*

Usually you will need between eight and twelve items in a fear hierarchy. Rarely are less than eight enough, and more than twelve are even less frequently required. You will probably find that you are able to continue to refine each item, to make it even more exactly descriptive of your fears, as you work through the systematic desensitization process in steps 4 and 5. It is unlikely that you will have to change the number of items in your original hierarchy, but it does occasionally happen that an individual finds that there is too big a gap between two successive items in terms of the relative amount of fear that they elicit. In this case, insertion of an intermediate item may be called for.

3. Inducing Self-Relaxation

Now you're almost ready to begin the actual desensitization process itself. Once you've broken the phobic event down into a series of graded experiences and structured these into a fear hierarchy, the next step is relaxation. Refer back to the muscle-tense-and-relax process described in Chapter 2 before continuing on with this chapter. It is fundamental to the self-treatment method set forth here. Do not proceed with the desensitizing process until you know that you can induce a state of relaxation in yourself thoroughly and quickly . . . in a matter of two to three minutes at most. After this step, we henceforth assume that you have thoroughly learned the muscle relaxation procedure.

But knowing how to relax is only part of this process. The other part is knowing how to apply it properly so as to block the fear response. Most people are relaxed at certain times, and some even work diligently at various formal methods designed to achieve deep states of relaxation—such as transcendental meditation or Yoga—but this in no way guarantees that such a state can be readily achieved and maintained *in the phobic scene*. Once you have learned to become thoroughly and quickly relaxed, what you need to learn next is systematic, specific methods for importing that relaxation into those special situations that evoke intense fear in you.

To refresh your memory, we explained in Chapter 2 that the underlying function of relaxation is to put you into a state that is incompatible with high sympathetic arousal, as occurs in states of extreme fear or anger. You cannot be relaxed and terrified at the same time. It's physiologically impossible. In fear states, the blood rushes to the center of your body, adrenaline courses through your vascular system, and your heartbeat and respiration rate soar. In relaxation, your vascular system dilates, blood flows readily to the periphery of your body, you feel warm and content, and your heart rate and breathing are slow, even, and regular. The goal of the next step is to help you learn to supplant your fear response with a relaxation response. When you can do this, your phobia will be under control.

4. Working on the Desensitization Process Itself

Your phobia, whatever its cause, has made you overly fearful of something. Your fear is extreme and serves no practical, adaptive purpose. To counter this, you need to reverse the process by learning how to desensitize yourself to the feared scene.

You are now equipped with the necessary tools to do this—a knowledge of what it is you fear, a hierarchy of increasingly threatening phobic scenes, and the ability to relax thoroughly and quickly. Desensitization is simply the process of combining these in a specific, systematic way so as to change your inappropriately learned fear responses.

The first step is to make yourself comfortable on a bed or reclining chair and work to achieve a state of complete relaxation. Remember to work through the muscle groups individually, as outlined in Chapter 2. Breathe slowly and deeply. Close your eyes, don't speak, and avoid interruptions. If you can, leave the room in semidarkness before you start. Sometimes counting backward slowly from 10, and imagining the numbers themselves as you do so, helps to take the state of relaxation deeper and deeper.

Once you are thoroughly relaxed, begin to envision the first scene in your fear hierarchy, that which has little or no power to induce a phobic fear in you. If your phobia is one of dogs, for example, your first scene may be no more than viewing a very small dog, far away, that is locked in a cage. You may want to tape a description of each scene and play the tape as you relax to help you imagine it. But if you do this, be sure that the motions of operating the tape recorder don't force you to disturb your relaxed posture very much.

As you imagine the scene, try to picture yourself in the phobic situation as vividly as possible. You may even want to start with a test scene, a completely unrelated neutral scene of something else entirely, just to be sure that you are relaxed and that other, unrelated anxieties aren't disturbing your ability to relax and concentrate. It is important to be sure to imagine that you are truly immersed in the scene and that *you are also very relaxed*. These are the key elements in this process.

Not only should you be totally relaxed in real life, as you recline on the couch and focus on this scene, but you should also *imagine* that you are just as relaxed in the fantasied scene that you are concentrating on. Envision yourself as behaving in a calm, relaxed, unruffled way. If you aren't completely relaxed, turn your attention back to your body, and work momentarily on becoming more relaxed by focusing on the areas of tension and by successively tensing, holding, and then relaxing those particular muscle groups.

You may be able both to feel relaxed and to imagine yourself remaining relaxed in the presence of the first scene on the fear hierarchy almost immediately, or it may take a while to achieve. If, after several minutes of relaxed concentration, you find that you cannot achieve a relaxed state or that you can achieve it but can't maintain it, you may have to begin by constructing an item on the fear hierarchy that is even less anxiety provoking than your first one and then starting all over again.

Once you've been able to maintain your relaxation while vividly imagining the lowest item on the hierarchy, stop thinking about that item, and direct your attention back to your state of relaxation. If it is still intact, good. If not, if any muscle areas seem to have tensed up while you were envisioning the phobic scene, work on relaxing them again.

Imagining a pleasant rather than a frightening scene as you work on relaxation can make the process easier. Pick one from your past, one in which you remember feeling especially happy and contented, and bring it to mind during the intervals in the desensitization process when you've turned your attention away from the fear hierarchy and you're concentrating on relaxing your tense muscle areas.

Once you're thoroughly relaxed again, go back to the same item, the first one, the one that you just worked through, and reenvision it once more. This will be the usual pattern in the desensitization process throughout this book: muscle relaxation, followed by a two-minute first exposure to the phobic scene, followed again by one minute of relaxation, then reexposure (two more minutes) to the same scene, and finally relaxation (one minute) once more.[3] To reiterate, the underlying process here is one of gradually learning to substitute relaxation for anxiety through systematic encounter with scenes of the feared experience.

Stay at one level in the hierarchy until you are able to maintain control over relaxation. Then and only then should you allow yourself to proceed to the next scene in the hierarchy. The systematic nature of this approach cannot be overstressed.

You should restrict yourself to working on no more than three or four steps in the fear hierarchy at any one session. A single session shouldn't last for more than thirty to forty

---

[3]You can vary the elapsed times for each step if they don't feel quite right to you, but you should follow this sequence.

minutes; some people find that twenty to thirty minutes is preferable.

You may wish to start by spreading the desensitization sessions out over time, so that you're only holding one or two per week. If, however, you want to make rapid progress, practice more frequently, up to two or three times a day.

To end each session, go back down one level from the highest item you reached on the fear hierarchy, and work through this scene one last time. This same scene, one below the highest you've reached is also where you should begin the next session.

COMMON PROBLEMS WITH THE DESENSITIZATION PROCESS

Bridging. It's normal for people to have problems at first with the desensitization process. A fairly typical one involves difficulty in moving from one item, say number 6 in the hierarchy, to the next highest, number 7. They complain that it is easy for them to stay entirely relaxed while envisioning item 6, but that when they try to move to item 7, they can't seem to picture it vividly without becoming so tense that they're constantly forced to go back to working on relaxation.

The remedy for this is simple. If it happens to you, just construct an intermediate item, or more than one if necessary, as kind of a bridge to help you get smoothly from item 6 to item 7. Your new intermediate step(s) should, of course, be more fear producing than item 6 and less fear producing than item 7. It may take some ingenuity to work out the right sequence of steps, so that the new scene(s) will both function as transitional scenes and will also fit midway between the other two items on the fear hierarchy, and it may mean adjusting some of the other items, on both the upper and lower ends; but this is the most effective way to overcome this type of obstacle.

Starting the Procedure. Occasionally people have trouble beginning the procedure at all. Usually the reason for this is that the lowest item on the fear scale—that which was supposed to have little or no fear-producing potential—actually does have a substantial amount of anxiety associated with it, and the individual hasn't designed a suitably tolerable starting point for the desensitization process. The remedy, then, is simply to reconstruct the bottom end of the scale. Add some scenes of even lower intensity, and try once more to begin the process.

Concentration. You may find that you have trouble holding the scenes in your imagination persistently and vividly. Or that your imagination strays elsewhere. Or that you can imagine the scene but you can't place yourself convincingly in it.

This is a common problem especially if you haven't learned to relax thoroughly. The solution is to work for more complete relaxation and for richer detail in your phobic scenes. First work on deepening your state of relaxation, and see if that doesn't stop your mind from wandering and make it possible for you to hold the scenes quite easily and vividly in your mind. Try talking softly to yourself as you imagine these scenes. Tell yourself that you're in the presence of the phobic situation, moving toward the phobic object, but you're staying relaxed. An example of this kind of internal monologue is included here:

SAMPLE INTERNAL MONOLOGUE
DURING DESENSITIZATION
PROCESS

"... Here I am, approaching this snake, I'm getting closer. It's in its case, coiled up, small, green. I know it's harmless and I'm not getting tense. I'm staying relaxed. My pulse is a little rapid, but there's no panicky feeling. I'm staying relaxed and calm.

"Now I'm near the case. The snake is moving slightly. I can see it slowly sliding across the bottom of the case. When I put my hand out, it senses the motion and watches my hand. I put my hand against the side of the case. Still I remain calm and relaxed. I check my muscles, and they are all calm. I know this is a new experience, remaining relaxed in this situation, but it feels good. I feel that I'm in control of myself. It's exhilarating. My pulse feels normal, my breathing is normal. I don't feel that old fear welling up in me. I'm relaxed and calm."

You may also want to try tape-recording your descriptions of each item to give them more persuasiveness. (Remember not to let the motions of operating the tape recorder disrupt your state of relaxation.)

A third method that can help focus your concentration is to sit down at a desk or table and use the process of writing to help you direct your attention. Begin to imagine the phobic scene, and write out in detail all your thoughts and emotions as you become more engaged in the phobic setting. Do this for each item on the hierarchy. Start at the lowest level, as before, and begin writing. At each level, whenever you feel yourself becoming tense, stop writing, and work on becoming relaxed again. Then, once you're relaxed, go back to writing.

Finally, try including scenes in which you picture yourself showing some hesitation and anxiety as you first approach the phobic object but then overcoming this moment of tension and showing instead a sense of confidence. This is a "coping" response, and it can provide an internal model for the process of transforming your real-life reactions to phobic objects.

As well as inadequate imagery, people occasionally find that the hierarchy is directed at the wrong fear, or that the phobic stimulus hasn't been quite accurately defined yet. The man with the elevator phobia may find that he's actually afraid of the dark, not small, enclosed spaces, and that he's really worried about the possibility that all the lights in the elevator will go out suddenly. If this happens, don't let it disturb you; just work on refocusing the hierarchy so that it reflects your phobia more accurately. The construction of an appropriate fear hierarchy is frequently an evolving process that may take some time to develop completely.

Once you have been able to progress *systematically* in your imagination through all the items on your fear hierarchy while maintaining your state of thorough relaxation, you're well on your way to curing yourself. As a last step in the exercise of imaginal desensitization, try this test. See if you can now imagine an item or two that exceed even the highest one on your fear scale in their ability to evoke anxiety in you. You've probably, up to this point, tended to restrict yourself unconsciously to scenes that are more or less realistic, even including those at the top of your hierarchy. Now try constructing a few that surpass what might realistically occur. Really let yourself go. Stretch your imagination to its limits to come up with these last few items. If, for example, your last item was "Walking down a dark street alone," add one now that reads: "Walking down a dark street at night alone in a big city during a blackout, seeing strangers heading in my direction."

Or perhaps you're a college student with test anxiety. Suppose the most anxiety-producing item you could come up with in your original construction of the fear hierarchy was handling a surprise quiz on assigned reading. Now, once you've been able to master that event, try constructing a new, even more extreme situation, perhaps one in which you imagine that you are highly prepared for an exam but when you read the questions, you suddenly realize that somehow you've studied the wrong material and in fact you hardly know any of the answers at all.

The idea here is that if you can train yourself to relax in *extreme* circumstances, you're far more likely to stay relaxed during the most common real-life situations that you may actually experience. And the more relaxed you can stay in real-life encounters with your phobic object, the more likely it is that you will be able to respond to them effectively, rather than freezing and becoming panicky.

Remember that the critical thing, throughout the process of imaginal desensitization, is *the amount of exposure you have to the phobic object while simultaneously remaining relaxed.* The greater this is, the more likely it is that this step will successfully prepare you for real-life phobic situations. At the end of step 4, you should have worked through the hierarchy several times, until you're confident that you can remain relaxed as you visualize yourself in all levels of the phobic scene.

5. Working on Real-Life Desensitization

The likelihood of your being able to confront calmly actual phobic scenes in real life has now been greatly enhanced by the preceding exercise with imaginary scenes. If you've been able to learn to relax successfully while working through the hierarchy of imaginary phobic events, you will find that the same relaxation response is now much more accessible to you in real-life situations. It won't be a snap—a great deal of diligent application and hard work is still left—but you're well on your way to being in control of your phobia.

Essentially, step 5 helps you transfer the learning experience you've just undergone in step 4 into less predictable and more demanding circumstances. This is a critical step. In many ways, gradual desensitization to actual events is even more effective than imaginary desensitization, as you might well imagine, but it's also harder to achieve, since life is harder to control than your imagination. The mixture of the two, as we present it here, allows you to rehearse relaxation in a secure, predictable setting, then to transport it carefully into the external environment.

You still need to adhere to a gradual, step-by-step approach. We can't overemphasize the importance of this fact. *It is critical that you not exceed your ability to stay relaxed as you move up the fear hierarchy, whether in your imagination or in real-life settings.*

The procedure itself of real-life desensitization is straightforward. Just refer back to the lowest item on your fear hierarchy, and to the extent that you possibly can, duplicate it in real life. Put yourself into the relaxation state, and watch a small dog, placed far away from you and locked in a cage, if that was item 1 on your fear hierarchy. Or, if the lowest item was "Walking through my dark house at night, but with someone else in the house," create that situation for yourself in real life.

However, there is one important difference between imaginal and real-life desensitization. In the latter, you need to be sure always to give yourself an out, a way to retreat if the phobic event suddenly becomes unbearable for you. Don't for example, drive onto a busy freeway at rush hour when you have only fifteen minutes to get to an important appointment if you have a freeway phobia. Instead, pick an uncongested area, a quiet time of day, and a stretch of freeway that has a lot of exit ramps along it within a short distance of the point where you plan on entering. That way, if the experience is too much for you, you won't be trapped right in the middle of it.

A few kinds of phobia are caused by vast, unpredictable events that are hard to duplicate on demand, such as thunder storms or sudden loud noises, but the vast majority are not. It is usually possible, we have found, for people to set up real-life hierarchies that are very much or even exactly like those that they have developed for imaginal desensitization.

In some cases, you may have to vary gradually some element besides the intensity of the phobic object or event. This is usually possible if you remember that it is your *exposure* to the phobic stimulus that needs to be systematically increased. For example, if you have a phobia of loud noises, you usually can't manipulate their relative intensity in real life as easily as you can in your imagination. But you can control your degree of *exposure* to a repeated loud noise, like a gunshot, by changing your proximity to it. Start the desensitization at a distance where you can barely hear it, then gradually move closer.

Or you can work to master a fear of heights by moving up only a few floors at a time in a tall building, or by selecting a very high floor and gradually approaching the window a few feet at a time, making sure that you stop and relax before going on to the next closest place. If you have a fear of crowds, try going to a large public event, like a concert or a sporting competition. This is a situation where there will be lots of people, but where you can control your contact with them by moving into the crowd until you get tense, then withdrawing, relaxing, and trying again. In one case, a lightning phobia was ingeniously treated with the help of a cooperative planetarium. In short, if you can't alter the *intensity* of the phobic event, you can usually alter some other element in it and achieve the same systematic result.

Don't worry about the fact that creating a real-life phobic hierarchy usually means that the phobic event loses some of its unpredictability. It's quite alright if, instead of simply waiting for a large, angry dog to come bounding toward you, you arrange with a friendly dog owner to help you out by placing his dog at closer and closer distances. The unpredictable quality of unexpected phobic triggers is not the major source of their power to cause intense anxiety. Working on a real-life hierarchy, even one that seems artificial and contrived to you, will help you learn to control your phobic reactions.

Remember to maintain as complete a state of relaxation

as you possibly can at all times. You won't be able to stay quite as relaxed as you were when you were reclining comfortably and securely in your own home, but as long as you're more relaxed than tense, you shouldn't let this bother you. The object now isn't exact duplication of the imaginal hierarchy in real life but rather replacement of your fearful reactions with the general one of relaxation that you have just predisposed yourself to produce in the phobic setting.

Again, if you find that you have trouble working through the entire real-life hierarchy, create a bridge between the highest item you can comfortably reach and the one you can't quite manage. Do not proceed up the hierarchy until you feel relaxed at each step. Remain patient and persistent.

If you should happen to encounter unexpectedly a real-life scene that is far higher up the hierarchy than you're prepared to tolerate comfortably and you experience your old panic again, don't get discouraged. This occcasionally happens. It will be difficult, when you are confronted in life with a scene that you haven't yet worked through, to remain relaxed. Don't expect to be able to cope with these levels until you've had the opportunity to work on gradually, systematically desensitizing yourself to them.

However, it's important not to let your fear ever reach an uncontrollable level at any time during the actual desensitization training process itself. As soon as this happens, your therapeutic progress, as measured by your ability to remain relaxed in situations that you previously found highly anxiety provoking, has by definition ceased.

If you find that you anticipate experiencing much more fear in these situations than what you actually feel once you're exposed to them, congratulations. You're making progress; step up your practice. The more you confront a potentially phobic situation and find that your fear is already under control, the more rapidly you will become completely desensitized.

You may, on the other hand, find that progress up the

imaginal hierarchy was quite a bit easier than real-life desensitization. Don't let this discourage you. It's quite common and only means that you need to keep practicing. The more systematically you practice, the sooner you will have vanquished your fears.

Most people choose to practice imaginal and then real-life desensitization in a strictly sequential fashion; only when they know that they can control their phobic reactions at every level of the imaginal hierarchy do they then choose to move on to real-life practice. However, there's nothing wrong with overlapping the two if this appeals to you. Once you've gotten two or three steps up the imaginal hierarchy, try practicing the lowest scene in real life. Then, if it suits you, continue to work on both simultaneously, but always lead by two or three steps with the imaginal hierarchy.

If you have difficulty keeping the practice up, whether it's because you don't have the time or are just having trouble summoning up the necessary self-discipline, try referring to Chapter 3 and working out a contract with yourself along the lines that we describe there.

Finally, if you discover that your anxiety is really quite generalized and this has never been characteristic of you before, be sure that your eating, sleeping, and exercise patterns are sound, and check with your doctor to be sure that there isn't an underlying physiological component, such as hypoglycemia, to your anxiety.

6. Monitoring Your Progress

Be sure, as you work through both imaginal and actual desensitization hierarchies, that you stop frequently and monitor your progress. Keep track, on written forms like that shown in Figure 5.1, of the date you started your self-modification project, how often you've practiced, how far you've gotten, and how much you have left to go.

Self-monitoring is a very effective type of reinforcement. It has been frequently and convincingly demonstrated in a variety of settings that this process works even better than praise as a motivator to encourage completion of the entire desensitization process.

	Imaginal Desensitization	Real-Life Desensitization
Date		
Length of session		
Level reached		
Level session ended on		

Figure 5.1 Desensitization Monitoring Form

7. Practicing Imaginal Flooding

Flooding simply means repeating the top item in your imaginal hierarchy over and over again until your anxiety begins to diminish. If gradual, systematic desensitization is not completely effective in diminishing your fears, consider flooding.

The approach here is very much the same as has already been described. First, be sure that you can effectively relax. Then construct a hierarchy as before. But now, instead of working your way systematically up the scale, lie down, relax, and plunge directly into full-blown, vivid imagery of your worst fear.

Naturally, you can experience strong anxiety during

imaginal flooding, but if you persistently concentrate on relaxing, the anxiety will subside, and you will feel relief as
your control builds. Your avoidance response, which you
can't control, will gradually begin to dissipate if you keep this
up, and your feeling of confidence at your mastery will grow.

It is essential when using flooding to hold the phobic
image in your mind until your fear begins to ebb. If you do
not do this, if you simply allow the imagery to evoke strong
anxiety in you and then give up or turn away from the desensitization process, you won't benefit from flooding. The object is to create an experience of anxiety arousal *followed by
anxiety subsidence.* The more you experience relaxation and
security during exposure to the worst scene you can imagine,
the sooner your fear will diminish.

We do *not* recommend attempting real-life flooding on
your own.

Phobias are distressing problems to live with, and they
can be tremendously disruptive of one's life, but they are
fortunately quite treatable through the processes described
here. However, if you have worked through the steps we've
described in this chapter, if you've practiced them patiently,
systematically, and diligently but there seems to be no improvement in your phobia, seek out a therapist (one who is
experienced in the treatment of phobias) and enlist his or her
assistance.

ANXIETY MANAGEMENT TRAINING

The systematic desensitization process just described is
highly appropriate and effective in treating phobia. But
many individuals suffer from more generalized anxieties
that are not triggered by a specific object or situation, and for
these people a slightly different approach is often more useful than that used to treat phobia.

Anxiety Management Training (AMT) was first developed and described in 1971 by Drs. Richard M. Suinn and Frank Richardson. Quite familiar with the benefits that could be gained from conventional systematic desensitization procedures, Suinn and Richardson became interested in seeing if these processes could be streamlined in such a way as to make them an efficient tool that could be successfully applied to a wider spectrum of anxiety problems.

The result of their clinical research is the AMT procedure, in which repeated visualization of a past anxiety-inducing event takes the place of hierarchy construction. The essence of the AMT process is that it transforms the first psychophysiological signs of anxiety into cues for relaxation, so that instead of becoming increasingly tense and fearful, the individual trained in AMT is able to abort the anxiety cycle automatically, before it can become firmly established, and is able to switch over to a relaxation response instead.

The AMT process can be described in three steps:

1. *Learn the muscle relaxation method explained in Chapter 2.*

2. *Monitor your emotions for one week, and make a list of the external events and the internal thoughts or feelings that immediately precede the onset of anxiety for you.*

3. *Instead of constructing a hierarchy, relax, and then train yourself to replace anxiety with relaxation responses by first visualizing an anxiety-provoking event, then shifting away from this scene to concentrate on relaxation. Repeat this procedure several times.*

1. Learning the PMR Process

Before you begin the AMT process itself, you must know how to induce a state of relaxation in yourself quickly and thoroughly. If you haven't already done so, go back to Chapter 2, and learn the PMR process described there.

2. Monitoring Your Anxiety Responses

The AMT process works in part by first making you much more acutely aware of the earliest signs of the onset of a state of anxiety. You become, through the steps we describe, much more sensitive to both the cues in your daily enviroment that cause you to feel anxiety and to the most subtle first signs of anxiety in your body and in your emotional and mental processes. Many people find that practicing step 2 alone helps a great deal in bringing nebulous and pervasive anxiety responses under control. Suinn and Richardson suggest that it may be that an individual may become

> overwhelmed by his anxiety simply because he has been unaware of it during the early stages of arousal; by the time the anxiety state is noticed, the level of intensity is so high that the client cannot possibly cope with it. Awareness training might help the client to recognize the early signs quickly enough to activate cognitive self-controlling behavior.[4]

In order to refine your understanding of the cues that elicit generalized anxiety responses for you, we recommend that you monitor your anxiety for one week, using a form like that shown in Figure 5.2. Keep track of all events, internal or external, that immediately precede increased anxiety for you. These are not necessarily anxiety *causes*, but they may well be associated with anxiety, as anxiety cues that act to trigger the onset of anxiety in you, probably without your being aware of it. Some common anxiety cues are listed below.

[4]Richard M. Suinn and Frank Richardson, "Anxiety Management Training: A Nonspecific Behavior Therapy Program for Anxiety Control," *Behavior Therapy*, 2 (1971), 507.

TYPICAL ANXIETY CUES

- *Driving.*
- *Being the object of someone else's anger.*
- *Visiting one's parents.*
- *Unresolved family problems.*
- *Not knowing what to do with one's time.*
- *Competing in sports.*
- *Being criticized.*
- *Being short of money.*
- *Going to a party where there will be a lot of strangers.*
- *Being in crowds.*
- *Being alone.*

Date	Time	How I felt (rate anxiety on a scale of 1 to 10)	What happened just before this anxiety in my immediate external environment	What I was thinking or feeling just before I noticed the anxiety

Figure 5.2 AMT Monitoring Form

3. Alternating Anxiety and Relaxation Responses

This step is the heart of the AMT process. Essentially, by first deliberately causing yourself to feel anxious, then halting that process and substituting deliberate relaxation, you gradually train yourself to react automatically to the first signs of anxiety *as though they were a cue for relaxation*. Thus you short-circuit your anxiety response and replace it with a much more useful and enjoyable relaxation response.

The process goes like this. First, lie down or sit in a comfortable chair and relax. Use the PMR method to put yourself in a quiet, peaceful mood. Then begin to envision a scene, drawn from the week of monitoring your anxiety arousal, that you are certain has the power to elicit anxiety in you. Make it vivid and as realistic as possible. Work at this for two to three minutes or until you feel yourself becoming more tense and distressed, which will probably begin to happen immediately. When you know that you have definitely begun to feel anxious, stop, let the scene dissipate, and return to the PMR process. Focus on recreating the condition of quiet, calm lack of arousal that you started with.

Continue doing this on an imaginal basis until you are able to call to mind, without getting anxious, scenes that you know from your week of monitoring were anxiety provoking for you. It takes a certain amount of diligent practice for most people who are anxiety prone to reach this stage, but most do in fact find that they are able to reduce arousal, and there is no need to first construct and then work methodically through an anxiety hierarchy.

Once you've mastered your anxiety responses in imaginal practice, begin to work on AMT training in real-life settings. This is harder, of course, because you don't always have the opportunity to bring an anxiety-inducing event to a halt once it has begun. But you *can* frequently remove yourself from it briefly, take a break, and focus on bringing forth relaxation responses. Remember two things: (1) Relaxation responses learned in imaginal practice *do* transfer to real-life practice quite well; and (2) the more adept you become at recognizing *early* signs of anxiety in yourself, the more effective you will get at shunting them off onto the relaxation circuit. Eventually, if you practice in a methodical, disciplined way, the relaxation override will become automatic. You won't even realize it, but you will notice that you're not feeling as drained and defeated at the end of the day, and that situations you once found difficult to bear have become much easier to handle.

six

Assertion
Expressing Yourself
Effectively

If you can keep your head when all about you
Are losing theirs and blaming it on you,
If you can trust yourself when all men doubt you,
But make allowance for their doubting too;
If you can wait and not be tired by waiting . . .

Or, being hated, don't give way to hating . . .

Yours is the Earth and everything that's in it.

—RUDYARD KIPLING

Susan K. is an attractive, well-educated woman in her mid-twenties who left a promising career in photojournalism a few years ago to marry Dan, an attorney. She's an exceptionally competent, efficient individual with an active social schedule and a number of close friends. Most people find her to be pleasant to be with, intelligent, and agreeable. Until recently, Susan prided herself on the fact that she virtually never raises her voice or lets herself get really angry.

But lately, some cracks have begun to appear in her composure. Her relationship with Dan is becoming strained. And it all seems to be due to a strange new tendency Susan has to explode violently, lashing out at Dan over absurdly trivial disagreements. Dan is concerned and puzzled, but he's also resentful. At these moments, Susan seems to feel deeply hostile toward him, but he honestly doesn't know why.

Let's watch them interact through a series of events in a fairly typical day.

Both Dan and Susan are early risers. Each likes to get out and get whatever they have planned for the day started before too much of the morning has gone by. But because they go their separate ways once they leave the house and because Susan does not work, Dan isn't usually aware of the details of Susan's schedule, and this morning, as on many other mornings, he takes his time about showering and shaving. Susan soon realizes that she probably won't be able to make her first appointment on time. But she doesn't say anything to Dan. She doesn't let him know that she too has to leave early that day.

Dan and Susan have agreed to share the household routines of cleaning, cooking, and maintaining the yard. One of Susan's responsibilities is preparing breakfast for both of them. Because on this day she had planned to leave early, she intended to fix only a very light breakfast, juice and cereal, so that she could spend some extra time getting dressed and made up, but as she pulls the milk out of the refrigerator, Dan calls out from the bedroom, reminding her that she agreed the night before to fix bacon and eggs with hash browns for them this morning. Rather than objecting and pointing out to him that she really cannot afford the extra time just then, Susan quietly puts the milk back and pulls out the frying pan.

By the time Susan gets to her appointment, a meeting with her church group, she is quite late and feels obliged to offer profuse apologies. At this point, she begins to feel upset and slightly depressed by the turn of events in her day. *Nothing seems to be going smoothly for me today,* she thinks. Her suppressed anger, which she isn't fully conscious of, begins to make her think generally critical thoughts about Dan. She vaguely feels that he is responsible for "making" her get off to such a bad start that day.

The church group meeting has been called to plan a large fund-raising dinner. Susan listens attentively to the plans for the banquet, and as she begins to become involved in the discussion, her spirits rise. At one point, as the proposed menu is being considered, she offers a suggestion that she has been thinking about for the previous two days. It's a good suggestion, but she makes it hesitantly, in a low, indistinct tone of voice, and she looks down at the table in front of her as she speaks, rather than directly at the leader of the group.

Before she can even finish her statement, another member of the group, Diane, interrrupts her and makes an entiely different recommendation. The attention of the group shifts to Diane, and the discussion moves on without any acknowledgment of Susan's contribution. She feels a moment of frustration over this indifferent response but then sets it aside and tries to concentrate on the next issue. The thought of raising her recommendation again or replying to Diane's intrusion with a defense of her own suggestion doesn't cross her mind. She feels instinctively that to do this would be pushy. Susan is vaguely annoyed at the way her day has gone up to this point, but she pushes her sense of displeasure out of her mind.

At lunchtime, Susan joins a friend in a busy restaurant. They chat, the waitress brings menus and then returns shortly to take their order. When asked whether she prefers soup or salad, Susan clearly says that she wants salad, and she asks for a glass of water as well. But when the meal is brought, it turns out that the waitress has mistakenly brought Susan the soup. Susan can't quite bring herself to correct the error—she feels that she might be causing a scene. So she sets the soup aside and grumbles to her companion about the poor service. No glass of water appears. When they leave, Susan stops her friend from leaving a tip and again makes a disparaging remark about the quality of the service.

Susan walks out of the restaurant angry. Her friend, who recommended that they eat there, feels embarrassed and uncomfortable. The waitress, unaware of the mix-up in the orders, is disappointed at receiving no tip. Had Susan been able to assert herself more effectively, she and her friend and the waitress would all have gotten what they wanted and could have ended the entire interaction on a much more positive note.

When Susan gets home late that afternoon, she is tired and irritated from the ups and downs of the day. Her schedule has been off since early that morning, so she still has errands and shopping to catch up on. She's about to rush back out to try to do them before dinner when a business associate of Dan calls. Even though she doesn't know him well, he's a very gregarious, talkative person, and he keeps her on the phone for a precious twenty minutes, talking about the last time they were all together, which makes her feel even more tense and pressured. Even though she's feeling acutely uncomfortable, Susan just can't bring herself to be "rude" and explain to him that she's sorry she can't continue their conversation just then because she has some urgent commitments she has to take care of.

By this point, Susan's actual level of suppressed rage and frustration are close to the boiling point. But since she's been holding them back all day, she isn't very clearly aware of this, only that it's been an extremely trying day. She denies these impulses so well and is so compelled to be pleasant that if asked how she was feeling at that moment, she would shrug, smile in a slightly tired way, and say that she was feeling "a little rushed." She is very reluctant to admit to negative emotions.

When Dan gets home that evening, he doesn't notice Susan's mood. She seems normal to him, though perhaps a little more remote than usual and just a bit sharper in her tone of voice and her motions and gestures. Blissful in his ignorance of her true emotional state, he delays helping her set the table and instead returns the call to his business partner. The call lasts for an hour, and Susan slowly feels herself becoming more and more impatient.

As Dan hangs up the phone, he turns to her and asks about his shirts, which she had agreed to pick up but hadn't been able to get to. This time, finally, her pent-up emotions are too much for her. They boil over, and she explodes into accusations and recriminations, stalking off into the bedroom in tears, slamming the door violently behind her.

Dan is, of course, bewildered by her outburst. And angered. But it will be very difficult for either of them to learn anything from her rage, since its very intensity will soon shock Susan into apology. She will try to dismiss the episode by saying something like "I just don't know what got into me," or "It's just that it's been such a lousy day." Out of affection, Dan won't want to force the issue, so nothing will change. Eventually, the strain may become too great for the marriage.

Susan's cycle of (1) submission to innocently unreasonable expectations, followed by (2) the accumulation of her suppressed rage, concluded with (3) her overreaction to trivial misunderstandings will continue unless she can learn to be more appropriately assertive. As things stand now, her responses are badly out of synch with the situations in which she finds herself. Either she's not quick enough in advancing her feelings, particularly the negative ones, or she is far more extremely and vehemently negative than the circumstances properly call for, lashing out at an innocent victim of anger displaced from other frustrations.

Susan's feelings of stifled rage may lead to other problems besides those she is experiencing in her relationship with Dan. She may find that as well as hindering her sense of personal and professional satisfaction, smothering her anger can also lead to somatic disturbances, such as headaches, hypertension, colitis, and ulcers. She may find herself avoiding social gatherings, or drinking too much, or overmedicating herself with tranquilizers.

People like Susan don't let themselves deal effectively with the real issues in their lives. Rather than expressing anger and irritation in a polite but firm manner, they prefer to bypass the threat of any sort of confrontation, even of the most trivial nature, instead of risking the chance that a conflict may arise. They tend to rationalize this pathological avoidance behavior by telling themselves that the disagreements are too trivial and unimportant to waste time over. But anger doesn't always just go away. It often builds and builds until it has to find an escape valve. By that time, the nonassertive individual is close to flash point, and then any argument, even the most insignificant, can touch off a monumentally inappropriate explosion.

Assertion is the proper balance between two unhealthy extremes: submissiveness and aggressiveness. Being overly submissive, as the foregoing example shows, means that you comply too readily in your actions and your words with the preferences of others. You may even seek out, somewhat unconsciously, clues to what others are thinking, so that you can conform to what they seem to want, thus preempting the anger that you fear will arise from even the smallest disagreements.

Submissiveness is far more than the normal acquiescence that goes along with the attempt to be a reasonable, civilized human being. It's a compulsion to please, coupled with a technique of yielding quickly to anyone else's preferences, of tacitly implying that your rights, thoughts, desires, and feelings are somehow not quite as valid as anyone else's.

Nonassertive people frequently excuse their overly compliant behavior by pointing out, with some bitterness, that the world would be a much better place to live if we were all "nicer" to one another. This is undeniably true. But, as with everything else, there is an appropriate time and place for being nice. To be accommodating and thoughtful to *everyone*, regardless of the circumstances, is to ask for trouble, since the unfortunate truth is that we do not live in a world where everyone has his or her fellow human being's best interests at heart. There are plenty of people around who are only too happy to take advantage of someone else— economically, politically, emotionally, sexually—if they see an opportunity to do so. Not only that, but it takes a modicum of assertiveness just to get things accomplished in this world. If we all hung back, waiting for someone else to make a move, state a preference, reach a decision, nothing would get done.

On the other hand, Diane, who interrupted Susan at the church meeting, may be acting in an overly aggressive manner. Aggressiveness, as unhealthy an extreme as submissiveness, is a state of borderline hostility involving a kind of combativeness that seems almost to invite conflict. Aggressive behavior is offensive—it tramples on the rights and feelings of others—and is often indulged in by childish and insecure people who achieve positions of moderate power. Anger in these individuals is often very personalized, expressed at any available victim, often in antagonistic and belittling terms. People who indulge in overly aggressive interpersonal transactions are like petty tyrants, emotional bullies who act out of their own feelings of suppressed, unacknowledged rage.

Balanced, reasonable assertiveness is, very simply, the relaxed, confident, and appropriate expression of an emotion or thought, positive or negative. According to Arnold A. Lazarus, a well-known psychologist, it also means being able to say no; being able to start, stop, and maintain a conversation; and being able to make requests and ask for favors.[1] The appropriately assertive individual speaks plainly and audibly, without prolonged hesitation or stammering. He or she invites open, candid communication by looking directly at the person being addressed, by adopting a relaxed and open posture, and by letting feelings show in gestures, in the tone of voice, and in facial expressions. He or she tends to move toward, rather than away from, the other person.

Being effectively assertive does *not* mean *always* expressing every feeling that can be detected at any single point in time. Quite the opposite: assertion can involve actively suppressing inappropriate and exaggerated emotional responses for the sake of getting what you want out of an interaction with someone else.

How assertive are you? Do you feel that you generally get what you want in your interactions with others? Do you

---

[1] Arnold A. Lazarus, "On Assertive Behavior: A Brief Note," *Behavior Therapy*, 4 (1973), 697–699.

feel you consistently give more than you get? Or do you feel that you get what you want but at the price of consistently alienating those you deal with?

If you're not quite comfortable with your level of inter-personal effectiveness, try taking Test 6.1 to check your re-sponses to a number of situations that nonassertive people often find difficult to handle.

Test 6.1 How Submissive Are You?

	Never	Rarely	Some-times	Usually
I would avoid rebuking someone who butted into a line in front of me.				
I consider myself to be shy.				
I don't think people make an effort to listen to what I'm saying.				
I don't like to criticize friends.				
I don't like to say no.				
I find it hard to hang up on sales people who call to sell me something.				
I find it hard to turn down requests for money from panhandlers on the street.				
I feel uncomfortable when I have to return things to the store.				
I don't like to complain about food or service in restaurants.				
I find myself saying "I'm sorry."				
I believe people's feelings are easily hurt.				

Test 6.1 (continued)

	Never	Rarely	Some-times	Usually
I try to qualify my statements so that I won't sound offensively dogmatic.				
I don't like to ask friends for favors.				
I feel uncomfortable asking people to be quiet in theaters.				
I have trouble telling people who are sexually attracted to me to leave me alone.				
I tend to like to be told what to do.				
I try to avoid arguments.				
I find it a strain to talk to people I've just met.				
I get very nervous in job interviews.				
I don't like to be the center of attention in public places.				
I don't like to feel foolish.				
I am afraid to get very mad.				
When I do get mad, I quiver like a leaf and become speechless.				
I am reluctant to ask people who owe me money to pay it back.				
I don't like to go into a grocery store or restaurant without buying something.				
I feel uncomfortable ending a conversation.				

Test 6.1 *(continued)*

	Never	Rarely	Some-times	Usually
I feel compelled to answer the doorbell/phone.				
I don't like to tell people who call at inconvenient times to call back later.				
I feel nervous about disagreeing with someone.				
I find it hard to tell friends and loved ones that I care for them.				
I feel compelled to try to please people.				
I don't like to interfere with other people's plans, even if they are quite inconvenient for me.				
I believe in trying to be nice.				
I feel uncomfortable when people compliment me or give me presents.				
I don't like to speak up if I'm passed over or ignored by a salesclerk.				
I don't like to complain about the service in a store, a bank, etc.				
I don't mind if other people interrupt me.				
I don't like to make phone calls to strangers.				
I don't like to feel that I'm asking stupid questions.				

	Never	Rarely	Some-times	Usually
I don't like to talk about myself or my accomplishments.				
I feel uncomfortable asking people to change their habits.				
I'm nervous when there's a lull in the conversation.				
I don't like to point it out when someone is being highly unfair.				
It's hard for me to make decisions.				
I get angry over trivial things.				
I find it difficult to maintain eye contact in a conversation.				
I find it particularly difficult to express and defend my viewpoint when I find myself in disagreement with a friend.				
I tend to get overcommitted in my work because I find it hard to decline requests from my colleagues and superiors.				

The process of becoming more effective in interpersonal exchanges really means being able to get what you want from others, which you can't do if you either alienate people or tend to be ignored by them. To take the first step in this process, you may have to be willing to make some changes in your own behavior, especially in the way you go about interacting with the people around you.

HOW TO BECOME MORE ASSERTIVE: THE TREATMENT PACKAGE

Learning to be more assertive means working through these steps:

1. *Identify your problem areas—circumstances in which you have trouble being assertive.*
2. *Arrange the situations in step 1 into a hierarchy, from the least to the most troublesome.*
3. *Practice relaxation training.*
4. *Work on imaginal rehearsal.*
5. *Work on role-playing rehearsal and modeling.*
6. *Employ real-life application.*
7. *Learn when to give in.*

1. Identifying Problem Areas

Most people who have problems with assertion find that these problems pertain to fairly specific settings. For example, they may have no difficulty expressing themselves effectively to their spouse but find it nearly impossible to refuse unreasonable requests from a superior at work. Susan is an unusual case in this regard, because her nonassertiveness gives her trouble in all phases of her life.

If you're not clear about which areas of your life are giving you trouble with assertiveness, try these techniques.

First, just look back at a recent event that you found particularly upsetting, one in which you didn't feel that you got what you wanted or where someone else took advantage of you in some way. Ask yourself whether you were able to deal with the real issue while the interaction was taking place. Or did you leave with that resentful feeling that Diderot called *l'esprit de l'escalier*, the spirit of the staircase, the thought of what you "should have said" that hits you on your way out the door and down the stairs after you've just come off second best in an emotional confrontation? This is a certain clue that you weren't able to get at what was specifically bothering you, that you somehow skirted around the problem instead of saying what it was that you wanted, how you wanted the situation to be different.

Second, if the first technique doesn't pinpoint your nonassertive trouble spots, you need to keep a continuous record of a week or so of your daily activities, specifically those that consistently make you feel angry, frustrated, and dejected. Use a chart similar to that shown in Figure 6.1. This will show you where you were, what took place, what your response was, and what you think it should have been. This last category—what you should have done or said—is especially important, since this will provide the basis for developing ways to become more effective at getting what you want out of these same situations in the future. And in fact, a number of careful studies have demonstrated that most nonassertive people *do* have the skills required to make a more effective response in situations that give them trouble, but they don't know how to go about applying them. Nonassertiveness tends to be a matter of inexperience, not ignorance or intrinsic inability.

If you keep this record for a week or two, patterns of ineffective response will become quite obvious; you'll begin to see clearly what kinds of interactions give you the most trouble with nonassertiveness.

Figure 6.1 Assertiveness Record

Date	Time	Place	Interaction /Event	What the Other Person Said/Did	What You Said/Did	How You Felt	What You Wish You'd Said/Done

2. Arranging the Hierarchy of Nonassertive Interactions

Once you know which specific situations in your life routinely tend to infuriate yet intimidate you, the next step is to arrange these into a hierarchy. Put those that are least troublesome at the bottom of the list and those that are most troublesome at the top. A typical list might look like this:

1. *Responding to criticism at work.*
2. *Getting the attention of salesclerks.*
3. *Refusing requests to work overtime.*
4. *Starting conversations with strangers at parties.*

As you begin, in subsequent steps, to work on changing your behavior in these targeted settings, you may at first find that people who know you and who are used to your customary nonassertive patterns of behavior react with surprise, confusion, and perhaps even anger and sarcasm as you move from being submissive to becoming assertive. Any time you begin, without much explanation or warning, to behave differently around people who know you well, you're going to get reactions like these for a while, largely because we're all more predictable than we might like to think. It doesn't matter what the difference in your behavior is; as long as you're breaking away from your usual patterns, your friends, acquaintances, and family will be startled at first. Even the simplest of differences, such as ordering a soft drink instead of something alcoholic or a salad instead of a large, calorie-laden dinner, can put acquaintances on the defensive, especially if they're a little insecure about their own habits or assertive capabilities.

Don't let these reactions discourage you. Be prepared for them. In the long run, your friends and relatives will get used to your new behavior, and you will become more effective; so don't cave in. It also often happens that overly nonassertive people tend to group together, perhaps because they share a common fear that if they voice their feelings and stick up for their rights, they will inevitably be punished in some mysterious way for doing so. By becoming more assertive yourself, you may be triggering this kind of defensive fear in some of your acquaintances.

Freud first suggested that nonassertive individuals may fear that acting more directly means that their impulses are getting out of control, that they are becoming too aggressive, and that this may bring about retributive punishment. And it is true that people who are habitually submissive can go overboard when they first practice assertiveness; they can become overly blunt and abrasive in their efforts to be more effective. Remember, as we said earlier, people respond to your emotional state, to *how* you say what you say, more than to the content of what you say. So, as we outline the steps below, keep in mind that the important thing is to learn how to express your wishes and your point of view firmly, confidently, and politely, but not aggressively. An overly aggressive or bullying tone of voice or manner of behaving is self-defeating. It only tends to elicit an equally aggressive or defensive reaction from others.

Though the people who know you well may be initially surprised at your change in manner, your true friends will respond positvely to your own sense of greater pleasure in becoming more effective and will be quite supportive. Also, they will find you more interesting and easier to get along with, because they will sense that you're more comfortable with saying what's on your mind, how you feel, what you want and don't want, what you like and don't like. Certainly Susan's husband, for example, would much rather hear that she, too, needs to leave early than face her overreactive and apparently irrational outbursts.

3. Practicing Relaxation Training

By now, you should be a veteran of the relaxation procedure set forth in Chapter 2. It is as important a basis for the change procedures to increase your assertiveness as it is for those described in any other chapter in *Spare the Couch*. Why? Because in order to behave the way you want to in these targeted situations, and to say the things you want to be able to say, you're going to have to be able to stay composed and alert. If you let yourself become angry and tense in one of these situations, that's exactly what you will produce in the other person—tension and anger. Coupled with the rehearsal and modeling techniques of the next step, relaxation will help you manage the tendency to get angry that can undermine your effectiveness in these settings. So, if you have not yet learned the relaxation procedures set forth in Chapter 2, do so now before going on to step 4.

4. Working on Imaginal Rehearsal

Now select the lowest event on your hierarchy, refer to the assertiveness records that you've been keeping to refresh your memory on the kinds of responses that you would prefer to have in this situation, and then create a state of thorough relaxation in yourself. Using the material that you've recorded, run through in your imagination, step by step, precisely how you would like to be able to behave in this setting. Carefully specify the exact words you would like to use, the kind and level of emotion you would like to allow yourself to feel, how relaxed you would like to be, how alert you would like to be, and the degree of combined friendliness and firmness you would like to be able to express. Focus on the mixture of words and actions that you believe would best serve to create just the right type of responsiveness in the other people involved in this hypothetical scene. Imagine the scene as vividly as possible; try to remain as relaxed as possible.

The process of constructing a hierarchy of nonassertive scenes and then envisioning them vividly while remaining relaxed is, as you will probably have recognized, similar to the process of systematic desensitization, which we described in the previous chapter as it is used for treating phobia. There certainly are clear-cut parallels between desensitization and the process described here, and you may want to refer to Chapter 5 to reacquaint yourself with many of the procedural details of hierarchy construction and the role of relaxation in imaginal exercises. However, the imaginal process described in this chapter is not strictly equivalent to desensitization; the object here is the creation and rehearsal of a pattern of behavior to be used as a model in problematic nonassertive settings. In desensitization training, the role of imaginal exercises is more of control rather than rehearsal. The two are very close, of course, but the desensitization scenes are used to allow a phobic person to learn to substitute relaxation for panic *gradually*. In assertiveness training, they are used, in conjunction with relaxation, to allow a nonassertive individual an opportunity to construct, rehearse, and master coping responses. In short, imaginal scenes are used *remedially* in the former case, *instructively* in the latter.

As we explained in Chapter 5, it helps in imaginal training to actually say your lines out loud or even to tape them or write them out. The idea here is not that you're programming yourself with automatic phrases that you will memorize and then produce on cue in the stressful setting itself, but that if you can practice in advance while also remaining calm, you will be less likely to lose track of your own naturally assertive responses when you're actually involved in the real-life setting.

5. Working on Role-Playing Rehearsal and Modeling

Ideally, the process of developing effective responses falls into three discrete steps, which you can follow either in a strictly sequential fashion or can overlap to a great extent. The first step is imaginal rehearsal; the second is actual role playing and modeling with a friend; and the third, which we describe next, is real-life application. If you choose to practice these in an overlapping manner, first begin with step 4, imaginal practice. Then, once you're well into step 4 and you've moved up the nonassertive hierarchy, begin also including some actual role-playing rehearsal and modeling of the lowest nonassertive scene in your hierarchy. Finally, as you near completion of imaginal practice for all nonassertive scenes and you're well along with step 5, begin trying to apply in real-life settings the responses you've acquired for the lowest scene on the hierarchy. In other words, if you overlap the three steps that constitute an ideal assertiveness training routine, make sure that you stagger the starting points for each stage.

You needn't feel obliged to follow the ideal three-stage process strictly, particularly if you don't have a partner to role play and rehearse with, or if you feel quite confident of your ability to move into real-life settings without first working through *both* imaginal and role-playing stages. The important point is to construct systematic ways to handle these problematic situations *before* they suddenly confront you and to work through them in advance so that you're equipped to respond more effectively to them.

For step 5, ask a friend to help you by playing the role of the other person as you rehearse your part. Write out a script if it seems to be called for, work your way through it, and focus on letting yourself experience only those emotions that will help you get what you want out of the hierarchy scene that you're practicing.

Always remember to stay at each level in the hierarchy until you feel completely comfortable with it. Whether you're working on an imagined, role-playing, or real-life level, don't move up the hierarchy until you've mastered your tendency to become overly submissive in lower level scenes. These procedures must be followed *systematically* for them to work.

If, as you're working through the practice session either by yourself or with a friend, you reach a point where you begin to feel uncontrollably anxious or blocked up, go back, rewrite the script, and start over again.

It's important to begin with as simple and manageable a setting as possible. For example, it's usually easier to practice what you want to say to your boss when asking for a raise than it is to rehearse what you will do when someone has just stolen your parking space, because your boss's responses are more predictable than a stranger's, and your part of the interaction with him or her is more subject to your control.

A friend cannot only help you role play but can also be quite useful as a model in actual and assertive scenes, to demonstrate for you the more appropriately assertive response that you want to learn. Select a setting that simulates one that you've practiced thoroughly with imaginal and role-playing techniques; then closely observe your partner as he or she behaves in the way you would prefer. Modeling is a technique with wide applicability; it can be used to help refine your imaginal and role-playing scenes and procedures, and it can be used as a bridge to real-life practice on your own.

The goal in every rehearsal setting is to reach a point where you feel that you are able calmly and precisely to say to the other person what you want to say—how you feel, what you think, and what you want from them. This way, you won't find yourself leaving interpersonal encounters feeling that there were things you needed and wanted to say but couldn't due to your own inhibitions.

6. Employing Real-Life Application

Once you feel that you've adequately rehearsed a particular scene in your hierarchy, whether through imaginal training, role playing, or modeling, begin applying your new responses in a real-life setting. If the scene is one that involves initiating conversations with strangers in social settings, you will have already rehearsed a number of alternative strategies for doing just that before you actually confront the real-life situation. You will have gone over and acted out precisely the kinds of things you want to say, how you want to feel, and the kinds of responses that you want to generate in another person. All this work will have prepared you for behaving effectively in the setting that you have identified as problematic for you. And you will find that your rehearsal responses *do* carry over into real-life situations. You will also find that practicing relaxation will have helped you to learn to remain calm and alert in these settings, so you will be able to draw more and more heavily on your own natural responses as you engage new acquaintances in conversation.

When you succeed in real-life application, give yourself credit. Even small changes are very significant when compared with years of giving in to powerful habits of submissiveness. Also, be prepared for occasional failures. Don't try to accomplish everything at once. You may find that it is now relatively easy for you to initiate conversations but that it suddenly has become harder for you to terminate them assertively and graciously. Don't let this frustrate you. You've added one new capability to your assertiveness repertoire— that of knowing how to strike up a conversation in a social setting—now all you need to do is apply exactly the same practices to learning yet another skill—ending them pleasantly. First successes will be followed by second, third, and fourth successes, until patterns of assertiveness have become second nature to you.

It's also good practice to begin to generalize from the specific scene. For example, if you have trouble talking to a stranger at a party, you probably also have difficulty talking to strangers in other settings. The degree of difficulty will vary with the situation, but chances are good that the essential theme of a nonassertiveness problem will appear across a wide spectrum of settings in the submissive individual's life. So begin to work on carrying your newfound skills into other settings as well; begin to change the overall way in which you habitually interact with strangers. Begin initiating contacts with people you don't know in a variety of new circumstances. For example:

- *Say hello to the checker in the grocery store, and chat with him or her briefly.*
- *Talk to the clerk in the bank for a moment or two.*
- *Visit an open house and converse with the real estate agent there about it.*
- *Price a new car in a sales showroom and spend some time discussing it with the salesperson.*
- *Go to a department store and shop for a new garment, engaging the clerk in conversation as you do so.*
- *Speak to the person next to you on the bus or subway.*
- *When you stop for gas, ask about a specific repair job for your car and then extend the conversation into more general areas.*
- *Respond to an appropriate employment ad in the paper, and learn all you can about the job from the person who answers the call.*

Remember as you work through the specific levels of the hierarchy that one of the most effective kinds of reinforcement, aside from the glow of successful change, is keeping very close track of your progress. This will give you a tangible record of your rate of improvement and will provide solid proof that the change is actually occurring.

Consider using a chart like that shown in Figure 6.2. The chart is divided into four zones, each representing a specific scene on this individual's assertiveness hierarchy. The numbers along the bottom of the chart represent days; each scene was practiced for one week before this person moved on to the next level in the hierarchy. Along the left side of the chart, she set up a scale showing the number of times each day that she successfully completed her real-life practice. As you can see, the lines drawn for each week represent steady improvement.

7. *Learning When to Give In*

As a properly assertive person, you will find that your behavior produces the desired response in others with minimum wasted motion, because you know where you stand, so do other people, and as a result, you then learn where they stand also. Communication is clear. Assertiveness cuts through ambiguity and hesitation between people. Definite, candid statements have the effect of requiring others to be more definite and exact in their interactions with you.

Fewer and fewer of your actions or statements will go unnoticed if you learn to deliver them forthrightly. People are far more likely to ignore and isolate submissive or aggressive individuals than firm, polite, explicit, yet relaxed individuals.

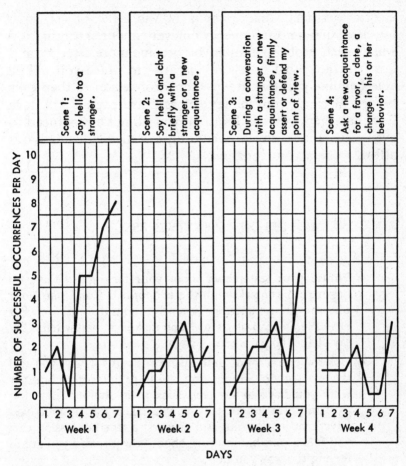

Figure 6.2 Progress Chart for Monitoring Assertive Behavior

However, do use some discretion in selecting the occasions for employing your strategies for more assertiveness. Try to assess in advance just how effective you think you can be—don't waste time and energy fighting a "no-win" situation. Don't be overly insistent if you're dealing with a particularly upset or distressed individual or if the annoyance is a very trivial one. Learn to give in to irrelevancies; this is an effectiveness tactic that can help you win the war by refusing to waste your time and energy on every minor skirmish. You will, in fact, probably find as you become more assertive and less frustrated that occasions will arise in which you will be able genuinely to tolerate greater inconveniences than ever before. Because your powers of assertive coping will have been enlarged, you will find that you do not always need to avail yourself of them. Authentically assertive individuals can afford to be accommodating.

SIX GENERAL TIPS ON ASSERTIVENESS

- Phrase your statements about your feelings so that you begin your remarks with the pronoun I. Don't start your phrase with the word *you*; it tends to sound accusatory. For example, instead of saying "You make me mad when . . . ," say "I feel angry when. . . ."

- Don't spend a lot of time giving reasons for why you feel the way you do. Simply jump ahead to the bottom line, say what you have to say, and stick to it. Rationalizing and explaining at length why you've taken the position you have is at best boring and at worst a tacit confession that you feel somewhat insecure about how justified you are in feeling the way you do.

- Move in closer to the person you're addressing. It will give you a greater sense of control over the situation.

- When you want to decline a request, do so directly but politely. Don't apologize, don't make excuses. Simply say "No, thank you." If the other person's response is one of enticement, cajolery, criticism, appeal to guilt, or sarcasm, just repeat your negative firmly until you've made your point. Repeating the refusal over and over, a systematic skill called "broken record," works like a charm. Ever been accosted by those so-called religious groups who persistently solicit your donation on the street? Simply say "Please leave me alone," repeatedly and emphatically until they do.

- Tell yourself that it's alright to fail. Everyone does, sooner or later. The important thing is to learn how to get what you want from your interactions with others, and you can't do that if your own emotions and desires are constantly being subordinated to theirs. You have a responsibility to yourself first, not to a mythical code of behavior designed to impress upon everyone how "nice" you are.

- Remind yourself of the price you pay for being inadequately assertive. If you deny small amounts of irritation, they accumulate until you're at an emotional flash point, and the next trivial incident will set you off like a barrel of gasoline. And it probably won't have anything to do with the real issue that you're upset about. You will eventually realize that your anger is displaced from elsewhere, that you're overreacting and being unfair, and this will just make you feel guilty. At the very least, submissiveness means missing a host of opportunities in life and tolerating greater and greater encroachments on your personal rights. It means withdrawal, hurt feelings, depression, lost relationships, dependency, and isolation—all of which are entirely unnecessary.

Remember our pervasively submissive friend Susan? It didn't take her long to realize what was wrong with her ways of interacting with others, especially once she began to read some of the literature that is available today on nonassertiveness and other self-imposed patterns of problematic behavior. A thoughtful friend gave her a popular book on learning to change and urged her to read it, and Susan's own native intelligence and determination took over from there.

Having read the book and examined her interpersonal difficulties at length, Susan acknowledged that a large part of her episodic rages was due to her own inability to speak up for herself, to get what she wanted when she wanted it. It took her some time to come to grips with the idea that it wasn't helping her to be compulsively nice, and that she didn't have to conform rigidly to a code of behavior that she learned as a child.

"Standing up for myself was scary at first," she says, "but after a few weeks the change felt good, really good. I surprised myself at how quickly I gave up the secret martyr role I was playing without even knowing it. But it took work, lots of careful, deliberate, thoroughly practiced trials and errors. And I'm still working on assertiveness . . . I probably always will be."

Once Susan sat down and explained to Dan what she thought she was doing wrong and how she wanted to change it, he was fully supportive of her. He's as delighted as she is with her new skills and very proud of her, too.

seven

Obsessive Thinking and Compulsive Behavior
Managing Useless Rituals

> We may say that . . . a compulsion neurosis [is] a caricature of religion.
>
> —SIGMUND FREUD

Jane K. is in her mid-fifties. She's divorced, and she has one grown daughter. She has had the same job, working as a dentist's office manager and lab assistant, for the last twelve years.

Jane is abnormally compulsive. She engages in repetitive, ritualistic actions that serve no apparent rational purpose but about which she feels extremely tense if she doesn't complete. For example, she checks her stove at least half a dozen times before she can feel comfortable about leaving the house. She tells herself that she's afraid the gas won't be turned off and that it will cause a fire, but she admits that one, or at most two, checks would be plenty to see that it was off. She also checks all the electrical outlets in the house before she goes to bed. If the plugs are not actually pulled out of the wall sockets and placed carefully on the floor, Jane can't get to sleep.

Jane balances and rebalances her checkbook each time she writes a check. When she goes out, she feels compelled to check, double-check, and then check again the doors and windows of her house to be sure that they are securely closed, even it she's only planning to be gone for ten minutes.

Jane also takes her compulsiveness to work with her. The furniture and instruments in the office must be in specific locations, or she isn't able to continue with the job at hand. All the accounts must be brought up to date at the end of each day, or she can't bring herself to go home. Jane even finds that some patients infuriate her because they seem so careless and disorganized; some are always late, some never pay on time, a few even forget to mail back the portion of the billing statement that she uses to post the day's receipts in the account book. Once or twice, her frustration with the patients has made her edgy and irritable enough to merit a reprimand from her employer, but on the whole, her compulsiveness stands her in good stead in the office, since it tends most of the time to translate into efficiency and neatness.

Jane has few friends, no hobbies, and almost never takes time off from work. The rare vacation she takes is as compulsively organized as the rest of her life. If she finds herself with nothing to do, even on a beautiful beach in Hawaii, she becomes agitated and nervous.

It's in Jane's personal life that her compulsiveness really takes its toll. She is literally so compulsive that she only has time to work, eat, sleep, and comply with compulsive rituals.

Jane is quite aware that her compulsive behavior is irrational and that she really has no control over it. She herself thinks of it as an addiction, but she knows that the anxiety she feels if she doesn't comply with her rituals is so strong that it is literally irresistible. She states, for instance, that she just can't drive away from the house unless she has first locked the front door, shaken it twice, paused, then twice more, paused again, and then finally twice more. Once should be plenty, she agrees, but it just isn't, and there doesn't seem to be anything she can do about it.

Most of us have found ourselves from time to time dwelling incessantly on a phrase, a thought, even a song or an advertising jingle that keeps running through our mind over and over again. Or we catch ourselves following a ritualized pattern of action, like reading all the signs we pass on the highway. We usually think little of these habitual routines, dismissing them as the product of boredom or maybe even acknowledging to ourselves that they may be very mild defense mechanisms, designed to ward off larger problems by diverting our attention to something more easily managed.

And it is true that these repetitive, magical kinds of thoughts and actions are frequently no more than a minor annoyance, easily dispelled when they become too intrusive or embarrassing. For most of us, most of the time, they don't last very long, and few of us would be inclined to take them very seriously. In fact, they can even serve a moderately benign purpose, helping us maintain a sense of control, particularly in times of stress, by focusing our attention on something trivial, thus quieting our anxieties in the same way that rubbing a worry bead over and over again can calm some people. Other obsessive habits may serve as mnemonic devices to help us remember something, such as when we subvocally chant "milk, apples, paper towels, bread, coffee" as we drive to the store.

But they can get out of hand. Rather than remaining means to any number of useful minor purposes, they can become ends in themselves, like any other addiction. All our energy and attention can become absorbed in complying with the demands of these compulsive actions and obsessive patterns of thought. Under stress, we are particularly liable to become more compulsive and more obsessive. We may eat more, drink more, smoke more cigarettes, and work harder with a kind of demanding, repetitive intensity, all as a response to the larger anxieties that we have trouble controlling.

Parents of very small children, for example, not infrequently find themselves entertaining unwelcome thoughts of harming their children. This is an appalling kind of fantasy for a new parent to have, of course, especially since it can be a very persistent one, which keeps returning again and again. They know consciously that they love their children and mean only to protect and nurture them, but anxiety over living up to serious parental responsibilities can take this horrifying form; not a few new parents have found themselves wondering if their obsessive fantasies indicate some kind of mental breakdown.

Others experience equally frightening obsessive images of a graphically aggressive or sexual nature. Exhibitionists feel an overwhelming compulsion to expose their genitals. Other individuals have reported imagining their bodies covered with excrement or eating filth off the sidewalk. And these are understandably highly intrusive patterns of thought.

Unfortunately, even the most minor and mundane compulsions can develop into elaborate, prolonged rituals with little or no apparent purpose. Two of the more common, for example—contamination and checking rituals—involve endless hand washing, cleaning, vacuuming, walking around the house in a certain pattern at certain times of day, inspecting furniture, clothing, appliances in patterned ways; perhaps adjusting their positions, or picking a garment up and shaking it, often a certain number of times in a set number of directions.

When such rituals—whether they involve compulsive actions or obsessive, ruminative thought patterns—become this time-consuming and exhausting, they can seriously interfere with their victims' domestic and vocational responsibilities. For example, people afflicted with the obsessive fear of causing an automobile accident often simply have to give up driving completely. There is no other way for them to assuage their anxieties. Others may develop compulsive facial tics, stammers, or other body motions that disrupt normal social interaction.

Underlying both the obsessive thought and its visible counterpart, the compulsive action, is a struggle for control over anxiety. The obsessive-compulsive person is possessed with the fear of *not*—of not complying with the ritualistic action or thinking through the obsessive routine. Though rational and clearheaded, he or she is emotionally convinced that terrible consequences will ensue unless the rituals of thought and action are performed. In the mind of the obsessive-compulsive person, they serve an almost magical purpose, like spells or incantations to ward off evil.

Like phobias, compulsions and obsessions stem from exaggerated and irrational anxiety. Unlike phobias, in which the anxiety is triggered by the thought of *approaching* or encountering the phobic object, the anxiety of obsessive-compulsiveness is caused by the thought of *not* engaging in the ritualistic thought or action. It is the *failure* to engage in the ritual that leads to anxiety. If Jane leaves her car without first checking the locks a certain number of times, she will find herself distracted with worry for the rest of the day, fearing that it will be broken into, perhaps stolen.

This is the payoff in the mind of the obsessive-compulsive person for continuing to devote the time to these rituals: he or she knows that doing so decreases the foreboding sense of worry and concern. And because a decrease in anxiety is an emphatically positive experience, it encourages continued compliance with the compulsion or obsession.

But this payoff is good only for the very short run. Anxiety builds up again; the need to ward off imagined disasters returns, and so inevitably does the need to repeat the compulsive action or the obsessive thought pattern. The process is an addictive cycle: anxiety and high arousal—followed by an urgent need for relief—followed by compliance with the obsessive-compulsive ritual—then short-term relief—gradually returning anxiety—and so on. Once this cycle has become firmly entrenched, it is very difficult to break up.

Over the long run, complying with obsessive-compulsive rituals brings negative results. As with Jane, one has less and less time to oneself. The compulsion or obsession becomes a cancer, consuming all one's available attention and energy. As it grows out of control, it becomes extremely exhausting. Because others become impatient with the disruptions that they are forced to tolerate, they withdraw from the compulsive individual, leaving him or her increasingly isolated.

Compulsions and obsessions are quite common. At the lower end of the spectrum, they are often nothing more than harmless annoyances. At the other end, however, they can become serious, unmanageable problems. Examine the diagnostic sheets in Test 7.1 if you feel that you may be more obsessive-compulsive than you would like to be. If your responses fall along the right-hand column, you may want to set up a self-treatment program along the lines we describe.

Test 7.1 How Obsessive-Compulsive Are You?

	Never	Rarely	Some-times	Usually
I have found myself needing to check repeatedly to see if the stove is off, the door is locked, the windows are closed, etc.				
I find that jingles from radio and TV run through my mind repeatedly.				
I make lists and follow them, crossing things off as I complete them.				
I wash my hands repeatedly.				
I clean the house repeatedly.				
I dislike using public bathrooms.				
I dislike touching banisters on public escalators and stairways.				

Test 7.1 *(continued)*

	Never	Rarely	Some-times	Usually
I keep the sharp knives safely shut up in a drawer.				
I find that alien, unwanted images come to mind.				
I'm tempted to shock people I know by shouting obscenities or saying something shocking.				
I tend to like to do things the same way.				
I put things away if I'm not using them.				
I follow recipes exactly when I cook.				
I like a clean, orderly desk top.				
I like to keep my possessions neatly stored.				
I like to follow a routine daily schedule.				
I check the alarm clock repeatedly before falling asleep.				
I keep my wristwatch tightly wound.				
I rinse the laundry repeatedly to get the soap out.				
I arrange the money in my wallet by descending denomination, all facing the same way.				
I set specific goals, quotas, and deadlines for my daily tasks.				

	Never	Rarely	Some-times	Usually
I know what time of day it is.				
I don't like to be without something to occupy my mind.				
I voluntarily work overtime.				
I like to answer my mail and pay bills as soon as possible.				

WHAT TO DO ABOUT YOUR OBSESSIVE-COMPULSIVE BEHAVIOR: THE TREATMENT PACKAGE

The key element in breaking up an obsessive train of thought, a compulsive ritual, or any other kind of addictive cycle is to learn to reduce the tension and anxiety that you feel when you *do not* give in to your obsessive-compulsive habits. The treatment steps summarized below are designed to help you learn to do this.

1. *Establish obsessive-compulsive hierarchies.*
2. *Learn relaxation/thoughtstopping.*
3. *Use imaginal desensitization.*
4. *Use real-life desensitization.*
5. *Try flooding procedures.*
6. *Employ paradoxical practices.*
7. *Develop social support systems.*

1. Establishing Hierarchies

As with phobia, the best treatment for obsessive-compulsive disorders is to establish hierarchies of feared experiences and then to learn to encounter these experiences gradually and methodically—first in your imagination, then in real-life settings—while simultaneously concentrating on maintaining a complete state of muscle relaxation. Unlike phobia hierarchies, these hierarchies should be built around the central obsessive-compulsive anxiety—the stress and tension you feel when you *do not* comply with your obsessive-compulsive urges.

Most compulsions and obsessions exist on a continuum—at certain times they are felt much more strongly than at others. Recognizing which occasions tend to evoke only mild obsessive-compulsive responses in you will provide the basis for constructing the first steps in your hierarchy. More stressful events, which provoke greater compulsive behavior, will then provide material for creating the higher steps. Remember that the treatment program is directed at controlling the fear that is aroused in you at the thought of *not* engaging in the obsessive-compulsive ritual. So your evaluation of the strength of an obsessive-compulsive urge should be based on how difficult it is to *refrain* from giving in to the urge—on how much anxiety it causes you to *avoid* following through with the ritual. The intensity of this reaction is what should be used as a gauge to decide where an action or thought falls in the hierarchy.

Two model hierarchies—one for a hand-washing compulsion, the other for a checking compulsion—are included here. We assume, as is true of most hand-washing compulsions, that certain events are regarded by this compulsive individual as being more contaminating than others and thus as requiring more hand washing.

DESENSITIZATION HIERARCHY:
HAND-WASHING COMPULSION

1. *Touching excrement, then not washing.*
2. *Touching soiled bandages, then not washing.*
3. *Taking the garbage out to the garbage can, touching the garbage can to lift the lid up and put it back, then not washing.*
4. *Handling the soles of muddy shoes without washing.*
5. *Touching handrails and banisters in stores and other public places without washing.*
6. *Washing my hands only once after a contaminating event.*
7. *Washing my hands only twice after a contaminating event.*
8. *Washing my hands only three times after a contaminating event.*
9. *Washing my hands only four times after a contaminating event.*
10. *Washing my hands only five times, instead of the usual six times, after a contaminating event.*

DESENSITIZATION HIERARCHY:
CHECKING RITUALS

1. *Not checking to see that electrical appliances are off.*
2. *Not checking to see if gas is turned off.*
3. *Not checking to see if keys are in purse at all.*
4. *Checking to see that keys are in purse only once after leaving home.*
5. *Locking doors and windows without checking at all.*
6. *Checking front door and windows only once.*
7. *Checking front door and windows only two times.*
8. *Checking to make sure the front door is locked and the windows all closed only three times instead of four.*

Note that in each case, the hierarchy starts with a simple reduction in the number of times that the compulsive action is performed. In the first case, for example, the compulsive individual typically needs to wash six times, more often after an especially contaminating event, so the hierarchy starts with a reduction of the ritual to five repetitions. Touching garbage and touching soiled bandages, for instance, are shown to be more contaminating than handling muddy shoes. Construction of a hierarchy based on a contamination fear requires this kind of discrimination between the types of events that elicit the hand-washing behavior, particularly with regard to their relative repugnance. Start your hierarchy with those that require the least amount of compulsiveness afterward, and progress to those that are considered most contaminating and that thus require most hand washing.

2. Learning Relaxation and Thoughtstopping

In order to apply relaxation in the desensitization process for obsessive-compulsive problems, it's essential that you first become quite competent in the PMR method first described in Chapter 2. If you haven't already learned it to the point that you are able to relax your entire body quickly and completely, go back now, and work on this step thoroughly before going ahead with the next treatment procedures described in this chapter. Breaking up obsessive or compulsive rituals is highly dependent on being able to learn to control your tendency to become anxious if they are not performed. You must learn to be able to induce and maintain a state of bodily relaxation even when you do not allow yourself the anxiety reduction that follows from complying with the compulsive action or the obsessive thought pattern. From now on, your sense of control will come more and more from relaxation and less and less from compliance with your obsessive-compulsive inclination.

The relaxation process can be supplemented with a technique called thoughtstopping, which we first described in detail in Chapter 3. This technique is particularly effective with obsessive tendencies, when the problem is frequently that anxiety, tension, and highly repetitive, obsessive thoughts feed on one another in a self-generating vicious circle. Breaking up the process can be done at the point of bodily tension through use of the PMR method, or it can be accomplished more directly at the point of the obsessive thoughts themselves using thoughtstopping. In any event, interference with the obsessive thoughts that almost always accompany compulsive behavior is quite important.

Thoughtstopping is very simple. When you notice negative thoughts intruding into your consciousness, stop what you're doing immediately, and imagine shouting STOP to yourself at the top of your lungs. Do this sharply and strongly, devoting your full attention to it. As simple as it sounds, you will find that it is quite effective in disrupting your train of negative obsessional thoughts. If you are in a setting where you can afford to scream STOP out loud, so much the better.

As soon as this obsessive cycle is disrupted, *substitute a positive train of thought for it.* Force yourself to think about something positive, a pleasant event that you've planned for the future, a happy memory, or a particularly rewarding fantasy. Describe it out loud to yourself if the setting permits. Don't let yourself return to the negative train of thought. Relaxation tends to dispell negative thought processes, but they must also be supplanted by positive thoughts.

The hierarchies you develop should be based on your own compulsive or obsessive experiences. They should contain between eight and twelve items. This is usually about the right number to begin with. Try to describe each step in vivid but concise detail.

If you have trouble finding items for the hierarchy, spend a week or so monitoring your obsessive-compulsive rituals. Keep track of these in written notes, and you will find that you soon have more than enough material for a hierarchy. Once you have the separate incidents collected, arrange them in order with the most compelling at the top—those that you know you feel *most* anxious about if they are left undone—and the least anxiety provoking at the bottom.

3. Using Imaginal Desensitization

Now set aside a time each day when you won't be interrupted, and begin working your way through the imaginal hierarchy. Remember to relax on a reclining chair or couch. Use the muscle relaxation program to be sure that you're fully relaxed; then begin imagining the first scene in the hierarchy. (You may want to try recording the hierarchy steps on tape or having someone else tape them so that the voice you hear is not your own. If you tape these items, be sure that the motion of operating the tape recorder won't disturb your state of relaxation.)

Begin by imagining the first item on the hierarchy, the one that is least anxiety provoking for you. Focus on imagining the anxiety that can be aroused in you if you do *not* comply with the compulsive inclination. Imagine this as vividly as possible while maintaining your state of muscle relaxation. Do this for two minutes; then turn your attention back to your body. Take one minute to check to see that you're still relaxed. Then go back to the same hierarchy item, the first on your list, and go through the visualizing process again for another two minutes.

Do not progress to the next item on the hierarchy until you are certain that you can remain relaxed in the scene of not *performing the compulsion or obsession throughout the entire process of imagining the current item in your hierarchy.*

If you find that you have trouble moving up the hierarchy, remember our discussion of desensitization obstacles in Chapter 5. You may need to refocus the hierarchy so that it is directed more accurately at your specific obsessive-compulsive fears. Or you may need to construct an intermediate item to bridge a gap between two hierarchy items. If you have trouble starting the desensitization process, you may need to practice becoming more fully relaxed, and you may also need to construct a hierarchy event that has even less anxiety than the one with which you originally began your hierarchy.

Use the technique of talking to yourself softly, reproducing the kinds of statements you ordinarily make in these situations. Write out all your anxiety responses in detail to make them as vivid as possible. Add coping scenes to your hierarchy, scenes in which you first falter and show some anxiety in the obsessive-compulsive scene but then overcome it and resolve the event with confidence. Remember always to practice desensitization as *systematically* as possible.

Work on two or three items each desensitization session. The sessions can be held two or three times a day or only two or three times a week; the more you practice, the sooner you'll gain control over your compulsiveness. End each session with practice of the item just below the highest you were able to tolerate while remaining completely relaxed during the session.

4. Using Real-Life Desensitization

Once you've been able to work your way completely through the imaginal hierarchy while remaining relaxed at each item, the next step is to desensitize yourself to real-life compulsive events. You can begin practicing real-life desensitization only when you've worked completely through the imaginal hierarchy, or you can overlap these two kinds of practice. If you decide to overlap them, however, always keep the imaginal desensitization several steps ahead of real-life practice.

You will probably find that some of these procedures, particularly those used for real-life desensitization, are quite anxiety provoking at times. But if you can work your way successfully through the imaginal hierarchy, you will also find that the substitution of relaxation for anxiety tends to carry over into real-life settings. Instead of feeling panicky, you will be able to feel much more relaxed than before, when you first began resisting your compulsive urges in the imaginal exercises.

It's important to try very hard not to give in to your tendency to go ahead and fulfill your compulsive or obsessive wish. As we already stated, the short-term consequences may seem positive, since your anxiety level will immediately decrease, but over the long run, all that will have happened is that you will have reinforced the hold that your compulsion has on you. During the first few times that you try to reduce the level of compliance with your compulsion and you feel yourself becoming more and more anxious, evoke the muscle relaxation process, and wait out the anxiety until you feel it passing away and your sense of confidence and self-control returning. Don't give in to it if you can possibly help it.

Since the problem with compulsion is breaking up the repetitive cycle and sticking with the new behavior long enough to get the anxiety to diminish, start with small, easy steps—those that assure you success, those that you feel sure you can handle—especially for the real-life desensitization process. This may be difficult for you to do at first, because it can feel very unnatural to break a habitual response into small segments, but it is essential to follow this systematic program to assure yourself of permanent change. Close the door only five instead of six times. Continue to close it only five times until this level feels comfortable. Then, and only then, reduce it to four times. Wash your hands only twice instead of three times. Don't try to start out by deciding just to drop the compulsion once and for all on the spot. Chances are, the anxiety will be too great for you if you try this, and you will fail to break the compulsive pattern. Take the program one easy, systematic step at a time.

> To get Jane to learn control over her checking compulsion, she was told first to learn the PMR method of inducing deep muscle relaxation. This took her a while to learn—about three weeks—but once she had the basic response available to her, it wasn't hard for her to begin applying it to some of her most compulsive actions. First she tried checking the stove only five times instead of her customary six. She began to feel a little tense as she left the house, but she stopped, concentrated on relaxation for a minute or two, and the anxiety ebbed away. Throughout the day, whenever she would think of her inadequately checked stove with anxiety, she would use the same procedure; a minute or two of relaxation was all it took to bring the compulsive anxiety back under control.

> Next she reduced the stove-checking ritual to four times, then three, then two, and finally one, where it remains today. It wasn't an easy, automatic process. It took time and steady, careful application of her attention and energy, but it succeeded.

5. Practicing Flooding

Once you've been able to work your way through both the imaginal and real-life hierarchies, you will feel that the compulsive pattern has begun to dissipate and that a great measure of your self-control has been regained. Now, to reinforce that sense of self-control and to wipe out any last lingering traces of compulsive tendencies, try working through first an imaginal and then, if practical, a real-life flooding procedure.

Flooding simply means exposing yourself for a prolonged period of time to one of the most anxiety-provoking scenes you can imagine—one that exceeds any of those on your hierarchies, even the worst. For example, if your compulsion is checking the doors of your house, then the most anxiety-provoking thing for you might be to imagine leaving your house for an entire day without locking doors and windows and coming home to find that it has been broken into and vandalized. This is *not* a flooding scene that you would want to reproduce in real life, for obvious reasons. When you make the transition from imaginal flooding to real-life approximations of the imaginal scenes, you must use good judgment about how far to go in duplicating your fantasies. Obviously, inviting vandals to break in is *not* a good idea. An example of a better transition between imaginal and real-life flooding can be constructed drawing from contamination fears and cleaning compulsions. If you're overly compulsive about cleaning your house and you've worked through appropriate imaginal and real-life hierarchies constructed around this theme, first try imaginal flooding with a scene that far exceeds realistic probabilities. Imagine, for example, allowing your bathroom to become thoroughly filthy: mold on the walls, stains in the bathtub, wastebaskets overflowing, and so forth. Be sure to practice holding the scene in mind *until you relax*. The desensitization process is of no use unless you can experience relaxation while simultaneously experiencing the event that has previously caused you extreme arousal and anxiety.

Once you've successfully performed the imaginal flooding exercise, recreate the scene in real life as much as possible. Allow your bathroom actually to become quite untidy, and once it is, practice full exposure to it all at once until you have the experience of feeling yourself relax. If you're working on a hand-washing compulsion and it is related to contamination fears, another example is to try first imagining

that you're playing with very repulsive substances—
excrement, garbage, and the like—and that you're not washing your hands afterward. (Again, you would have to modify
this and exercise good judgment in your analogous construction of the real-life flooding scene; garbage alone would
probably be repulsive enough for desensitization purposes.)

As you expose yourself to the flooding scene, whether in
your imagination or in real life, remember to hold it until
you can produce and maintain your state of relaxation. The
experience of remaining relaxed while you encounter these
once highly anxiety-provoking events is the heart of the process of eradicating a compulsion. *Hold the scene until the anxiety
begins to diminish and your body begins to relax, until you begin to
experience the ability both to confront that which you most fear,
without submitting to your compulsive defensive rituals, and to remain calm.* If you give in before you become relaxed, it won't
help. You must wait until you feel the relaxation response
replacing your tension.

If flooding is done successfully with scenes that are more
anxiety provoking than those on the desensitization hierarchies and that are drawn from likely situations, chances are
good that you will have no trouble remaining relaxed in the
real-life situations that you are actually likely to encounter.

6. Employing Paradoxical Practice

Paradoxical practice means that instead of constructing
procedures like the desensitization hierarchies already described, which are designed to *reduce* your obsessive-
compulsive behavior, you intentionally *increase* it to the point
that it becomes obnoxious and boring rather than rewarding.
This is especially useful if, while you're working on the imaginal desensitization process, you succumb in real-life situations to a compulsive or obsessive urge. This is a difficult

moment, because you can render ineffective your relaxation and desensitization practice if you give in to the obsessive-compulsive inclination, find relief from your anxiety, and thus reinforce your first decision to give in to the compulsion. Rather than allowing the feeling of relief after such a transgression, paradoxical practice utilizes the idea that the last emotion associated with the compulsive act should be negative, not positive. So if you can't resist and you find yourself giving in, then go ahead and make the compulsion irritating and tedious by forcing yourself to overdo it. If you ordinarily check your car locks six times, check them twelve times. Keep going until you *really* don't want to continue; then keep on just a little more.

This procedure works as well for obsessive thoughts as for compulsive actions. The next time during the treatment program that you slip and begin ruminating about the most disastrous possibilities that you can imagine—losing all your possessions, being cast out into the street, having to beg for a crust of bread—go beyond reality to the worst you can possibly conceive. Eventually it will come to seem absurd and ludicrous to you rather than threatening.

7. Developing Social Support

Many of the steps in this process, especially those involving real-life desensitization, can be made much easier if you have another person along to help you out and give you support. Depending on your living situation, you may want to explain to your spouse, roommate, or friend that you're working on a program to help you lose your obsessive-compulsive tendencies. Assure them that the program is important to you, and ask them to help you with it. Then explain specifically what kind of help you need. If, for example, you've decided to work at a certain level of not engaging in your compulsion but your anxiety is mounting, and you're beginning to feel more and more panicky and more and more inclined to give in to the compulsive wish, it's important that others help you get through that particular stage and, inasmuch as possible, prevent you from giving in to your wishes. It's especially important to try not to give in to obsessive-compulsive inclinations once you've started on this program, and others can help you with this.

It can also be quite persuasive to watch someone else, someone you trust, model the desired responses for you, behaving as you would if you were free of your obsessive-compulsive drives. For example, if you have a checking compulsion, get a friend to leave her house with you, lock her door, and walk off without a second glance or other sign of anxiety about the security of her home.

An effective tool to use to block obsessive-compulsive tendencies is to develop satisfying social interactions, which will compete with the time you've tended to devote to your magical rituals. Don't let yourself become isolated. See friends. Enlist their help. Compulsive kinds of behavior are harder to maintain if you're in the company of other people, who can provide a kind of support and reassurance that will substitute for the relief that you get from your compulsiveness.

There will be times, of course, when this program will seem difficult for you. But if you can get through the first step, the second will be easier, the third easier still; and eventually your obsessive-compulsive responses will be mangageable.

Remember Jane, our compulsive friend from the beginning of this chapter? She was successsful in ridding herself of her compulsions—so successful, in fact, that a pleasant and somewhat ironic new problem emerged—what to do with all the free time she found she had once she liberated herself from her magical, addictive rituals.

eight

Stress

Letting the Rat Race Get to You

The bow too tensely strung is easily broken.   —PUBLILIUS SYRUS

Stress is perplexing. We all need some stress in life to stimulate us, to keep us alert and active and thus healthy. But as with too much of any good thing, an excess of stress can be very unhealthy, even fatal. Heart disease, for example, is very closely linked to stress and to how we cope with it.

This chapter is divided into five subsections, each one dealing with a common, dysfunctional response to stress: insomnia, headache, menstrual discomfort, Type A behavior (which Dr. Meyer Friedman has demonstrated to be a precursor of coronary heart disease in some people), and hypertension. None of the first three is fatal, of course, but all are good indicators that their victims are too tense, that they're letting stress get to them in unhealthy ways. Thus, they are part of an overall behavior pattern, one that can also include

155

Type A behavior and hypertension, one that signals a need for better adjustment to the inevitable stress of life's demands.

INSOMNIA

If you're not sleeping well, it's because you're letting something block your natural sleep cycle, and it's consequently up to you to alter that pattern, to keep problems from preoccupying you when you should be getting some rest. Although it is true that there have been a few documented cases of individuals who function perfectly well and with no apparent discomfort on as little as an hour or two of sleep each night, most of us need to spend one-third of our lives asleep in order to feel well. And sleep is not only a necessity for most of us; it's also very pleasurable. The relaxation, contentment, and escape from daily pressures that sleep brings is like the relief from pain and anxiety of a powerful narcotic.

Extensive research performed in the last decade on sleep disorders has shown that sleep can be divided into several major phases, two of which are Rapid-Eye-Movement (REM) sleep and Non-Rapid-Eye-Movement (NREM) sleep. These are so different that it seems as if humans have three distinct modes of existence: wakefulness, REM sleep, and NREM sleep.

In REM sleep the body is still, the closed eyes move rapidly back and forth, and the heart beats at its normal daytime level. The activity of the brain, as indicated by its patterns of electrical discharges, may reach and even surpass waking levels.

NREM sleep, on the other hand, is divided into four somewhat arbitrary stages, which broadly correspond to steadily diminished activity as the sleeper progresses through them. As we move from stage 1 through stages 2 and 3 to stage 4, our muscles become more and more relaxed, the brain becomes very inactive, the heart begins to beat more and more slowly, and our breathing grows deeper and more regular. During the night, we pass through several sleep cycles as we move through short REM to NREM states and then back again. A complete cycle containing both REM and NREM stages lasts from one to more than two hours. As the night progresses, these cycles get longer, and we experience proportionally less NREM sleep and comparatively more REM sleep during each cycle.

Sleep patterns are only one of many body processes, both physiological and psychological, that follow a daily (or *circadian*) cycle. Our body temperature, our alertness, our motor reactions, our endocrine functions, the formations of biochemicals in our blood, even the volume of fluid in our bodies—all seem to follow patterns that last about one day. Circadian cycles vary among individuals. Some people find themselves at their sharpest in the morning. Others don't hit their stride until late afternoon or evening. Similarly, some people find that they're ready for sleep much earlier in the day than others. Younger people tend to need much more sleep than others; with increasing age, a kind of natural insomnia sets in.

Although disruptions of the circadian rhythms of the body, such as occur in long-distance jet travel or in insomnia, are probably not medically harmful, they can lead to a very unpleasant listlessness, a fuzzy, inert kind of feeling, and they can make one more susceptible to accidents and diseases. Sleeplessness won't kill you, but good rest is essential to health and well-being.

Most researchers divide insomnia into three types, each of which can be represented by a unique pattern of brain waves. First, there is the insomnia of simply not being able to fall asleep. If you get into bed feeling tired and sleepy but find that you only lie there in the dark, unable to relax and prevent your racing mind from going over the trials and stresses of the past day or those to come, and if this state lasts for at least half an hour or so, you can consider yourself to have one of the three kinds of insomnia. (However, each of the three types must be accompanied by a feeling of fatigue and lethargy on the following day, or it cannot really be considered insomnia. You don't have insomnia just because you don't sleep very much. You also have to feel distinct negative effects from your loss of sleep.)

The second kind of insomnia occurs when you find yourself waking up in the middle of the night and not being able to return to sleep within half an hour or so. It's so normal as to be commonplace to wake up once or twice in the night but only if you then fall asleep again almost immediately and feel no ill effects from your wakefulness the following day. This type of insomnia also stems from an abnormal, obsessive type of concern about a difficulty or problem.

Finally, if you find yourself waking up at five in the morning or earlier and being unable to fall back to sleep, followed by the distinct sensation of fatigue during that day's activities, you are suffering from the third variety of insomnia.

Nearly all of us, as an inevitable consequence of life's pressures and challenges, will find ourselves encountering occasional bouts with insomnia. And as a response to severe disruptions in the normal routine and circumstances of one's life, insomnia is predictable and normal. As many as one out of every seven Americans, however, suffers from chronic insomnia, which lasts at least six months and sometimes up to several years.

This kind of insomnia is frequently associated with other chronic mood disorders, such as depression and anxiety. Americans spend vast sums of money annually—nearly $200 million or about $1 for every man, woman, and child in the population—for medications intended to aid sleep. And there is convincing evidence that all this expenditure is unnecessary and even dangerous. Many sleep medications interfere with REM cycles, suppressing them while the medication is in use, which causes them to return much more intensely when the medication is stopped. The effect of these intensified REM cycles that follow cessation of sleep aids can be unpleasant, restless sleep and nightmares, which can then in turn cause an individual to return to use of the sleep medication. Furthermore, once an individual has become tolerant of sleep medication, it can take some time—as long as five or six weeks—to return to normal sleep cycles once the medication is stopped. Most sleep researchers feel that there simply are *no* good sleep drugs on the market today.

---

1. Date:_____.

2. I got to bed last night at_____.

3. I got to sleep at_____.

4. Just before I went to bed, I was doing_____,

   and I was thinking about_____.

5. My mood was one of_____.

6. I was alone/talking to_____ about_____

   _____.

7. During the night, I woke up_____times, for about_____

   each time.

8. I woke up at_____.

9. I got up at_____.

10. I would estimate that I was asleep for_____hours and awake

    for_____ hours.

Figure 8.1 Sample Sleep Record

WHAT TO DO ABOUT INSOMNIA: THE TREATMENT STEPS

Insomnia can be readily cured in the vast majority of cases by following these six simple treatment steps:

1. *Carefully observe and record your mental and physical state just prior to going to bed for a week or two.*
2. *Prepare for sleep.*
3. *Learn and apply the progressive muscle relaxation system described in Chapter 2.*
4. *Strengthen the potential of your bedroom setting to serve as a sleep cue.*
5. *Do not take naps.*
6. *Substitute positive thoughts and pleasant fantasies for the obsessive concerns and doubts that are blocking the onset of the natural sleep response.*

1. Observing Sleep Antecedents

The first step in alleviating insomnia is to monitor carefully all the thoughts and activities that immediately precede your usual bedtime. What are you customarily doing and thinking just before you go to bed? Organize a record like that shown in Figure 8.1, and keep it faithfully for two weeks. This will give you a record of the antecedents to your insomnia. Chances are good that disruptive patterns will become clearer to you just through the act of keeping this kind of record, and before you even start working on specific insomnia remedies, you will already have a good idea of what the underlying problems to be eradicated are.

Keeping this kind of record is extremely important. People suffering from insomnia find that the simple act of recording, in a regular and organized fashion, the physical, social, and mental conditions that precede insomnia is often sufficient, in and of itself, to identify *and alleviate* the factors that are inhibiting their sleep response. Most people find, after keeping this kind of record, that the reason they can't get to sleep is because they're letting themselves obsessively worry about something, some event or problem in their lives. Clearly, one part of the effective response to stress is to keep yourself from losing sleep over it.

2. Preparing for Sleep

It's important to let yourself wind down in the evening before you actually go to bed. People who are prone to insomnia often tend also to be those who have trouble letting themselves relax. They tend to stay keyed up all evening, right up to and including the moment they get into bed. Then they lie there sleepless, and they begin to worry about falling asleep. Fears about not being able to fall asleep lead to fears about not being able to resolve problems or to meet the next day's demands, and the whole obsessive circle of anxieties begins to grow and feed itself until the nervous system is so worked up that there's no hope of getting to sleep soon.

Don't put yourself in this rut. Pick an activity you know you find relaxing—such as watching TV or reading a book—and *routinely* indulge in this relaxation cue *every* evening before you go to bed, whether you feel that you need it or not that night.

Also, don't stimulate your system with caffeine or other energizing drugs late in the evening. Don't take over-the-counter sleep aids. A little alcohol may help you feel drowsy, but more than a little can interfere with your REM and NREM sleep stages.

3. Practicing Relaxation

If you haven't already become thoroughly adept at the relaxation method described in Chapter 2, refer back to it now, and get it down cold. Numerous experimental studies have shown that practice of the PMR method all by itself is quite effective in dispelling insomnia and inducing sleep.

You should actually work through the relaxation process while lying in bed on your back. You will notice that some parts of the procedure, such as the foot and leg exercise, will be harder to accomplish when you're flat on your back, but follow the entire process just as you would as part of any other treatment method described in this book. Do this *regularly* every night, whether you think you need it or not, to get used to associating a state of deep muscle relaxation with your bedroom, your bed, and sleep.

An additional technique that many people find effective is to use a metronome to help bring on sleep. Buy the windup kind, place it where it can be heard but not too near the bed, since most are a bit loud, and set it for sixty beats per minute. The sound of the *tock . . . tock . . . tock* is inherently relaxing. You can also tape-record soft, muffled beats at that same rate—sixty beats per minute—if you don't want to buy a metronome; the tape recorder should be one that shuts off automatically.

You can adjust the rate of beats somewhat, but don't set it too high or too low. A high rate, like 120 beats per minute, is more like the rate of an alarm clock and will prove distracting. Setting the rate too low won't be very effective either.

4. Strengthening the Sleep Cues in the Physical Setting

One problem with insomnia is that the more often you lie awake at night, tossing fitfully in your bed, the more you begin to associate the bed and the bedroom with a state of wakefulness rather than sleep. To counter this tendency, you need to manage the physical environment of the bedroom so that its association with sleep is reemphasized. There are a number of ways to do this:

- Eliminate bright lights and noise in the bedroom. As you wind down in the evenings, avoid things that will stimulate you into greater alertness.

- Rearrange the furniture in your bedroom, so that you start out with a fresh sleep setting.

- Go to bed only when you feel that you're beginning to unwind, to relax. Try to sense when your body feels the need for sleep; then respond by heading for the bedroom.

- Begin getting up at the same time every morning. As well as going to bed only when you feel sleep beginning to come on, you should leave the bed and the sleep setting when it's time to wake up and to become alert and active again. By making your wake–sleep cycle more regular in this way, you give your body's natural circadian rhythms a chance to stabilize. This is especially important if you've been taking sleep medications.

- If you don't fall asleep within half an hour, get up and leave the bedroom. Do something else for a while. Make sure that it's relaxing, but don't do it in the bedroom.

- The same is true if you wake up in the middle of the night. If you can't get back to sleep within ten to fifteen minutes, don't just lie there. Get up. Break up the wakefulness cycle. Get a glass of milk from the refrigerator. Read the paper. Get your mind off your problems. Then go back to bed, and work your way methodically through the muscle relaxation procedure.

5. Avoiding Naps

Napping during the day is another way to disrupt your natural sleep–wake cycle by giving your body confusing signals about the right time to go to sleep. Napping is fine for some people, those who have no trouble falling asleep again at night, but not for those having trouble with insomnia. Avoid it.

6. Replacing Obsessive Anxieties with Positive Thoughts and Fantasies

You will find that the muscle relaxation technique tends to dispel automatically the tension-producing doubts and fears that are disturbing your sleep. Because it tends to bring the parasympathetic division of the autonomic nervous system into dominance, it will help induce an attitude of calm and serenity in you.

Supplement this peaceful mood with pleasant scenes, fantasies, and memories. You will notice that as you practice this more and more, there comes a time when the mental image begins to take on a life of its own, to become vivid and real and quite absorbing. This is usually the prelude to falling asleep.

Some people focus their thoughts on a simple image, like a candle flame. As they watch it flicker and burn, they feel themselves growing drowsier and drowsier.

Others like to imagine happy memories of friends or family members. One man reported that he liked to imagine being lost in a blizzard, with cold snow and ice swirling around him, then stumbling into a snug, warm cabin where he could settle down into a deep, peaceful rest.

Some people successfully focus on their breathing. They

breathe deeply and slowly, counting the breaths to themselves and visualizing each number as they count. They tell
themselves they're becoming just a bit more relaxed with
each breath they take.

If you can't free yourself from negative thought processes, you may need to refer back to our previous discussions of depression and phobic anxiety in Chapters 4 and 5
and work on applying the techniques we outline there.
People who tend to lie awake at night worrying about their
problems often find it helpful to desensitize themselves to
their doubts and fears by setting up an imaginary hierarchy
for the stressful situation and methodically working through
it while simultaneously remaining calm and relaxed. The
sense of control this brings is a highly effective soporific.

7. Paradoxical Therapy: Staying Awake

The steps we've described work well in helping most
people dispel bouts with insomnia. They do take practice,
and they do require a few days to take effect. If you're feeling too impatient to begin a gradual treatment program—
maybe you've already been up for three nights running and
you're dead on your feet—try this simple procedure before
you break down and go to a doctor for a barbiturate or an
antihistamine injection. Try staying awake. Tell yourself that
you're not even going to plan to go to bed. Go on with your
usual routines, and try to ignore your body's demand for
rest. Don't worry excessively about physical fatigue. Just
lying in bed will give your body about 75 percent of the rest
that sleep will. Do *not* drive, however, or put yourself in other
situations where drowsiness could be dangerous or harmful.
Stay home, and stay awake.

The idea underlying this technique is that the anxiety

that is overriding your normal sleep response is evidently so powerful as to block it completely, and you will have to let yourself become more fatigued before your need for rest will be strong enough to make you set this cause of concern aside long enough to get some rest. So don't fight it . . . go with it. One or two more sleepless nights won't hurt you. And they will make your sleep response more irresistible as you become more and more tired. One researcher even believes that a night or two of sleeplessness is a good remedy, when used with other treatment techniques, for mild depression and anxiety. It seems to bring on a slight euphoria with the growing sense of weariness.

But one caution: don't push it too far. If you've gone for two or three nights involuntarily unable to sleep, followed by one or two more intentionally trying to stay awake, and you still haven't gotten to sleep, see a physician.

HEADACHE

One of the most common kinds of reaction to stress is headache. If the sales of aspirin and acetaminophen are any indication, headache is probably the single most common stress-related physical complaint in the United States.

Headaches can be divided into three broad, somewhat overlapping categories: tension headaches, migraines, and a third catchall category that includes headaches resulting from accidents and head injuries as well as those that are symptomatic of other physical disorders such as tumor, stroke, or allergy.

If you are having routine, relatively severe headaches and they do not respond to aspirin or to the treatment we outline here, be sure that you check with your physician for a complete medical diagnosis of the possible underlying causes.

WHAT TO DO ABOUT HEADACHES:
THE TREATMENT PACKAGE

The majority of commonly experienced headaches are tension headaches. Both tension headaches and migraines are amenable to the treatment process outlined in the following steps:

1. *Diagnose the headache type.*
2. *Monitor the frequency and duration of the headache.*
3. *Refer to and learn the PMR method described in Chapter 2.*
4. *For tension headaches, apply PMR specifically to neck and shoulder muscles.*
5. *Continue monitoring.*
6. *For migraines, learn the autogenic hand-warming process.*
7. *Learn to apply treatment procedures preventively.*

1. Diagnosing Your Headache Type

The checklist shown in Test 8.1 will give you a general idea of the kind of headache you're having. Fill it out before continuing with the rest of the chapter, so that your responses won't be biased by what you read later.

Test 8.1 What Kind of Headaches Do You Have?

	Yes	No

Migraine

The pain is usually on one side of my head.

The pain throbs like a pulse.

I get nauseous shortly after the headache starts.

Nausea and vomiting are often associated with my headaches.

My vision changes when one of these headaches is coming on.

I often got carsick as a child.

There are typical warning signs other than pain that tell me when one one of these headaches is coming on.

A blood relative in my family gets migraines.

Alcohol makes my headaches worse.

My headaches come on just *after* a stressful situation, when I should be starting to feel relaxed.

They're usually gone within twelve hours.

Tension Headaches

My headaches start *during* or *before* the stressful situation, when I'm most tense.

They can last for days at a time.

The pain is steady, not pulsing, and is more generally located in my head, not in one particular spot or on one particular side.

Aspirin/acetaminophen help.

My neck and shoulders have been getting stiff and sore frequently.

Alcohol relieves the headache pain.

Test 8.1 *(continued)*

	Yes	No
Other		
Sometimes vomiting associated with these headaches begins so suddenly that I have no warning that it's coming.		
There doesn't seem to be any connection with stress; they can hit me even when I'm asleep.		
I've suffered a serious head/neck injury in the past year.		
The headaches seem to be most often associated with reading.		
I have a morning postnasal drip condition.		
I've had trouble holding things recently.		
I've had trouble walking recently.		
My speech is slurred recently.		
I've been told I have arthritis.		
I sometimes see double.		
I have had a seizure.		
I feel short of breath sometimes.		
My fingers feel numb and tingly now and then.		
I have blacked out.		
I have frequent toothaches.		
My headaches start suddenly and vanish just as suddenly.		
I've had sudden weaknesses in one part of my body.		

As you can see, the checklist is divided into three sections: migraine, tension headache, and other. If a majority of your *yes* answers falls into the first grouping, you probably have migraines. If in the second group, you have tension headaches. (It is possible to have combined migraine-tension headaches.) If most of your answers fall into the third grouping, your headaches may be a symptom of a more serious disorder, which should be diagnosed by your physician.

TENSION HEADACHES

Tension headaches arise from muscle contraction, particularly in the neck and shoulders. You may feel the pain in your forehead, but it's originating from your neck, shoulders, and scalp. Because muscle tension plays a critical role in instigating tension headaches, the method for relief focuses on helping you learn to exert enough control over the tension in your neck and shoulder muscles that you can prevent the onset of tension headache by simply eliminating the muscle tension that brings it on. We don't tell you how to eliminate the stress itself or the anxieties and frustrations that cause you to react to stress by getting tense. To work on these, you may want to reread Chapter 6 on assertion and Chapter 5 on managing fears and anxiety to help you cope with the underlying situations that actually bring excessive tension into your life.

The procedures set forth here are special applications of the PMR method described in Chapter 2 that have been successfully applied in Dr. Tasto's clinical practice. In a group of people suffering from tension headache, these methods have been able to reduce the average weekly cumulative duration of their headaches from thirty-eight hours to almost nothing ... nearly complete relief!

As with all the self-management procedures detailed in *Spare the Couch*, the process must be followed diligently, step by step, to insure that you receive the maximum benefit from them.

2. Monitoring

Once you know what kind of headaches you have, the second step is to monitor them for one week before actually beginning the self-treament program. This will give you an exact idea of the number of hours per week that you actually suffer from headaches. It will also give you a benchmark, an initial level against which you can measure your progress as the number of hours of pain drops lower with each passing week. Knowing how much progress you've made is one of the strongest forms of encouragement you can give yourself in this type of treatment program.

Figure 8.3 shows a typical daily monitoring chart. We've provided you with eight of these, one for each day of the monitoring week plus a spare to keep for future reference. If you cut out all seven and staple them together, you will have a convenient pretreatment monitoring booklet that you should carry with you during the day.

During the measurement week, whenever a headache seems to be coming on, just note the time under *Time Onset*. When the headache ends, jot down the time under *Time Finished*. Calculate the length of time elapsed between *Onset* and *Finished*, and you will have the *Duration* of the headache. If you have more than one headache in a day, total all the lengths together, and put down the combined amount under *Duration*.

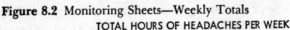

Figure 8.2 Monitoring Sheets—Weekly Totals

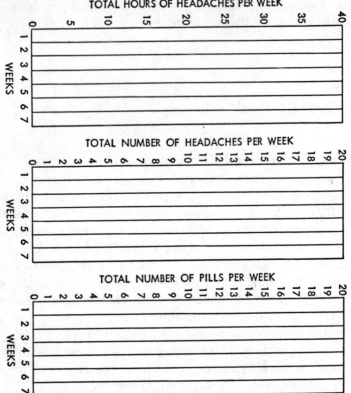

If you take any kind of medication for your headaches, write down the type and amount every day, so that this can also be measured before self-treatment begins.

The totals, shown in Figure 8.2, can be plotted at the end of each day. As the treatment program progresses, continue to keep track of your headaches with these sheets. You should notice decreases soon, probably first in the amount of medication you need, then in the total number of hours of headache you experience in a week, then finally in the total number of headaches you have. In other words, headaches usually first become a little less severe in this program, then

Figure 8.3 Daily Monitoring Chart

Date: _____

Time Onset: _____ _____ _____   Medication: _____

Time Finished: _____ _____ _____

Duration: _____ + _____ + _____ =   _____
                                       Total hrs/day

Date: _____

Time Onset: _____ _____ _____   Medication _____

Time Finished: _____ _____ _____

Duration: _____ + _____ + _____ =   _____
                                       Total hrs/day

Date: _____

Time Onset: _____ _____ _____   Medication: _____

Time Finished: _____ _____ _____

Duration: _____ + _____ + _____ =   _____
                                       Total hrs/day

Date: _____

Time Onset: _____ _____ _____   Medication: _____

Time Finished: _____ _____ _____

Duration: _____ + _____ + _____ =   _____
                                       Total hrs/day

Figure 8.3 Daily Monitoring Chart

Date: _____

Time Onset: ____ ____ ____   Medication: ____

Time Finished: ____ ____ ____

Duration: ____ + ____ + ____ =
                                            _____
                                            Total hrs/day

Date: _____

Time Onset: ____ ____ ____   Medication: ____

Time Finished: ____ ____ ____

Duration: ____ + ____ + ____ =
                                            _____
                                            Total hrs/day

Date: _____

Time Onset: ____ ____ ____   Medication: ____

Time Finished: ____ ____ ____

Duration: ____ + ____ + ____ =
                                            _____
                                            Total hrs/day

Date: _____

Time Onset: ____ ____ ____   Medication: ____

Time Finished: ____ ____ ____

Duration: ____ + ____ + ____ =
                                            _____
                                            Total hrs/day

they become of increasingly shorter duration, and finally you just don't get them at all. That is the overall pattern of headache reduction, but a decrease at any time in any of these three variables—number, length, or medication use—is a sign of progress.

3. Practicing Relaxation

Once you've charted the week of premeasures, you're ready to begin the therapeutic procedure. If you haven't already done so, turn to Chapter 2, and work through the directions once more for learning muscle relaxation. It is fundamental to this treatment process that you know how to relax your entire body and how to do so quickly. At first, practice the entire PMR procedure at least once a day for a week or until you feel you have it under control. Work on achieving this ability as you proceed with the specific exercises for relaxing muscle areas related to tension headache.

4. Learning to Relax Shoulder and Neck Muscles

In addition to the overall exercises set forth in Chapter 2, you need to focus on the muscles of the back of the neck and the shoulder areas. Set aside time to work on these exercises when you are not practicing the procedures of Chapter 2. Ideally, these specific relaxation exercises should be done several times a day. Because we tend not to use these muscles very much, they get stiff and lose their tone. So, to set the blood flowing again, it's essential to practice the procedures described next regularly.

To relax the neck area, begin by dropping your head forward so that your chin touches your chest. Then begin rotating your head to the right, so that your right ear sweeps down across the top of your shoulder. Continue this motion around in as complete a circle as you can manage, letting your head roll loosely around the pivotal point of the neck. Keep this motion up continuously until your neck muscles begin to feel loose and maybe even a bit numb.

After working on head and neck muscles, focus the relaxation practice on your shoulders. In either a standing or a sitting position, bring your shoulders up toward your ears. Then begin to draw them backwards, almost as though it were possible to touch them together behind you. Continue then to let them drop back down toward your waist. Then move them forward and upward, as though trying to bring them together in front of your chest. Continue to draw them up toward the original position of trying to touch your ears with them. Work on the entire motion until it becomes continuous and smooth. Do this until your muscles feel relaxed and loose. Then reverse the direction, and again develop your proficiency at making the motion smooth and fluid until these muscles feel relaxed.

Both these exercises can be performed quickly and without much trouble several times each day. You will find that they help you relax and tone up the muscle areas that play a central role in the development of tension headaches.

5. Continuing to Monitor the Headaches Each Week

Throughout the treatment program, which can last for eight weeks or more, continue to keep close track of the number and length of your headaches, as well as the amount and kind of medication you take for them. Seeing these levels drop over time is an excellent reward for following the relaxation exercises diligently. The best reward, of course, is the cessation of the headaches themselves.

Once you know how to use both overall relaxation and specific head, neck, and shoulder relaxation to moderate your headaches, the next step is to learn to relax your muscles automatically at the first sign of tension. The technique is simple, but it is extremely important that you carry it out faithfully. The time to stop a headache is before it actually comes on. Once a headache can be felt, even if it is only mild, it's much more difficult to eliminate it than it is to prevent it before it ever really gets started.

Pay attention to physical and situational cues. Most people can learn to sense when they're about to get a headache, and monitoring them will make it even clearer to you what kinds of events can give you a headache. Every time you notice the slightest indication that a headache may be coming on, stop what you're doing, and work on letting yourself become relaxed. This will mean interrupting some fairly demanding tasks at times, but it is essential that early in the treatment process, you take the time to focus consciously on relaxation. Though you will have to think carefully about the procedure at first, it soon will become almost a natural, automatic response to the first signs of muscle tension, and you will eventually find that you do not actually have to pay much conscious attention to relaxing your neck and shoulder muscles.

A conditioning process is at work here. If the slightest indication of a headache is paired often enough with muscle relaxation, then these headache precursors become a signal to elicit automatically the right kind of preemptive muscle relaxation. A neat little shortcircuit is built into the stress response cycle that will protect you from headaches as long as you remain just vigilant enough to cue in the relaxation response before the headache can get started.

As you work on this method, be sure to keep track of your progress with the monitoring sheet we described earlier.

Should you find that you have trouble learning the relaxation procedures or applying them successfully, consider seeing a professional therapist. Many are well trained in the application of a number of relaxation procedures, including those useful in preventing headache.

If for some reason the headaches do not diminish or if they seem to be getting worse, see your doctor.

6. Hand Warming for Migraines

Migraines are not as simple to treat as tension headaches; nor are they as well understood. They are often more severe than tension headaches, and they typically involve nausea and changes in vision. There is also a pattern of changes in blood flow and blood vessel size associated with migraine headaches that appears to be much more complex than that associated with tension headaches.

Before a migraine attack, there is vascular constriction of the arteries along the outside of the skull, along the sides of the head, followed by vascular dilation. The temporal artery pulse increases, and the elevated pounding or throbbing sensation is usually quite evident to the migraine victim. The dilation and expansion of the arteries in the head result in a greater amount of blood in the head, which is in part responsible for the pain. Relaxation exercises have been shown to be effective in disrupting this vasoconstriction–dilation cycle.

Migraines are an ancient affliction. Reports of their treatment appear in historical records that date back some 2,000 years. In many people, migraines are precipitated by stress, but they differ from tension headaches in that they tend to come on *after* the stressful incident, during the cooling-off and settling-down period. Tension headaches, on the other hand, usually develop *before* or *during* the stress. Those migraines that are not stress induced may be caused by certain smells, such as petrochemical odors, or by allergies to specific types of foods, such as bananas, sharp cheese, red wine, or chocolate. Currently they attack approximately one out of every ten individuals and are most often treated with ergotamine tartrate (or one of its derivatives), a drug that has the effect of constricting blood vessels. But the value of migraine medications varies from person to person, and they can produce some undersirable side effects. A number of intriguing experiments have demonstrated that placebos are also effective in relieving migraines, which strongly indicates that the process of controlling migraine pain may be primarily dependent on the internal resources of the victim.

For example, research conducted over the last decade by Joseph D. Sargent, M.D., and Elmer Green, Ph.D., at the Menninger Foundation in Topeka, Kansas, has indicated that migraines can be very successfully treated by a process that teaches people to raise the temperature of their hands. It's not yet entirely understood just exactly what biochemical mechanism is involved when migraine sufferers learn to relieve and then prevent their headaches by warming their hands, but the process goes like this.

First relax your entire body. Relaxation, as we explained in Chapter 2, is associated with greater flow of blood to the periphery of the body, including the hands and feet. (Most migraine sufferers regularly or intermittently have very cold hands.)

Once you're relaxed, you can help disrupt the vasoconstriction–dilation cycle by willing your hands and feet first to become *heavy*, then *warm*. Imagine, for example, that you have a lead glove on your right hand, a very heavy but comfortable glove. Instead of trying to pull your hand up, to resist the feeling of heaviness and sinking, let it just drop.

Allow the sensation of heaviness to flood into your hand. Feel it climb up to your elbow.

Imagine a heavy weight attached to your right forearm, pulling it down. Don't fight it. Let the arm sink heavily.

Do the same with your left hand. Then your left arm. If you're sitting, let your feet become very heavy, as if encased in lead shoes.

This will dilate the arteries in your hands and feet and will impede the dilation cycle in your extracranial arteries. As the blood comes into your hands, you will feel them become warmer. Encourage this process, and practice it until you can let your hands warm up quickly. Soon you won't need to make them feel heavy first, and they will rapidly become warmer almost as soon as you start to think about warming them up.

Any time you feel the *slightest* indication of a migraine, sit back and think in a relaxed way of how your hands are starting to feel warmer. Then your feet.

You cannot get the same effect simply by putting your hands in hot water. In fact, you may get just the opposite effect, since this will tend to drive the blood *away* from your hands into cooler parts of your body. The dilating process must be produced internally by innate physiological mechanisms that will bring about expansion of peripheral arteries. It can't be achieved by external processes.

With repeated practice, you will find that you can produce a feeling of heaviness in your hands and feet rather easily.

7. Applying the Treatment Preventively

As with any headache treatment, it is important to begin the treatment process at the first sign of the onset of a headache. Do not wait until the migraine has become severe before you try to manage it with this technique. When you think you feel the first signs of a migraine, try to remain relaxed, cease the activities that you're engaged in as much as possible, and concentrate in a calm, somewhat detached, but alert manner on allowing your hands, arms, feet, and legs to become as relaxed, heavy, and warm as possible.

DYSMENORRHEA

Dysmenorrhea is pain or discomfort felt during or just prior to menstruation. Its symptoms can include: abdominal cramps, nausea and vomiting, headache, backache, leg ache, dizziness, weakness, diarrhea, facial blemishes, irritability, and depression. Recent research conducted by *Spare the Couch* coauthor Donald L. Tasto and Margaret A. Chesney has confirmed the theory that there are two distinct kinds of dysmenorrhea—spasmodic and congestive—and that the former can be treated effectively with relaxation and imagery exercises.

The difference between the two kinds of dysmenorrhea can be summed up as follows. *Spasmodic dysmenorrhea* is characterized by fairly acute, cramplike pains, similar to labor pains, that start on the first day of menstruation, often soon after the first signs of menstruation appear. They tend to come at fifteen- to twenty-minute intervals. The pain is worst on the first day and then may last for one or two more days or may not reappear at all on following days. It is restricted to the lower abdomen, back, and inner thighs and may be severe enough to cause vomiting, fainting, or dizziness. Its victims often attempt to reduce its intensity by bending, reclining, curling up in a ball, lying in a hot bath, or hugging a heating pad or hot water bottle.

Congestive dysmenorrhea begins less dramatically, with a feeling of heaviness, lethargy, and possibly even depression, *before* the actual onset of menstruation. It is also usually accompanied by dull, aching pains in the lower abdomen. Occasionally, women suffering from this type of dysmenorrhea also experience nausea, irritability, loss of appetite, fatigue, and constipation, as well as headache, backache, and sore or tender breasts.

Researchers feel that dysmenorrhea is related to imbalances in the relative levels of two kinds of hormones—estrogen and progesterone. They theorize that spasmodic dysmenorrhea is related to a raised level of progesterone and, conversely, that congestive dysmenorrhea is linked to a raised level of estrogen. In the case of spasmodic dysmenorrhea, it is also thought that the elevated progesterone level may cause a smaller cervical opening, and that the characteristic cramps may result from contractions of the uterus working to force menstrual material through this decreased opening.

If you're not certain which of these types of dysmenorrhea you may be experiencing, take the Dysmenorrhea Symptom Test (Test 8.2) and see if it helps clarify whether you have spasmodic or congestive dysmenorrhea. The test is designed so that you can determine, by adding up the numbers that you mark for each question, whether you have spasmodic or congestive dysmenorrhea. For each question, mark *two* numbers, one in the congestive group on the left and one in the spasmodic group on the right. For question 25, if the first description fits your dysmenorrhea, add five points to your score. If the second description is more appropriate, add only one point. Once the test is entirely completed, if your total score is over eighty, you probably have spasmodic dysmenorrhea. If it's seventy or below, you probably have congestive dysmenorrhea.

In view of the ideas about the underlying cause of spasmodic dysmenorrhea, it follows that a relaxation method—one that may work either by subduing the sympathetic division of the autonomic nervous system (as we explained in

Chapter 2) or by actually directly relaxing the muscles of the abdomen—might help alleviate the discomfort of this type of menstrual distress, and actual experimentation has borne out the efficacy of relaxation processes in treating spasmodic dysmenorrhea. Because there has not yet been a successful attempt to apply behavioral methods to congestive dysmenorrhea, we can only recommend the procedures described here for use in treating spasmodic dysmenorrhea.

Test 8.2 Dysmenorrhea Symptom Test

	Congestive					Spasmodic				
	Never	*Rarely*	*Sometimes*	*Often*	*Always*	*Never*	*Rarely*	*Sometimes*	*Often*	*Always*
	1	2	3	4	5	1	2	3	4	5
1. I feel irritable, easily agitated, and am impatient a few days *before* my period.										
2. I have cramps that *begin* on the first day of my period.										
3. I feel depressed for several days *before* my period.										
4. I have abdominal pain or discomfort that begins one day *before* my period.										
5. For several days *before* my period, I feel exhausted, lethargic, or tired.										
6. I only know that my period is coming by looking at the calendar.										

	Congestive					Spasmodic				
	Never	*Rarely*	*Sometimes*	*Often*	*Always*	*Never*	*Rarely*	*Sometimes*	*Often*	*Always*
	1	2	3	4	5	1	2	3	4	5
7. I take a prescription drug for the pain *during* my period.										
8. I feel weak and dizzy *during* my period.										
9. I feel tense and nervous *before* my period.										
10. I have diarrhea *during* my period.										
11. I have backaches several days *before* my period.										
12. I take aspirin for the pain *during* my period.										
13. My breasts feel tender and sore a few days *before* my period.										
14. My lower back, abdomen, and the inner sides of my thighs *begin* to hurt or be tender on the first day of my period.										
15. During the first day or so of my period, I feel like curling up in bed, using a hot water bottle on my abdomen, or taking a hot bath.										
16. I gain weight *before* my period.										

	Congestive					Spasmodic				
	Never	*Rarely*	*Sometimes*	*Often*	*Always*	*Never*	*Rarely*	*Sometimes*	*Often*	*Always*
	1	2	3	4	5	1	2	3	4	5
17. I am constipated *during* my period.										
18. *Beginning* on the first day of my period, I have pains that may diminish or disappear for several minutes and then reappear.										
19. The pain I have with my period is not intense but a continuous dull aching.										
20. I have abdominal discomfort for more than one day *before* my period.										
21. I have backaches which *begin* the same day as my period.										
22. My abdominal area feels bloated for a few days *before* my period.										
23. I feel nauseous *during* the first day or so of my period.										
24. I have headaches for a few days *before* my period.										

25. *TYPE 1* (5 points)

The pain begins on the first day of menstruation, often coming within an hour of the first signs of menstruation. The pain is most severe the first day and may or may not continue on subsequent days. Felt as spasms, the pain may lessen or subside for a while and then reappear. A few women find this pain so severe as to cause vomiting, fainting, or dizziness; some others report that they are most comfortable in bed or taking a hot bath. This pain is limited to the lower abdomen, back, and inner sides of the thighs.

TYPE 2 (1 point)

There is advanced warning of the onset of menstruation during which the woman feels an increasing heaviness and a dull aching pain in the lower abdomen. This pain is sometimes accompanied by nausea, lack of appetite, and constipation. Headaches, backaches, and breast pain are also characteristic of this type of menstrual discomfort.

Total Score: _____

80 and over: spasmodic dysmenorrhea
70 and below: congestive dysmenorrhea

If you've determined that you have spasmodic dysmenorrhea, you should now take a second test, shown in Figure 8.4, to establish a pretreatment baseline score for the relative severity of your symptoms. For each of the fifteen descriptive items listed in the left-hand column, assign a number to the severity or incidence of the symptom, giving it a higher number, the more severe or frequent it is. Then add up the numbers you've checked. This isn't a diagnostic tool; there's no range of numbers to compare it with to find out how severe your symptoms are relative to other women's. It's purely relative and is included here so that you can judge your own personal progress as you work through the treatment program. Once you've begun to practice the steps we describe, take the test again each time you have your period, and compare the scores you get. If the program is working, you should get progressively lower scores as time passes.

Figure 8.4 Dysmenorrhea Symptom Scale

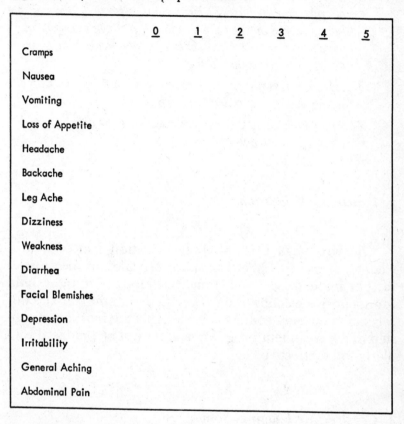

	<u>0</u>	<u>1</u>	<u>2</u>	<u>3</u>	<u>4</u>	<u>5</u>
Cramps						
Nausea						
Vomiting						
Loss of Appetite						
Headache						
Backache						
Leg Ache						
Dizziness						
Weakness						
Diarrhea						
Facial Blemishes						
Depression						
Irritability						
General Aching						
Abdominal Pain						

WHAT TO DO ABOUT
SPASMODIC DYSMENORRHEA:
THE TREATMENT PACKAGE

Treating this type of dysmenorrhea is quite simple. It can be described in four steps:

> *1. Review the PMR muscle relaxation process outlined in Chapter 2.*

189

2. *Develop a number of imaginal scenes (three to four) that characterize the onset of menstruation for you. They do not have to focus on the pain symptoms, just what runs through your mind in a typical setting as you realize that you're about to begin menstruation.*

3. *Practice remaining relaxed as you vividly imagine the scenes you've constructed in step 2.*

4. *Apply the relaxation imagery exercise to the actual, real-life onset of menstruation.*

1. Practicing Relaxation

As you work through the relaxation procedures in Chapter 2, pay special attention to relaxation of the muscles in your upper thighs and stomach. Pull them in tight, hold for about five seconds, then relax them. Let the sensation of relaxation envelop you. This is probably the most important step of the treatment program, and it must be practiced regularly to be effective.

2. Constructing Imaginal Scenes

Remember, these are to be associated with the *onset* of menstruation. Sample scenes follow:

EXAMPLE SCENES:
THE ONSET OF MENSTRUATION

1. *You are in your home, seated at your kitchen table. You look at the calendar and see that you are due to start your period this week. You also notice that you've got a number of things*

scheduled for this week–an office softball game on Wednesday, a concert on the weekend, and a meeting with an important client the following Monday. Because your period is coming, you wonder if you will feel uncomfortable this week and not be able to do all that you have planned. But you are able to think about all this and to remain calm and comfortable.

2. *It is the first day of your period. It began this morning, and you're now driving to work. You have four important calls to make today, and you had planned to walk downtown to shop for clothes at lunch. Now that you have started your period, you wonder if you will experience any pain today and if it will interfere with what you have to do. As you walk from your car to the office, you are able to continue thinking about the pain, but feeling calm, you think about the shopping you will do later also.*

You can use these just as they are presented, you can adapt them to suit your own setting and personality better, or you can construct entirely new scenes.

3. Practicing Imaginal Relaxation

Once you've constructed three or four imaginal scenes in step 2, work on simultaneously remaining relaxed and vividly developing these scenes in your imagination. Practice this twice a day for a week. Choose a comfortable, reclining chair or couch, pick a time and place where you won't be interrupted, then proceed through the PMR process. Once you're fully relaxed, allow the first scene to come to mind. Picture it as vividly as possible. Do this for two minutes, then let the scene slip away from your mind, and focus on the state of your muscle groups, especially those in your chest, stomach, buttocks, and upper thighs. Have they tensed up?

Work on relaxing them for a minute or so. Now go back to the scene. See if you can identify the particular part of the scene where you begin to tense up. Try to stay relaxed throughout it.

These scenes do *not* need to be arranged into a hierarchy for imaginal desensitization to be effective in treating spasmodic dysmenorrhea. You may in fact find that learning to relax thoroughly in just one typical premenstruation scene is all you need to do in order to alleviate your dysmenorrhea symptoms. However, if they do naturally fall into a hierarchical arrangement and you wish to work through them on this more structured basis, remember that you should start with the least arousing scene, and you should practice remaining relaxed in it until you can do so consistently and completely before moving on to the next scene in the hierarchy.

4. *Using Real-Life Application*

The basis of this treatment procedure is that effective relaxation of muscles in the stomach, gut, pelvic, and buttock areas will relieve the muscle cramping of spasmodic dysmenorrhea. Working with the PMR method described in Chapter 2 and the premenstrual imagery just given will help prepare you to apply relaxation to the actual onset of your next period.

It's important, when working on a program to prevent dysmenorrhea, to catch it *early,* to anticipate the onset of menstruation, and to use these relaxation techniques before actual muscle cramping begins. If you wait until you actually start to feel cramps, our method will probably not be of much use to you. It is a *preventive, rather than a remedial,* procedure.

So prepare yourself for your next period by remaining alert to the first twinges, the first signals of even very slight muscle tension or other spasmodic symptoms. Then stop what you're doing, and begin working on PMR exercises, even if you feel that the problem really hasn't actually appeared yet. This will prepare for the gradual displacement of your spasmodic responses with those of relaxation, and you will find, as you go back each month to the symptom severity test, that the problem is becoming more and more manageable.

CORONARY-PRONE TYPE A BEHAVIOR

What Is Type A Behavior?

The theory that an individual's personality and how it predisposes him or her to react to life stresses and demands plays a more significant role in the formation of heart disease than diet, exercise, smoking, or any one of numerous other factors was first scientifically articulated by Meyer Friedman and Ray H. Rosenman, two eminent cardiologists practicing in the San Francisco Bay Area.[1]

Stated very simply, the central idea underlying the work of Friedman and Rosenman is this: We all face stress in our lives, but we have a choice in how we structure our response to it. Though stress is inescapable, some of us manage to experience it without developing cardiovascular disease or suffering coronaries. Why? Because of the differences in our reactions to stress, differences that are as varied and numerous as are the individuals in the world but, according to

[1]Friedman and Rosenman have described their theory of Type A and Type B behavior and its connection to cardiovascular disease in a well-known book, *Type A Behavior and Your Heart* (Greenwich, Connecticut; Fawcett Crest, 1974), which we urge you to read for a comprehensive understanding of the connection between certain kind of behavior and attitudes and the development of heart disease.

Friedman and Rosenman, differences that tend to fall into one of two broad, general classes: Type A and Type B.

Basically, the Type A response is one of aggressive, hard-driving, impatient urgency. The Type A individual is highly aware of time and tends to overload his or her schedule, as well as to set very exacting standards and to expect himself and others to conform to them rigidly. Type A's also tend to alienate others; driven by needs to compete, to peform, to acquire, and to succeed, they often become brusque and even hostile in their interpersonal interactions, in their futile struggle to live harder and faster. Here, in detail, is how Friedman and Rosenman characterize Type A behavior:

YOU POSSESS TYPE A BEHAVIOR PATTERN:

1. If you have (a) a habit of exposively accentuating various key words in your ordinary speech even when there is no real need for such accentuation, and (b) a tendency to utter the last few words of your sentences far more rapidly than the opening words. The vocal explosiveness betrays the excess aggression or hostility you may be harboring. The hurrying of the ends of sentences mirrors your underlying impatience with spending even the time required for your own speech.

2. If you *always* move, walk, and eat rapidly.

3. If you feel (particularly if you openly exhibit to others) an impatience with the rate at which most events take place. You are suffering from this sort of impatience if you find if difficult to restrain yourself from hurrying the speech of others and resort to the device of saying very quickly over and over again, "Uh huh, uh huh," or, "Yes yes, yes yes," to someone who is talking, unconsciously urging him to "get on with" or hasten his rate of speaking. You are also suffering from impatience if you attempt to finish the sentences of persons speaking to you before they can.

Other signs of this sort of impatience: if you become *unduly* irritated or even enraged when a car ahead of you in your lane runs at a pace you consider too slow; if you find it anguishing to wait in a line or to wait your turn to be seated at a restaurant; if you find it intolerable to watch others perform tasks you know you can do faster; if you become impatient with yourself as you are obliged to perform repetitious duties (making out bank deposit slips, writing checks, washing and cleaning dishes, and so on), which are necessary but take you away from doing things you really have an interest in doing; if you find yourself hurrying your own reading or always attempting to obtain condensations or summaries of truly interesting and worthwhile literature.

4. If you indulge in *polyphasic* thought or performance, frequently striving to think of or do two or more things simultaneously. For example, if while trying to listen to another person's speech you persist in continuing to think about an irrelevant subject, you are indulging in polyphasic thought. Similarly, if while golfing or fishing you continue to ponder your business or professional problems, or if while using an electric razor you attempt also to eat your breakfast or drive your car, or if while driving your car you attempt to dictate letters for your secretary, you are indulging in polyphasic performance. This is one of the commonest traits in the Type A man. Nor is he always satisfied with doing just two things at one time. We have known subjects who not only shaved and ate simultaneously, but also managed to read a business or professional journal at the same time.

5. If you find it *always* difficult to refrain from talking about or bringing the theme of any conversation around to those subjects which especially interest and intrigue you, and when unable to accomplish this maneuver, you pretend to listen but really remain preoccupied with your own thoughts.

6. If you almost always feel vaguely guilty when you relax and do absolutely nothing for several hours to several days.

7. If you no longer observe the more important or interesting or lovely objects that you encounter in your milieu. For example, if you enter a strange office, store, or home, and after leaving any of these places you cannot recall what was in them, you no longer are observing well—or for that matter enjoying life very much.

8. If you do not have any time to spare to become the things worth *being* because you are so preoccupied with getting the things worth *having*.

9. If you attempt to schedule more and more in less and less time, and in doing so make fewer and fewer allowances for unforeseen contingencies. A concomitant of this is a *chronic sense of time urgency*, one of the core components of Type A Behavior Pattern.

10. If, on meeting another severely afflicted Type A person, instead of feeling compassion for his affliction you find yourself compelled to "challenge" him. This is a telltale trait because no one arouses the aggressive and/or hostile feelings of one Type A subject more quickly than another Type A subject.

11. If you resort to certain characteristic gestures or nervous tics. For example, if in conversation you frequently clench your fist, or bang your hand upon a table or pound one fist into a palm of your other hand in order to emphasize a conversational point, you are exhibiting Type A gestures. Similarly, if the corners of your mouth spasmodically, in ticlike fashion, jerk backward slightly exposing your teeth, or if you habitually clench your jaw, or even grind your teeth, you are subject to muscular phenomena suggesting the presence of a continuous *struggle*, which is, of course, the kernel of the Type A Behavior Pattern.

12. If you believe that whatever success you have enjoyed has been due in good part to your ability to get things done faster than your fellow men and if you are afraid to stop doing everything faster and faster.

13. If you find yourself increasingly and ineluctably committed to translating and evaluating not only your own but also the activities of others in terms of "numbers." [Pp. 100–102]

We suggest that once you're read this description, you have a friend, a colleague, or a member of your family read it and tell you how descriptive it is of your behavior and in what specific ways. We have found that it is exceptionally difficult for many Type A's first, to recognize and, second, to admit to any characterization that sounds as though it might cast them in an unfavorable light. Other people's ratings of an individual's Type A behavior are much more predictive of that person's heart disease risk than are his or her own self-ratings of Type A qualities.

Type B behavior, on the other hand, is exemplified by an attitude of relaxed efficiency. Type B people do not drive themselves as relentlessly as Type A's, though they are just as successful and accomplish just as much in their lives. The major difference is that they are able to take time out for other things than acquisition, achievement, and conventional success. They're well rounded. They listen well. They're calm. Here's how Friedman and Rosenman describe the Type B individual:

YOU POSSESS TYPE B
BEHAVIOR PATTERN:

1. If you are completely free of *all* the habits and exhibit none of the traits we have listed that harass the severely afflicted Type A person.

2. If you never suffer from a sense of time urgency with its accompanying impatience.

3. If you harbor no free-floating hostility, and you feel no need to display or discuss either your achievements or accomplishments unless such exposure is demanded by the situation.

4. If, when you play, you do so to find fun and relaxation, not to exhibit your superiority at any cost.

5. If you can relax without guilt, just as you can work without agitation. [P. 103]

By contrast, probably the single most characteristic sign of the Type A person is that he or she is chronically engaged in a *struggle*—whether it's a struggle with time, with other people, or with self-imposed expectations and standards. Physiologically, we know that the Type A struggle leads to an increase in the level of noradrenaline (the "struggle" hormone) is the bloodstream, as well as changes in other aspects of the body's biochemistry—changes that pave the way for coronary heart disease—including higher levels of serum cholesterol, insulin, testosterone, and various other hormones, all of which expose the delicate inner walls of the coronary arteries to unusually high levels of substances that cause thickening and deterioration in them. Eventually, the artery can become blocked. Well over half of us have some degree of blockage in our coronary arteries already. The more serious it gets, the closer we are to heart trouble.

As one of a series of continuing studies designed to refine our understanding of the relationship between heart disease and Type A behavior, Dr. Friedman has selected a sample of heart attack survivors from San Francisco Bay Area industries and corporations and, in collaboration with Dr. Tasto, has devised a number of recommendations for altering this attitude and behavior pattern. The intention of these recommendations, which are currently being discussed with these individuals in small group meetings, is to prevent a recurrence of heart attack. A number of these same treatment strategies are presented next.

WHAT TO DO ABOUT TYPE A BEHAVIOR: THE TREATMENT PACKAGE

All of us must, of course, struggle to some degree simply to keep on living. But most of us also know how to take time out, to let the struggle pass us by for an hour, a day, a week, so that we can renew ourselves and can return to it refreshed. Most of us . . . but not the Type A person. He or she always struggles. Type A's may even struggle in their sleep, grinding their teeth and thrashing about uneasily.

The first step you need to take, if you share a preponderance of Type A qualities, is to realize that some things can be changed and others can't. For example, most of us are not in a position to change certain aspects of our occupations very easily, such as where we work, who we work for, or the type of work we do. Or, to take a more graphic example, if you get on the freeway to go home after work and find within five minutes that you're stuck in the middle of a massive traffic jam, there really isn't much you can do about it. In situations like these, we really have no choice but to *adapt*, and the body of this chapter is devoted—through a discussion of the seven steps shown in the list that follows—to outlining how Type A's can learn to improve their adaptation to life's demands.

Other aspects of life, however, can be changed, and doing so is primarily a matter of organization. For example, Type A's love to set up totally unrealistic timetables for themselves. They take on far too many commitments, this leads to conflict eventually, and they find themselves futilely struggling to catch up.

The remedy is simple: cut down on your commitments, schedule your affairs realistically, leaving room for error, and learn to say *no*, something that Type A's find very difficult to do. Start leaving a little earlier than necessary for your appointments, so that you don't have to rush constantly from place to place. If you're afraid you'll have to sit around with time on your hands because you arrive early somewhere, take along something to read while you wait. Avoid taking on extensive extracurricular commitments outside those involving your job, family, and friends. Accepting a position on a church committee or as an officer in a homeowners' association, for example, can be harder on you in many ways than coping with job stress, because the people in these settings are often strangers to one another; and since they aren't used to interacting together smoothly, it is easier for them to step on one another's toes and to generate exhausting conflicts. Avoid potentially explosive and draining groups or meetings, especially if you've already had a heart attack or know that you have cardiovascular disease. Also, avoid individuals who tend to make you feel frustrated and distressed.

Those, in a nutshell, are the choices for the coronary-prone Type A person: adaptation and reorganization. If you can't learn to accept the unchangeable and change the unacceptable, you're laying yourself open for heart trouble.

So, anything you can do the enhance your adaptability to stressful situations will help prevent cardiovascular disease. Begin to work on these habits:

1. *Learn to slow down and relax.*

2. *Avoid setting perfectionistic standards for yourself and others.*

3. *Remain calm in interpersonal conflicts.*

4. *Work on developing better social support and more positive responses from others.*

5. *Substitute positive for negative scanning.*

6. *Prepare yourself for unexpected stresses.*

7. *Set specific goals; don't always escalate your expectations.*

1. Learning to Relax and Slow Down

Type A's aren't necessarily any more efficient or effective than Type B's, in spite of the fact that they are definitely far more infected with a sense of chronic urgency. They consult their watches constantly and work against a demanding schedule. They eat fast, walk fast, and drive fast. They talk fast, and they wish others would too. They tend to be very intolerant of standing in lines, and they can't stand getting stuck behind slow drivers. Rarely do they feel that anything is getting done as fast as it could and should be.

If this sounds like you, it's essential that you *learn* to slow down. Go back, reread Chapter 2 *slowly*, and work your way through the PMR system described there. Set aside a specific time, perhaps every other day or so, to practice relaxation. Commit yourself to doing this. If you have trouble concentrating on the instructions or find that you tend to work through the PMR procedure too quickly (a common problem for Type A's), tape the instructions, or have a friend tape them so that you have something to pace yourself with.

At the same time that you practice progressive muscle relaxation, develop three separate imaginal scenes, each one depicting a typical situation that tends to upset you. The first should be one of mild upset—perhaps like filling out a bank deposit slip—some slightly boring routine task that tends to make you *mildly* impatient. The second should be a scene in which you become *moderately* upset. Perhaps one like this: you've called a meeting for 9:00 in your office, and your employees are not all there until 9:10 or 9:15. The third should be a scene of *severe* upset, one in which you get boiling mad. Pick as typical a scene as possible in each case, one that you actually encounter in your life. An example of a frustrating scene of this intensity for many Type A's is being stuck on a narrow, winding mountain road behind a very slow driver—a driver who is apparently oblivious to your presence.

Now, as you work on muscle relaxation, try at the same time to envision the first of the foregoing three scenes, that in which you become slightly upset. The object of this exercise is to practice staying relaxed under imagined conditions that you know have the potential to upset you, to get your noradrenaline going. Stay with the imaginary scene for five minutes; then focus your attention on your state of relaxation. Have any muscle areas become tense? If so, work on relaxing them. Then go back to the imaginary scene once more, and redevelop it in detail as vividly as possible in your mind. It will help to picture yourself remaining calm and relaxed, even under stressful conditions. This in turn, as we discuss later, will help elicit different responses from others when you find yourself actually experiencing a potentially distressing event.

Stay with imaginal practice at the mild-upset level until you can remain relaxed and calm throughout this scene. Then and only then should you move on to the moderately upsetting scene. Follow the same procedure—first vividly imagining the scene in explicit detail, then refocusing your attention on your muscle groups, working to rerelax any that may have become tense. Then go back to the moderate scene. In it, introduce new patterns of behavior in which you remain calm and unruffled. Finally, once you can remain relaxed in the moderately upsetting scene, work through this same procedure with the most upsetting scene. Repeat it as often as necessary until you find, upon checking your state of relaxation, that you're able to remain physically relaxed even under the most extreme conditions you might plausibly encounter. We predict that if you stick to this process, you will find that your newly learned ability to lower your level of tension under upsetting imaginary circumstances will begin to transfer to real-life situations. It will take work, of course, but you will find that you have learned to exert greater control over your urgency responses through imaginal rehearsal.

Type A individuals frequently live with the mistaken assumption that in order to be mentally alert, they must also be physically tense. This isn't true. You must learn just the opposite, to remain mentally alert while staying as physically relaxed as possible. You must learn to "uncouple" cognitive processes from physiological ones, especially those linked to states of chronic tension and stress and thus to cardiovascular disease.

Once you feel that you've gotten the knack of using relaxation to uncouple physical stress from mental stimulation, try applying this process to some very simple, common, real-life situations such as driving or writing. As you sit, concentrating on one of these functions, note your general level of muscle tension. It will almost invariably be much higher than it needs to be. If it is, take each muscle group separately—your shoulders, arms, hands, stomach, thighs, calves, feet—and slowly relax it. Work to reduce your physical tension as much as possible without actually going completely limp, of course. You will find that your overall tension level can be dramatically reduced without impairing your driving, writing, or thinking ability in the least. In fact, you may also find that your effectiveness at any of these or similar tasks actually increases, the more you practice this uncoupling process.

2. Avoiding Perfectionistic Standards

Most Type A's tend to expect far too much of themselves and of others, and they tend to expect far too perfect a fulfillment of their expectations. Unfortunately, when others do inevitably fall short of meeting these standards, it is the Type A man or woman who becomes frustrated and upset, *not* the others upon whom he or she has imposed perfectionistic expectations. That's the problem with unrealistic standards: when they aren't met, the Type A person is the one who suffers, not those for whom the expectations are established.

Consider the example of Tim H., the owner of a small plastics firm. Tim has angina[2] and has been warned by his doctor that he must learn to take it easier if he wants to avoid heart trouble. Tim likes punctuality and insists on it in his employees. Up to a point, this is a reasonable and prudent expectation for any independent businessman to have. But Tim carries it to an extreme. When he sets a meeting for 9:00, he expects everyone to be there precisely at 9:00, and he gets extremely upset if anyone is even a minute or two late. This is not reasonable, and the only individual who really suffers from the frustration and anger that this expectation arouses in Tim when it isn't met is Tim himself, since he is unwilling to go so far as to fire an employee for being 10 minutes late to a meeting.

Tim has realized that if he is going to avert heart trouble, he is going to have to change his Type A behavior patterns, starting with his excessively exacting demands for punctuality at meeting times. It took him quite a while and some conscious effort to revise his unrealistic expectations, but now Tim simply assumes that a meeting scheduled for 9:00 will actually start at 9:10. And it usually does. This way, he saves himself the stress of unrealistically perfectionistic standards, and he saves his employees the annoyance of his bad moods.

Tim also used to set these same demanding kinds of standards for his family. For example, when he used to find that his kids had left things like clothes, or tools, or toys lying around the house, he would become extremely annoyed and would try to outwait them, hoping that they would eventually come looking for whatever it was that they had carelessly dropped, knowing that he would then be able to rebuke them for not keeping better track of their possessions. But he was

[2]Angina pectoris is a type of pain, usually felt in the chest, that is caused by a lack of adequate oxygen in the blood in the coronary arteries. It is probably the most common symptom of heart disease.

the only member of the family who was ever really aggravated by their lack of organization, and he found he was spending days on end fuming over a jacket left on the stairs or a hammer left out in the yard.

Finally Tim agreed that since it was only upsetting to him, he would just go ahead and pick these things up himself. It was difficult at first, since he felt as though he was spending his evenings and weekends doing nothing but picking up after his kids, but eventually they began to respond to the example he was setting, and the entire problem no longer exists. They responded much better to his quiet, relaxed example than to his pent-up fury.

Tim has also changed his expectations of himself. There was a time, in the not-too-distant past, when he was flatly unable to limit the amount of work he would try to accomplish in a day. He was a workaholic. And this, coupled with his extreme sensitivity to deadlines and to the passage of time, made it impossible for him to get through a day without experiencing an incredible sense of stress. Now he focuses on the essentials and refuses to let himself get involved in tangential concerns. For example, instead of calling up subcontractors and suppliers that he's angry with and spending half an hour barking at them on the phone, now he has his secretary send them a terse note, and he spends his time on the phone promoting new business. Tim finds that he's easily more efficient than he used to be, back when he felt compelled to watch even the tiniest detail like a hawk waiting to pounce. And he feels much healthier.

Is the Type A behavior pattern necessary for success? We think not. Certainly those components of this behavior pattern that are most risky in terms of heart disease—the chronic sense of time urgency, the free-floating hostility, the polyphasic activity patterns, and the general aggressive irritability—are as counterproductive as they are helpful. Tim, for one, has no doubt that he's twice the businessman now that he was only a few months ago.

3. Remaining Calm in
Interpersonal Conflicts

Driven as they are by their overwhelming sense of inner urgency, Type A's tend to revert very quickly to anger, hostility, and frustration when they are confronted with interpersonal conflict. They also tend to be uninterested in small talk, feeling that it is essentially a waste of time.

Tim was like this, too, until his enlightened doctor convinced him that his behavior was putting him at risk of an early heart attack. For example, in meetings with his two business partners, disagreements among the three of them almost always led to red faces and a shouting match. It wasn't that the outcome was especially significant in any of these arguments; instead, it was that a rational discussion had turned into a power struggle, and Tim felt that if he gave in on even the smallest issue, it was tantamount to losing control, to defeat.

Tim felt that he was in an unresolvable dilemma. He put it this way: "I'm not sure I know what to do in these situations. If they make me angry, shouldn't I blow up and get it out of my system, or should I do nothing and just ignore it?" His doctor explained that these were not Tim's only real alternatives. There was a third: deal with the problem in a relaxed, effective way. Don't let your anger get out of control, but don't attempt to pretend simply that the problem doesn't exist either—neither of these alternatives will satisfy you. Deal with issues that must be dealt with, so that the outcome will be to your satisfaction, but keep cool. Practicing relaxation and preparing for these stressful events will help.

Once Tim began to see that remaining calm and relaxed could be a superb technique for gaining the upper hand and paving the way to more effective interaction over truly important issues, he was won over. One day, during a meeting on an especially critical topic, Tim said virtually nothing to either of his partners, though he knew without a doubt that they were in fact wrong on a number of points. Instead of fighting them on the spot, Tim remained calm. He even made a point of agreeing with those statements that he knew to be correct. Both of Tim's partners were astonished by this change in his tactics. They kept looking at him oddly, waiting for him to explode.

The next day, at the continuation of the same meeting, Tim calmly and quietly listed his criticisms of the points that had been raised in the previous meeting. He was careful to remain relaxed and to communicate an emotional state of cooperation, not tension, but to say precisely what it was that he wanted to get across rather than duck the issues. His partners were, as you might expect, stunned, but more important, *they listened.* Tim did not have to repeat himself, nor did he have to raise his voice once. They agreed with every point he made. When he left the meeting, he felt great. For once, he had been able to be persuasive and to communicate effectively without having first to become furious.

Once a Type A person like Tim is able to move beyond an initial reaction of hostility in interpersonal conflict and to remain calm instead, it becomes possible to appreciate the essential value of human relationships.

4. Developing Better Social Support

Opportunities for generating much more positive social responsiveness abound in nearly everyone's daily environment. If you want to break up patterns of social interaction that tend to alienate others and to keep you isolated, try spontaneously acting in a more positive manner toward those with whom you come into casual contact during the day. Say something pleasant to the clerk in the grocery store, the waitress in the restaurant, the teller in the bank, and the attendant at the service station. Pay attention to the response you generate.

> Tim, for example, used to sit habitually grumpy and withdrawn, over his morning cup of coffee at a small donut shop near his plant. He almost never said anything to the waitress and rarely even really looked at her. But when he began trying to restructure his social interactions so that he got more positive feedback, Tim vowed that he would start with Judy, the waitress. Noticing the next morning that her service was as prompt and cheerful as usual, he complimented her. She was a little surprised at his gesture at first, but she responded warmly, and a very pleasant conversation ensued. Tim reports that he left the shop that day feeling much more optimistic, cheerful, and relaxed than usual.

> The same thing happened with Tim's family and friends. When he began to smile more, to stop and chat pleasantly, to show an interest in them, they were surprised at first, but they quickly began to respond in kind.

Social interactions are to a great extent under your control. If you initiate them and follow through, they will flourish. If you never initiate them and never try to keep them up, they will lapse. You can't simply wait until you "feel like it" before you start acting more pleasantly and positively to the other people in your life. It doesn't work that way. First, you must begin to change your patterns of behavior—it will feel uncomfortable and artificial to do this at first—then you will find that the positive responses you elicit will become self-sustaining, that it will become easier and easier and more and more rewarding to engage in these contacts. It helps to learn to listen to what others are saying and to ask them questions about themselves, questions that show that you have been taking an alert interest in what they've been telling you. Type A individuals, as Dr. Friedman points out, tend to fail to pay real attention to those with whom they converse. Instead, they tend to concentrate only on what they themselves want to say and to block out what they're being told by others. They tend to talk *at*, rather than *with*, others.

Take advantage of opportunities to get to know new people. Set aside work for the time being, or at least make it a secondary consideration, and just try to relate to others as fellow human beings rather than colleagues, clients, or competitors. Try to relax with them, and you'll soon find that their interest in you will grow. If you've been a hard-core Type A person for some time, you will find that it is surprisingly difficult and even uncomfortable to do this. The reason is that you feel you're letting your guard down and losing control when you try to be friendly. Try not to let this feeling inhibit you—it isn't accurate. You're not going to lose control simply because you become friendlier with people.

> Tim found that this technique worked well for him even under unexpected, stressful conditions, conditions that he couldn't prepare for by relaxing beforehand. For instance, his son backed rapidly out of the driveway one day somewhat carelessly and hit a car parked across the street. Normally, Tim would have become enraged, would have chewed his son out and punished him, and they probably wouldn't have spoken to each other again for days. This time, however, he checked himself, knowing that his son would already be feeling guilty and scared. He remained calm and did not explode, and they looked both cars over together. As a result, his son remained calm and did the right thing—volunteered to see to it that the other car's owner was informed of the details of the accident, that the insurance company was notified, and that both cars were properly repaired. At the end of the discussion, Tim and his son actually felt closer than they had for some time.

5. Learning Positive Scanning

Type A people tend to be hypercritical. In stressful settings, they allow themselves to react initially with strongly negative perceptions. As soon as one negative thought arises, it generates a second, which generates a third, and so on. In retrospect, the entire experience seems intolerable and oppressive.

The antidote to this behavior is intentional positive scanning. All of us, Type A's included, have had so many experiences, both positive and negative, that we are entirely free to choose which kind we will allow ourselves to dwell on. If we *choose* to react to a setting with a positive memory or expectation or comment, we are far more likely to generate further positive responses, both in ourselves and in others, and therefore to predispose ourselves toward enjoying the entire experience.

The next time—in any setting, whether familiar or strange—that you find yourself assuming a distinctly negative bias, *stop* for a moment, and deliberately redirect your thought patterns. Pick something positive in the surroundings, and force yourself to consider it, to make a remark to yourself on it. Note the effect on yourself and others. Continue in this positive vein, and you will probably find that you can transform your negative expectations into positive ones.

If you find that you *habitually* react to certain settings with negative thoughts and comments, work on altering those responses at home. Using the PMR method described in Chapter 2, put yourself into as complete a state of relaxation as you can. Now imagine the typical negative responses you'd like to change. Notice the tension they produce in you. Think about the feelings and mental processes that you associate with this situation. Analyze them in detail.

Then remodel them. Create a set of positive attitudes, thoughts, and actions appropriate to the same setting. In your imagination, practice experiencing these in the same setting as you remain relaxed. This may not be as easy as it sounds. You will feel that you're letting go of something, and you will resist the change from negative to positive. But continue anyway. Once you can experience relaxation concurrently with what have been negative cues for you, you'll find that this sense of uneasiness vanishes. Check your state of relaxation occasionally to be sure that you can maintain it and that no specific muscle groups are getting tense. If they are, focus on relaxing them.

Next, apply this to the real-life situation. As we have stated before, this won't be an automatic transference from imagination to actual experiences. There will probably be a lag between the progress you make imaginally and in real life. To start with, pick a setting that is relatively easy to control, such as in your car. As we've mentioned earlier, a common situation in which people—particularly Type A's—find themselves becoming overly tense and negative is while driving. Pick a pleasant scene, an expectation, a fantasy, or a memory, and direct your thought processes to it instead of to the negative topics and attitudes that you ordinarily allow yourself to dwell on. Both the muscle-relaxation process and the positive-scanning technique will help you feel calmer, better, and less tense even under the moderate stress of driving.

6. Preparing for Unexpected Stresses

Many Type A's find that they can alter their habitual patterns of behavior to many of life's routine stresses, but they aren't so sure about their reactions to unexpected events.

When Tim first started working on reducing his Type A reactions, he found that they were most obvious to him at the office, so they were naturally the most quickly altered there.

But he kept running into other situations that he hadn't anticipated in other settings that also provoked his Type A behavior. One day, for example, he went out to work on the yard and got so involved in it that he just couldn't stop. Instead, he drove himself harder and harder, trying to accomplish more and more, until he finally began to feel the familiar, unmistakable pain of angina. He simply hadn't expected yard work on the weekend to evoke Type A responses.

On another occasion, Tim found himself experiencing the first signs of chest pain while he was organizing material and forms so that he could begin working on his income tax returns. It wasn't paying the taxes but the work involved in planning all the details and the steps of calculating them that provoked his Type A reactions.

When you know that you're going to be encountering a stressful event, you can prepare yourself for it by relaxing, by planning and rehearsing your thoughts, your comments, and your actions in your imagination; by positive scanning, and by using social support systems. You can even rehearse just what you want to say aloud, as people often do who are invited to give public speeches. These kinds of preparation are valuable and effective.

But when you're thrown into a situation that you hadn't expected would be stressful and you suddenly find yourself with all your struggle responses in full cry, it can be doubly hard to return to a sense of calm and relaxation. This is one reason why it is very important to practice the PMR method regularly, until you reach a level of ability with it that allows you to relax yourself quickly and completely.

Under these circumstances, your goal should be first to identify those commonly recurring situations when you could be better prepared for the stresses they involve but ordinarily aren't. Second, when you do find yourself in a stressful event that you could not have foreseen, don't add to your tension by worrying about your stress levels at that moment. Wait until the event is over, then concentrate on reducing the amount of time that you remain at a high level of stress afterward. In other words, dampen down the emotional reverberations as quickly as possible. And use this same tactic on subsequent occasions when you find yourself in the midst of unexpected stress: wait until after the occasion is over, then focus on countering the nervous system arousal it evoked in you.

7. Setting Goals

The reason that most of us struggle to some degree—and Type A's to an excessive degree—is a desire for some kind of attainment, whether material, professional, or even artistic.

Too often we delude ourselves, telling ourselves that the struggle is temporary, that once we've attained our goal—whether it's a first million dollars by the time we're thirty-five, tenure and chairmanship of the department, or publication of the first book—we'll relax, we'll be satisfied. But then, once we've accomplished what we set out to do, we often find that as rewarding as the sense of accomplishment may be, it's temporary; and it soon subsides, leaving us feeling a little hollow, a little empty, wishing for another success, and ready to take on the next challenge that life holds for us.

To a degree, this desire for achievement is necessary and healthy. Carried to an extreme, it is a disease . . . and a deadly one. It must be halted at some point.

This is the value of setting firm goals for yourself and of learning early in life to pace yourself at whatever you do. Goals should be milestones. They should allow you to direct your efforts toward specific ends, and more important, they should prevent you from taking on every attractive opportunity or challenge that comes your way. Opportunity, it is said, is the enemy of commitment. Goals help you learn to say no, and you have to learn to say no in order to survive and prosper, particularly if you're a Type A person.

An important part of arriving at the goals you've set for yourself is pacing the work you do to get there. You must learn how much struggle you'll allow yourself before you back off, take a break—*even when you don't feel like it*—and get involved in something else for a while before you come back to work again.

Most of us pace ourselves automatically. We stop work and go out for a cup of coffee. Or we go talk to a friend in the next office. It's a healthy pattern of behavior. Type A's tend to be far more compulsive. If they do set up a schedule, it's apt to be a highly regimented one, with each box filled in for weeks in advance. And if it is interrupted, they are likely to become extremely upset and highly conscious of the passing of "wasted" time.

Then, on the other hand, if they work efficiently and get ahead of their own self-imposed deadlines, instead of relaxing and letting demands catch up to them again, they're far more likely to pile on extra projects, to assume new obligations, to escalate continuously their level of activity and commitment.

Learn not to respond to every demand. Don't answer every phone call, every letter. Allow yourself to be imperfect, even to make mistakes and to fail now and then. Accept the fact that some things simply won't be completed and that life itself is largely a process of unfinished efforts.

Try also to devote some part of every week to interests that have no practical, direct application Art, gardening, sports, reading . . . there are thousands of things you can do to distract yourself, for a refreshing moment, from the urgent struggle to which you're all too susceptible under ordinary circumstances.

Finally, do be sure to acknowledge your successes in

changing your behavior patterns, even if they seem very slight to you. Driven as they are by the never-ending challenge of new worlds to conquer, Type A's tend to underestimate their own accomplishments. And because they are so tenacious, they may not even pause to congratulate themselves on major achievements. In the context of cardiovascular risks, however, even the slightest alteration of Type A patterns is a triumph. Don't ignore it. Celebrate it.

HYPERTENSION: THE SILENT KILLER

Like Type A behavior, hypertension (high blood pressure) is a serious risk factor in the development of heart disease and stroke. In many ways, hypertension is the more insidious of the two, since it is impossible to detect externally; there are few if any visible manifestations of hypertension in the great majority of cases. Although medications have been developed that do control hypertension, thus reducing the risk of developing cardiovascular disease, if these drugs are not finely tuned to the metabolism of the hypertensive individual, they can result in unpleasant and adverse side effects such as nausea, fatigue, and impotence. Often there is also an understandable problem of noncompliance with the physician's instructions to take the medication. For example, Alfred is hypertensive. He feels fine, but his doctor tells him that he is sick; then, ironically, once Alfred starts taking the prescribed medication, he begins to feel sick, but his doctor now tells him that he is actually getting well. This is the kind of contradiction in normal body signals about health and disease that is very difficult to adjust to.

Fortunately, there are, in some cases, alternatives or adjuncts to medication. Research work conducted over the last decade or so in the United States and England has demonstrated that a number of behavioral techniques, including biofeedback and progressive muscle relaxation, can be effective in reducing blood pressure levels for many mild and moderate hypertensives, both in the laboratory and under real-life conditions. For example, it has been recognized since the late 1930s that decreases in muscle activity are associated with decreases in blood pressure for most people. Certain of the newer studies in this area have also shown that after following a program that combined relaxation training with meditation practice, approximately half of a sample population was able either to reduce substantially the amount of hypertension medication they were taking or to eliminate it altogether. Research conducted by Donald L. Tasto and James E. Shoemaker has demonstrated that the higher the original hypertensive blood pressure level, the more effective relaxation is in reducing it to a normal range. In other words, the higher a person's blood pressure is when relaxation practice begins, the greater the drop will be as a result of relaxation training.

These methods take practice, of course; one can't just spend an hour or two learning this new behavior pattern and then expect immediate change without further effort. It's not as simple as popping a pill, but it may result in more pleasant side effects.

It is particularly important in learning to control blood pressure levels in this manner to identify the particular events and types of situations in your life that tend to get you upset (see Chapter 2), especially those situations in which you typically tend to become overly frustrated, tense, anxious, hostile, and so forth. Bringing relaxation to bear on these particular moments of stress can be tremendously effective in reducing your overall hypertension level. And if you can learn first to relax and then to apply this response to these stressful events in your life, you will not only be able to supplement the effects of pharmacological interventions, but you will also generally feel better.

WHAT TO DO ABOUT HYPERTENSION: THE TREATMENT PACKAGE

1. *See your physician.*
2. *Learn the PMR method.*
3. *Monitor your blood pressure.*
4. *Construct a hierarchy of upsetting situations.*
5. *Practice relaxation in imaginal stresses.*
6. *Apply relaxation to real-life stresses.*
7. *Check your blood pressure levels again, while you continue to apply relaxation.*

1. Consulting Your Physician

Anyone whose blood pressure tends consistently to be higher than 140/90 is hypertensive.[3] However, you shouldn't try to diagnose your own blood pressure, even if you know

---

[3]The higher of these two numbers is the systolic pressure level, which is the reading taken as the heart cavities contract, pumping the blood out along the arteries. The lower number is the diastolic level, which reflects the reading taken as the same cavities expand, allowing blood from the veins to rush in and fill up the heart again. The diastolic level is generally considered to be the more reliable figure in diagnosing hypertension.

that it consistently tends to remain above that level. For one thing, a small proportion (perhaps 10 percent) of hypertensive problems are due to organic causes, and it will take a physician's knowledge and experience to determine if this is the case for you. It probably isn't, since the great majority of cases of hypertension are those called *essential* hypertension (meaning nothing more than that their cause is unknown). Discuss the dangers of hypertension and the side effects of the medications available for it with your physician, as well as the advantages of a relaxation program if you wish. Not every doctor will be aware of the research that has been performed on reduction of blood pressure levels through relaxation methods, but all will be able to give you additional information on the effects of high blood pressure on the cardiovascular system and on the best ways to go about monitoring your own blood pressure.

2. Learning to Relax

For step 2 of your hypertension program, go back to Chapter 2, reread it carefully, and begin to learn the PMR method that we describe there. If you've already worked at the PMR method and you're competent at muscle relaxation, or if you've already begun to combine it with some form of meditative practice, so much the better.

Becoming proficient at the PMR method requires practice. Hypertension is a chronic problem, and its treatment must necessarily be chronic as well. Most people find that it helps to schedule a regular time of day to work through the process, one in which they can take their time and not feel rushed. Use a taped instruction procedure if you find it hard to pace yourself, particularly if you find that you tend to rush through the program too rapidly. Try to practice at least once a day for at least a two-week period before you begin applying relaxation to the real-life events that you identify as upsetting in step 4.

3. Monitoring Your Blood Pressure

A number of stores, including large variety stores as well as many local pharmacies, now carry fairly inexpensive ($20–$30) blood-pressure testing kits that can be easily operated by you or a member of your family. Obtain one, and begin to monitor your blood pressure at regular intervals throughout the day, perhaps every three or four hours or so. When you know that you're approaching, are in, or have just left a particularly stressful situation, check your blood pressure. It will tend to rise with stress, and with time as the day wears on, but only if the average reading over the entire day is more than 140/90 should you consider yourself hypertensive.

Do this for two weeks, at the same time that you practice relaxation and identify typical upsetting and stressful events in your home and work environment (step 4). You may notice some drop in the daily average blood pressure level over these two weeks as you become more adept at relaxation and as you become accustomed to the very minor stress involved in taking your blood pressure and in thinking about your hypertension. Keep track of the daily averages on a self-recording form like that shown in Figure 8.5. This will provide valuable baseline information for comparison with your blood pressure levels once you have spent some time working on imaginal and real-life application of the PMR method.

Figure 8.5 Blood Pressure Self-Monitoring Form

	7:00 A.M.	12:00 NOON	6:00 P.M.	11:00 P.M.	AVERAGE
Day	Syst/diast	Syst/diast	Syst/diast	Syst/diast	Syst/diast
1					
2					
3					
4					
5					
6					
7					
8					
9					
10					
11					
12					
13					
14					

4. Establishing a Hierarchy of Upsetting Events

Obtain a notebook—one that you use only for this hypertension intervention program—and keep it with you for two weeks. In it, note any event that makes you feel tense, angry, hostile, nervous, upset, and so forth, and give each event a rating of how upset it made you on a scale of 1 to 10, 10 being livid with rage and 1 being mildly annoyed.

When the two-week period is over, look back through your notebook, and review which of these upsetting events occurred most often and which evoked the most extreme response in you. Chances are, you will already have a good idea of just which upsetting events in your life tend to take place most often and which tend to upset you the most.

Once you've reviewed the notebook, create three imaginal scenes using material that corresponds closely to the real experiences that you've been recording. One should be a scene of mild upset, in which you become annoyed but not outraged and which you are able to forget quickly. The second should be a more seriously upsetting scene, one in which there is some clear outward sign of your stress—a change in your voice, heavier perspiration, faster breathing, shakiness, or the like but not outright rage. The third should be a scene of violent upset, one in which you're as furious as you ever get.

Some people find that there are typically only a few very specific scenes, settings, or events in their lives that have the power to cause them severe emotional stress. Others find that some level of upset is almost chronic in their lives, that practically everything they do or encounter has some potential to cause them to become tense or angry or "concerned." In either case, a three-scene hierarchy will properly represent these stresses for the next step in the treatment program.

5. Practicing Imaginal Application of Relaxation Under Stress

When the hierarchy of step 4 has been established and the scenes have been described in concise, realistic detail, practice applying relaxation under imaginal stress. Find a

comfortable place, one where you're not likely to be interrupted, and put yourself into a relaxed state using the PMR
method.

When you're thoroughly relaxed, begin to imagine the
scene of mild upset. Concentrate on recreating, in your
mind, the sensations that you felt at that moment and the
emotions that you typically experience. Do this for two minutes. If you have trouble concentrating, try taping the description of the scene, or have a friend read it onto the tape
for you.

At the same time, remain relaxed. After two minutes, let
the scene slip from your mind, and check your relaxation. If
any muscle areas have become tense, work on relaxing them.
Then return to the imaginal scene for another two minutes.
The second time around, imagine that you behave differently in the upsetting situation, that instead of becoming
irritated or annoyed, you stay unruffled. You respond appropriately, but you do not let your negative emotions or
your physiological reactions to stress come into play. You
remain relaxed.

When you're able to work through the first scene—that
of least emotional intensity—without becoming tense, go on
to the next scene—that of moderate distress—and follow the
same procedure. Concentrate on it in detail for two minutes,
check your relaxation for one minute, then go back to the
imaginal scene for two more minutes. As before, the second
time you work on this scene, substitute imaginal responses of
effective coping and of relaxed mastery for your previous
reactions of tension, fear, and anger.

And finally, apply the same procedure to the scene of
most stress for you. The more arousing the scene becomes,
of course, the more work it may take for you to learn to relax
through it. If you find that you just can't seem to make the
transition between two scenes, create a bridge as we discussed
in Chapter 5—a scene of intermediate intensity—and work
with it until you've mastered it; then go on to the most difficult scene.

6. Applying Relaxation to Real-Life Stress

Relaxation techniques *will* lower dangerously high blood pressure levels for many people, but for this technique to be truly effective, these levels must not only be lowered but must also be *kept* lowered throughout days full of typical stresses. This is why it is *essential* to learn how to cue relaxation into the routines of daily living. It can't just be practiced for fifteen- to twenty-minute periods once or twice a day and left at that.

One series of research studies at Stanford University found that if hypertensive subjects were *not* taught to apply relaxation to real-life settings, their blood pressure levels would initially drop but would then gradually rise to dangerous levels again. However, when these subjects were then taught, in a more carefully designed follow-up study, to cue their relaxation responses into stressful situations regularly, there was not only an initial drop in blood pressure levels but also a continuation of the reduction in these levels.

So the important thing—once you have become well versed in overall deep muscle relaxation, have monitored and ordered your daily stresses into hierarchies of progressively greater potential to cause you to become tense, and have begun the imaginal rehearsal process—is to learn to cue relaxation into those daily situations that make your blood pressure levels start to climb. Again, let us reiterate that this is not a simple or automatic process. It takes commitment and deliberate, systematic practice. But, performed properly, it works.

We described building one hierarchy, but the process needn't stop there. Continue to scan your daily routines for additional stress-inducing events and interactions; then work these into new imaginal rehearsal scenes. Also, pay closer attention to the aspects of your environment that have the capacity to make you even *slightly* anxious and tense. Too often, we tend to ignore these, since they may seem to be very trivial, taken one by one. But they can become cumulative, each one contributing just a bit more to our overall level of arousal. So become alert to even the minor stresses in your life. Relaxation works best as a preventive technique, at *low* levels of physiological excitement. Once your blood pressure levels have risen to moderate or high levels, relaxation will be less and less effective at managing it.

Finally, you may want to refer to the Anxiety Management Training process that we described at the end of Chapter 5 to refresh your understanding of how best to cope with the anxiety cues in your environment. As we stated there, the essence of the AMT process is learning to use the actual signals of stress, tension, and anxiety as *cues* for relaxation. To learn this, you alternate imaginal scenes that cause you to become tense with relaxation practice until you've connected the two in such a way that tension itself becomes an automatic trigger for the incompatible state of relaxation.

7. Continuing to Monitor Blood Pressure Levels

You will find that concrete evidence of the effectiveness of this hypertension program is easily the best kind of support and reinforcement for continuing it that you could have. Even if you've managed to reduce your blood pressure levels back down to normal ranges for your age, continue to check yourself periodically, particularly before and after stressful events.

nine

Couples

Making Close Relationships Work

> There is nothing nobler or more admirable than when two people who see eye to eye keep house as man and wife, confounding their enemies and delighting their friends.
>
> —HOMER

Some dissatisfaction is inevitable in any long-term, intimate relationship. Eventually, one partner will always find some aspect of the other partner's behavior displeasing. How a couple handles its antagonisms and disagreements can make or break the relationship.

Communication, negotiation, and compromise can render harmless the threat of implied criticism and rejection and can transform the presentation of mutual dissatisfactions into an opportunity for learning and mutual growth. On the other hand, coercion and withdrawal, insults, and sarcasm will only exacerbate the pain of an already troubled relationship and probably will hurry it toward its end. Couples who cannot learn to express their dissatisfactions to one another in reasonable, balanced, and effective ways either break up or tend to bury their differences under a largely contrived pose of superficial amiability—one that may serve to block off any threatening discussion of serious issues but that also condemns each partner to the claustrophobic nausea of a relationship grounded in avoidance, withdrawal, and isolation. Unhappiness doesn't just go away; either it gets dealt with, or it remains—just under the surface of the relationship, slowly corroding the bonds that may once have held two people together.

In this chapter, we discuss the best ways to acknowledge and manage the difficulties and petty little hatreds that inevitably beset any arrangement that involves two human beings sharing domestic routines, mutual economic and emotional responsibilities, and sexual intimacy. Though we recognize that there are numerous other expressions of the universal human desire for companionship, marriage, of course, has historically been by far the most prevalent expression of this kind of human pairing, and it remains so today. As well as the usual stresses and strains that are encountered in any pairing context, marriage usually also adds the element of child rearing and the assumption of parental roles to the relationship. Because it is the predominant form of pairing, we focus our remarks on the interaction between heterosexual, married couples.

One advantage of dealing with the stresses of a relationship is that you have a partner to help you work out your problems, one who in most cases is as interested as you are in seeing difficulties overcome so that the relationship can succeed. Although you may at moments find yourself regarding your partner as the cause of your distress rather than as a source of help in alleviating it, try to bear in mind that you can't make the partnership function rewardingly without his or her active participation.

If you find, upon reflection, that your interpersonal anxieties do not stem from your close relationships but rather from encounters with people at work or in other more public situations, and that there is in fact very little if any likelihood of enlisting the cooperation of the other party to the distressing interactions, refer to Chapter 6 on learning to develop more assertive behavior rather than continuing here. This chapter is designed to help you manage interpersonal anxieties by involving another person—one who is an intimate partner in the problem areas that concern you.

A number of basic principles should be covered first. Probably the most important one is that your own behavior plays the most important role in determining how others, especially those who are closely involved in your life, respond to you. Their actions, words, and gestures are less a function of their own predetermined attitudes and personality types than they are a function of how you behave toward them. What you say, how you look and act, whether you carry out your intentions or not, all the observable manifestations of your thoughts, moods, and attitudes are the factors that exert the most powerful influence on determining what your spouse's attitudes and actions toward you will be.

An important corollary to this point is that it is next to impossible—as well as being an enormous waste of time—to try to guess or assume what your partner or spouse is thinking. Don't mind read. Give up all your efforts to psychoanalyze your partner's actions and words, to fit them into some overall psychological pattern that will reveal hypothetical underlying motivations or attitudes. Forgo asking yourself or your partner "why" events have taken place or "why" changes are desired; the fact that they are desired is sufficient.

Instead, direct your efforts toward identifying—in concrete, here-and-now terms—what it is that your spouse does or says that you dislike and, even more important, what he or she doesn't do or doesn't say that you would like to see more of in your relationship. Concentrate more on the absence of mutually rewarding behavior than on the presence of mutually frustrating behavior.

It is an unfortunate truth that in troubled relationships,

the proportion of negative interactions, of conflicts, jumps dramatically as the proportion of positive interactions and pleasant gestures drops. Irritating contact soon far outweighs rewarding interaction. The first and most important effort is to bring the proportion back into balance, into a position where each partner feels that the pluses outweigh the minuses.

Furthermore, there is an inevitable decline in distinct pluses over the long run in any well-established relationship, as positive interactions tend to be taken for granted. So when conflicts arise, their impact is often exaggerated, since the counterbalancing positives and pleasures in the relationship have already tended to fade into the woodwork.

To avert the fatal erosion of a relationship, the two most elementary things you need to learn are: (1) positive scanning—that is, how to resensitize yourself to your partner, so that you once again notice rewarding features of your relationship that you may have begun to overlook; and (2) how to cast your requests for a change in your partner's behavior in terms that ask for an *increase in positive activities* rather than a decrease in negatives. Since negative interactions already predominate in troubled relationships, requests for a change that can be misread as implied criticisms or subtle forms of rejection are treacherous. The last thing you want more of is interactions that only escalate the pain and distress already present in a troubled relationship.

You must also learn the art of deliberate negotiation and contracting for change. Most relationships of any kind are based on self-interested exchange—a *quid pro quo*. Each partner gives, each gets, and each strives to reach a comfortable balance point where he or she is satisfied that the gain outweighs the cost. Otherwise, the relationship is based on neurotic needs and will probably never succeed except in neurotic terms.

WHAT TO DO TO MAKE
YOUR RELATIONSHIP WORK:
THE TREATMENT PACKAGE

The treatment package for reviving a dying relationship takes these seven steps:

1. *Open up communications.*
2. *Define what needs to change, in terms of desired increases in specific positive or pleasant actions.*
3. *Write down and rank the desired changes by importance and level of difficulty.*
4. *Learn the PMR relaxation technique discussed in Chapter 2.*
5. *Present the desired changes to your partner in a relaxed, step-by-step manner.*
6. *Plan specific change contracts.*
7. *Monitor the change as it takes place.*

1. Opening Up Communications

The first step in changing some area of a relationship is to lay the foundation for discussions about desired changes. Asking someone else—even someone as intimate a partner in life as a wife or husband—to do something differently can be extremely difficult to do, not only because of a natural desire in close relationships to avoid hurting one another's feelings,

229

but also because such a request can touch on topics that have become so sensitive there is a virtual conspiracy of silence about them.

Frequently, long-standing interpersonal anxiety in long-term relationships has had the effect of placing whole subject areas off limits for discussion, and each partner can only speculate on what the other's reactions would be to these issues. Avoiding them altogether is the only way that some couples have of managing their anxiety at discussing them. You may in fact feel quite unhappy with the way your spouse handles money, or cooks, or dresses, or makes love, or ignores the children; but if you don't communicate fully and openly your point of view and reach some negotiated change, all you have is a constant level of irritation and hostility, as well as a strong and pervasive sense of loss of control over some very important areas of your life.

So it can be surprisingly difficult just to begin to alter the normal patterns of communication and noncommunication in a relationship, particularly if the level of disruption has reached a stage where statements that one of you intends as positive are understood by the other as bearing only negative connotations. This kind of defensive misinterpretation is often a severe problem in very troubled relationships, and it can be very difficult to dispel sufficiently so that candid, uninhibited communication can take place without evoking a great deal of negative conversational fallout.

You may be telling yourself as you read this that every time you try to talk to your spouse about the things in your relationship that displease you, the conversation seems to degenerate into an unpleasant fight, that it just isn't worth the aggravation for you, that you've given up trying to change things in the areas that seem to be especially sensitive. If that's true, you're faced with a difficult choice: either you tolerate, for the life of the relationship, the frustration and anger that constant exposure to a displeasing pattern of behavior on the part of your spouse brings you, or you develop a methodical, rational way first to talk about the changes you desire and then to structure ways actually to bring them about. We're interested in helping you with the second option.

However, before going on with a discussion of actual strategies for relaxed discussion and negotiation of change, we want to acknowledge that some relationships are hopeless. It does happen, not all that infrequently, that an immature and dependent man or woman develops an intimate, long-term relationship with a far more self-sufficient and mature partner, often as a way of escaping the anxieties that are an intrinsic part of true autonomy. In our view, these relationships are poor imitations of the kinds of interaction that is ideally possible between two mutually responsive adults. Unfortunately, however, these crippled relationships frequently are perversely hard to change, perhaps because both partners tacitly understand the enormous fear that one of them has of being left alone. Both become so paralyzed by this prospect that they essentially engage in a collusion to protect him or her from life itself. There is nothing noble or heroic about this; it is one of the most pitiful and devastating ways conceivable to destroy human dignity. Feelings can become so exhausted and corroded by one partner's insatiable need for security that eventually the other gets completely burned out and has nothing left to give.

The procedures we discuss here are unlikely to work in these cases, since the health of the relationship has been irrevocably subordinated to the futile effort to satisfy one individual's neurotic needs. Instead, we assume the involvement of two more or less reasonable individuals, both of whom want to see their relationship maintained and improved because of the very real, identifiable rewards and gratifications that they realize from it. If one partner cannot succeed, at the outset, in translating his or her sense of dissatisfaction with the relationship into eight to ten *specific* kinds of behavior that the other should change, go no further. A dogged adherence to remote, abstract protestations that "she doesn't really understand me" or "I never know what he's thinking" is a dependable sign that the speaker is operating on a level that is very resistant to rationally based strategies for change.

However, it should also be understood that sheer intensity of feeling in and of itself is no indication that a relationship is doomed. There may be a high level of hostility and anger between you at the outset, but this doesn't have to be a barrier to making the partnership work. If you don't shy away from it, you'll find that intense negative emotion can be transformed totally into intense affection, even devotion, as long as it can accommodate realistic discussions of change.

2. Defining Desired Changes

The second step in changing some area of a relationship is to define *concretely* what it is that needs to be changed. Often the largest problem in a relationship is that neither partner has the patience to define what it is that he or she wants to change. Everything that isn't right in the relationship is left on a very general, very abstract, very foggy level. One partner may simply complain that the other has lost interest in the relationship or may feel that the other is an "inadequate" parent, or housekeeper, or wage earner, or lover.

It's easy to define one's dissatisfactions negatively and abstractly. The critical step here, at the outset of your attempt to improve your relationship, is to define as specifically and as positively as you can those things that you wish your partner would do differently. And the best way to do this is to identify what it is that you think should increase in your partner's behavior and what you're willing to exchange to get more of these things.

Naturally, not *every* dissatisfaction can be defined in positive terms. If your partner picks his feet, for example, and it drives you crazy, you're going to have to tell him just bluntly—but calmly—that you'd like him to stop. However, we find that the kinds of dissatisfactions that couples tend to have with one another can usually be divided into two major types: (1) criticisms of a few specific, relatively minor but irritating personal habits; and (2) a number of major problem areas, often dealing primarily with expressions of support for and interest in one another, all of which can be couched in terms of a desire for an increase in positive behavior.

Frequently there is a connection between the two types. A man who is feeling hostile toward his wife because of the way she rebukes their son may find it easier to berate her for some relatively trivial behavior, like leaving wet towels on the floor of the bathroom, than to ask her to change the way she treats their children. This is one reason we urge you to concentrate on requesting *increases* in *positive* behavior; requests for *decreases* in minor irritants are often displaced substitutes for more basic issues.

Begin by trying to identify between eight and ten changes that you would like to see in your spouse. Keep this list to yourself for the time being. Don't worry if these desired changes seem small or petty when you first think of them; if they're having a negative effect on you, then they are not insignificant. The cumulative impact of even minor irritations can be severe. Include them, don't avoid them.

To help you pinpoint the kinds of problems that typically surface in a deteriorating relationship, we have composed a general checklist (shown in Test 9.1) of the kinds of questions you should ask yourself. Mark down your answers. See where the answers tend to fall. If they're predominantly in the yes column, you should have gained a sharper idea of the areas of criticism that you have of your partner. Both individuals in the relationship should take this test.

Test 9.1 How Troubled Is Your Relationship?

Is your spouse spending more and more time out of the house, away from you?

Is he or she refusing to talk about problems that you consider serious?

Does it seem that your common finances have become much more of an issue lately than ever before?

Do you find yourself wondering more and more what your spouse is thinking?

Do you feel that you are less free than you used to be to discuss ways you'd like to see the relationship change?

Do little things seem to be getting to both of you much more often lately?

Has your spouse stopped giving you feedback about what he or she likes and dislikes about you?

Would you call your spouse "nonresponsive"?

Does it seem to you that he or she has been a lot less responsive sexually lately?

Are you both disagreeing and fighting more now, without any resolution of the underlying problems?

Would you say that mutual anger and irritation are beginning to outweigh positive interaction?

Does your spouse seem to be taking you for granted more lately?

Do you feel that your spouse has become much more critical of you lately, that he or she tends to see only the flaws in you, not the strengths?

Do you feel rejected by him or her?

234

	No	Yes
Do you have the feeling that, although you don't know what specifically should change in your relationship, something has to?		
Do you feel that your spouse is an inadequate parent?		
Do you have the feeling that you're trapped in the relationship?		
Do you feel that your spouse is an inadequate wage earner?		
Do you feel that he or she is an unsatisfying and insensitive lover?		
Do you feel your spouse is passively aggressive, or hostile?		
Do you feel that he or she is unnecessarily sloppy?		
Do you feel that your spouse handles money badly?		
Do you feel that your spouse has lately begun to misconstrue what you say, to misinterpret it defensively, so that it comes out sounding much more critical than you intended?		
Do you feel that there are things you can't discuss with your spouse?		
Do you feel your spouse is insensitive to your needs?		

Another exercise that can be very useful at this stage is to compare your current relationship with an imaginary one—a perfect, ideal relationship that you make up to suit your every specification. Tape it or write it out in some detail, concentrating fully on how the partner in fantasy would behave and what he or she would be like. Remember, though, that this is an *imaginary* relationship and that this exercise is only designed to help you pinpoint areas where your real-life relationship could be improved. It very definitely is *not* intended to set up expectations that no human being could possibly ever fulfill.

3. Ranking the Changes by Importance

Once you have identified eight to ten specific changes that you want to see take place in your partner, write them down in a simple, clear, understandable way, and rank them according to which is the most anxiety provoking for you to discuss and which is the least. An example follows:

A SAMPLE RELATIONSHIP
CHANGE HIERARCHY

1. *Be more communicative about feelings (both positive and negative).*
2. *Spend more time with the kids.*
3. *Let me know when you will be late.*
4. *Don't interrupt me when I'm talking to someone else.*
5. *Be willing to talk to my mother on the phone.*
6. *Stop picking your fingernails.*
7. *Help clean up after dinner.*
8. *Pick up dirty laundry each day.*
9. *Offer to make me a drink when making one for yourself.*

4. Practicing Relaxation

If you find that even contemplating the process of discussing one or more of these issues with your spouse causes you distress, refer to the chapter on relaxation. Once you've refreshed your memory and your body on the PMR method that we discuss in Chapter 2, try to employ it to keep your overall level of somatic tension at a minimum as you work toward inducing a calm state in yourself.

It makes a tremendous difference if you remain as relaxed and confident as possible when you begin to talk about matters that have remained unspoken—possibly for years—because they are laden with potential anxiety. Allowing yourself to become too distressed, anxious, or angry as you discuss these issues with your spouse will almost invariably provoke a negative reaction. None of us likes an unpleasant surprise, particularly if it means confronting criticism or anger or sorrow; it makes us nervous. If you can keep from getting angry, you will have a much better chance of succeeding in your efforts to improve your relationship.

5. Presenting Desired Changes
to Your Spouse

When you know what it is that you want to change and you feel comfortable about bringing up your first requests, about presenting them to your spouse, make an appointment with him or her for a specific time when you can both relax for an uninterrupted half hour or so to exchange views on these issues. Don't pick an inappropriate time when your partner is already involved in something else or has other distractions to contend with. Wait until the occurrence of whatever it is that you're disturbed about passes; but don't wait until the next time you actually find the wet towels on the floor to rush off, find your wife, and then angrily insist that you sit down and talk. If you don't schedule your time for discussion in advance, when you're calm and collected, you lessen your chances of winning an approving and cooperative response. Most couples pick a time in the early evening, perhaps just after dinner when they feel most re-laxed, to discuss contemplated changes.

A number of simple, basic ground rules should be fol-lowing during these discussions. These are listed here and are discussed in more detail below. Each of you should read these ground rules separately before actually beginning the discussion. It's best *not* to have one partner read the ground rules out loud to the other.

GROUND RULES: COUPLES

1. *Stay relaxed—don't let yourself get angry.*
2. *Don't interrupt while your spouse is talking.*
3. *If possible, phrase your requests for change with considera-tion, so that you're asking your spouse to* increase *some* aspect of positive behavior *rather than decreasing negative behavior.*
4. *If you find you're getting upset and you can't control your emotion by relaxation, stop the discussion.*
5. *Acknowledge those things that you do appreciate about one another.*
6. *Face each other and speak audibly.*
7. *Start your requests and your descriptions of your feelings with "I . . . ," not with "You make me. . . ."*
8. *Don't mind read.*
9. *Focus on the future.*

10. *Be specific.*

11. *Admit that you are imperfect, and mean it.*

12. *Discuss each item on the list only when you find that you can discuss all previous items comfortably and thoroughly.*

Expect that you both will feel some discomfort at first. After all, if you're trying to alter a situation that you've both lived with unhappily for some time, there's bound to be an accumulation of worry and frustration associated with the topic. Chances are, it will come as no surprise to either one of you that there is dissatisfaction in the relationship and that it involves the topics you have both identified, but if you're both careful to phrase your dissatisfaction in terms of specific changes that call for an increase in some positive aspect of your partner's behavior, the likelihood of avoiding the futile recriminations that so often occur in these sensitive conversations is high.

Do not expect change to occur instantaneously. Start by telling your partner that you'd like to talk more about [name of problem] and that you feel you have some specific ideas about what changes you would like to see take place. Say that you want to consider these first discussions to be practice sessions, in which you both see if you can't develop some better, more effective ways of talking about your mutual dissatisfactions and your ideas for improving the relationship. This will seem somewhat artificial and strained to you, but that is mostly because you are anxious about raising these issues at all.

If, during the discussion sessions, either one of you feels too strongly moved to continue—whether by anger, sorrow, fear, or other strong emotion—stop the conversation, and try to relax. You may want to talk about something else briefly, or you may even want to leave the room. You should both understand at the outset that leaving the room does not mean a refusal to confront the issue and deal with it; it just provides an escape valve for emotions that can be truly overwhelming. If one of you does leave, be sure to agree to resume the conversation again within a reasonable length of time—a day or so—so that your efforts to open up communication aren't lost.

As you begin these discussions with your spouse, try to start out by summarizing sincerely the qualities about him or her that you genuinely appreciate and enjoy. Don't do this just to soften the blow of your implied criticism—try to mean it. Some individuals, more often men than women, have as difficult a time expressing positive as negative feelings; it's necessary to be able to do both with ease and directness. Also, it's typical in troubled relationships that the conflicts and difficulties seem far to outweigh the benefits and advantages, so it's useful to try to put things into a more balanced perspective. Recall what it was that first attracted you to one another. Take some time to identify carefully just what it is that you still do appreciate about one another. Too often, these qualities are taken for granted.

When you talk together at these problem-solving sessions, face each other, and look directly at one another. Speak distinctly and audibly. Sound as though you mean what you say. As you describe your emotions, try to refrain from making statements that attribute your feelings to your partner, like "You make me angry." Instead, phrase these statements in such a way that you first acknowledge your own primary responsibility for your feelings and second refer to specific actions by your partner that upset you. For example, begin your statements with the pronoun I, and specify what it is that your partner does that you wish to change: "I feel angry when you make fun of the children by mimicking what they say."

During these sessions, do not interrupt one another. Because the urge to defend yourself or to respond to what may seem to be veiled accusations can be overwhelming, you may need to use a token symbol, such as a card or a poker chip, to indicate who has the floor. The other person is not to speak until the person holding the token or card is finished and indicates a desire for a response by relinquishing possession of the token. Careful, attentive, prolonged listening is a necessary part of making any relationship work.

Be polite and sincere in your conversations. Unfair criticism, snide comments, insults, sarcasm, put-downs, and extraneous remarks are out of bounds. Be especially careful to avoid global comments that attack your partner's entire character. "You're careless" and "you're selfish" are castigations that only attack; they don't imply clearly what specific changes are desired. "I feel upset when you don't fasten your seat belt" and "I get irritated when you take the paper away to work before I've read it" are statements that give your partner an idea of what it is you want him or her to do differently, and they avoid blaming one's entire personality or attitudes, which are harder to change than one's actions. Concentrate on changing your partner's behavior, not his or her identity.

It's also patronizing to assume that you know what's on your partner's mind, so don't act as though you do. Try to hear what is being said objectively or at least without the usual orientation that you have unsuccessfully brought to these statements so far. Thinking that you know your wife or husband so well that you can't learn anything new from him or her is a foolish and potentially fatal error. No one ever completely knows or understands another human being.

These sessions should focus on the future, on how to work with the positive elements in your relationship to improve it. Frequently, couples are tempted to ruminate about the past, to dissect it and complain about it. Avoid this. It may not be as difficult as working on plans for the future, but it's also far less productive. Avoid dredging up and sandbagging your partner with long histories of past complaints. Stick to the change areas that you have identified as being most essential to the enhanced quality of the relationship. This process of specifying your wishes will make it crystal clear to your partner what you want him or her to do differently. Thus, you give your spouse a highly increased chance of pleasing you by trying to conform to your wishes. You will find that few things in a relationship are so gratifying as having a spouse's behavior change to suit your wishes more closely. And as you strive to do the same, an exciting sense of intimate interdependency can grow.

Finally, don't try to characterize yourself as blameless, pure, and innocent. No one is. All troubled relationships are the result of the interaction of two people's intentions and actions. Portraying yourself as a saint puts your partner in an impossible position, because he or she is thus always at a disadvantage. Who can compare with a saint?

You may tend to be angered—most people are—when you hear criticisms of yourself, no matter how positively they may be phrased. Suppress this anger. Accept the criticism even if you feel like snapping back. You may not *feel* that it is accurate or merited, but the point here is to open up communication, not to defend the integrity of your personality and character. If your real objective in these discussions is to try to absolve yourself of the slightest hint of guilt, imperfection, or wrongdoing, you might as well give up trying to have a vital and successful relationship with a real, live, warm-blooded, and highly imperfect human being.

Be particularly suspicious when you hear yourself describing first a negative action by your spouse, followed by a positive or "normal" one on your part, then concluded by a second negative one on your spouse's part. These little tripartite vignettes almost never accurately reflect the whole story. Instead, they are a selective, heavily biased attempt by you to portray your spouse as an unreasonable persecutor and you as the innocent victim. This is *not* sincere negotiation. It is not designed to enhance your relationship; instead you're trying to escape any possibility of blame or complicity by shifting it all onto your partner's shoulders.

Try to hear what it is that your partner feels you do to precipitate the behavior that you don't like in him or her. Remember that people in unhappy relationships sometimes become involved in a subtle, unspoken conspiracy to try to bring out the worst in one another, so that they can have a focus and a reason for their own unhappiness. It is simply the unfortunate truth that people who are feeling unhappy often find it easier to turn their partners into scapegoats than to admit to unpleasant behavior of their own.

If you have been on the receiving end of a spouse's attempts to bring change into your relationship by communicating in an honest, sincere, and earnest way, don't let yourself become angry or withdrawn because you feel threatened. You won't be able to avoid feeling somewhat upset—it's normal—but you need to respond as generously and positively as you possibly can to these attempts to make your relationship work. Keep in mind that it is difficult for your spouse to bring up sensitive issues in the first place, and if you react to those efforts with defensive anger, he or she will react to your reaction, you will precipitate an argument, and nothing constructive will come of it. So you must both concentrate on staying relaxed, open-minded, and appreciative.

First, listen carefully to what your spouse is telling you. When he or she finishes, paraphrase it back, emphasizing your comprehension of the kinds of changes in your behavior that you understand are called for. If you feel that there is an underlying problem, a hidden agenda, bring it forth, but don't intellectualize or interpret what your partner is saying according to an abstract theory of motivation.

You will probably both need to exchange feedback on one another's suggested change strategies for a while—over a number of discussion sessions perhaps—before you will be able to reach agreement on the specific kinds of changes that seem called for.

And when you're talking, remember that *how* you present your desired changes is at least as important as just *what* it is you're requesting. Remain positive, relaxed, and amicable, and you will elicit far more cooperation than if you let yourself get tense and hostile. Remember the importance of relaxation.

Take only one or two items on your respective lists at a

time. Move up to progressively more distressing issues *only* when you can talk about *all* the previous issues without getting upset. This is very important. If you don't get all the tension associated with previous items cleared away, it will make the next step, engineering actual changes, much more troublesome. If you try to do too much at one time, you will place your entire change program in jeopardy.

Also, you may find that if you take change in small steps and each step is managed with calm and clarity, you will begin actually to look forward with excitement and anticipation to discussing the next items on your lists. Rather than dreading interaction on these topics, you will begin to enjoy it.

Continue these sessions until you feel that you both understand what changes are desired by each partner. Then and only then should you begin to plan how the change is to take place. When you reach this stage, you're ready to begin the phase of planning a change that involves contracting.

6. Planning Specific Change Contracts

The word *contracts* may have an unpleasantly legalistic overtone to you, and you may find yourself asking why anyone should have to resort to such impersonal and "businesslike" methods to change relationships that are supposed to epitomize trust and close, understanding rapport. *Contracts,* in the sense that we use the word here, are not devised primarily for the protection of each individual, as they often are in the legal sense of the term. Here we use the term to refer to a clear agreement that focuses mutual attention on a kind of preferred exchange that you and your spouse wish to develop, and it acknowledges the view that marriages are built on mutual reinforcement—you *give* in order to *get.*

Change is made easier when you both know in advance what reward you will get from altering your own behavior as well as what penalty you will suffer for not altering your behavior.

Contracting behavior is natural to personal relationships, whether we are consciously aware of it or not. For example, we frequently use a kind of tacit, negative contracting when we feel that our partner has let us down by not carrying out some agreed-upon arrangement. When a husband forgets for the third night in a row to bring home the stationery that his wife needs for thank-you notes, and she is so angered by this repeated injustice that she decides to retaliate by "forgetting" to have his tennis shoes resoled—determined to wait until he's finally remembered his part of the deal—then you're into a negative, withholding type of contractual interaction. Unfortunately, this kind of contracting is nonproductive, first because its objective is punishment, not gratification, of mutual needs and second because it isn't usually very effective punishment, since one partner is typically not even aware of the contractual understanding. Don't use contracts in this way—as a passive aggressive weapon. Get your wishes out in the open; then work out positive contracts designed to facilitate smooth personal interaction with your partner rather than obstruct it.

Contracts don't necessarily have to be written out, but doing so helps to make them into an objective reference point, available to each partner, just as it helps to keep an actual written record of any behavior that you're trying either to increase or diminish. It serves to focus attention in a powerful way.

There are a couple of ways to structure a contract. The first is simply a straightforward exchange: one partner agrees to change something, say, "wash the dishes three nights a week by seven," if the other also agrees to do something, maybe "walk the dog before going to work every morning."

In these cases, if one party fails to keep his or her end of the bargain, the penalty is simply that the other person's end of the bargain doesn't have to be kept either. But these kinds of contracts can be tricky, and devising them properly can be something of an art.

First, in this example, the person who agrees to walk the dog really can't refuse to keep his or her end of the bargain. The dog has to be walked by somebody regardless of what happened to the dishes the night before. So it's important to choose actions that can be made dependent on other actions rather than tasks that must be done no matter what else happens. In this case, a better alternative might be something like "clean up the yard once a week."

But there's also a second kind of contract, called a "parallel contract," that often works better, because it offers a little more flexibility. Let's say you want your husband to talk to you more in the evenings after dinner. And he wants you to come with him when he plays golf on Saturdays. In this case, rather than working out an agreement that says something like "George agrees to talk to Maria for at least one hour each evening, four evenings a week, if Maria agrees to take six golf lessons within the next three months," you separate each action from the other and then associate different rewards with each one. In this example, a parallel contract would read something like this: "George will talk to Maria for at least an hour four evenings a week if Maria will rub his back for fifteen minutes afterward, and Maria will take six golf lessons in the next three months if George will clean up the yard once a week." This way, if one half of the changes aren't made, the other half can still continue unimpeded.

The important thing to remember in planning for change is that change must be rewarded (or punished) if it is to be maintained. If you are expected to do something differently, it must be made clear what benefit you will realize for changing, and the same holds true for your spouse. It is easy to start with good intentions and to change for a short

period of time, but if the effort doesn't bring about any rewarding difference in the other person or the environment,
if it seems to make no difference, you will tend to fall right
back into the same old patterns. The perfect example of this
is the New Year's resolution. Most fail because they require a
good deal of effort but bring no immediate payoff.

To apply this now to your situation, you should contract
with your spouse to change the easiest of the eight to ten
behaviors you have listed. For the first week, work only on
one behavior. Each time your partner lives up to his or her
part of the contract, you must live up to your part. Each time
your partner fails to live up to his or her part, you are not
obliged to keep your half of the bargain.

As you begin implementing the contracted changes during this first week, you will quickly discover unforeseen details of the agreement that need further definition. How
much talk is enough? Who gets to decide? Does cleaning up
the yard include trimming the hedges? How often? These
are the kinds of details that must be worked out as the
change process takes place. Devising practical contracts is a
continuous process, and you will need to try out various approaches and set provisional standards for one another until
you have some experience with it. Refining a contract—
particularly when it is a change tool that you aren't used
to—takes time, which is one important reason why it's best
not to work on more than one change item during the first
week. Trying to change too much at once is an invitation to
failure, to rejection of the change process, and to further
deterioration of the relationship.

Also, maintain a positive and constructive attitude during this refining stage. Don't nitpick or belittle one another
for specifying what seem to be trivial changes. Even seem-
ingly insignificant dissatisfactions can be the seeds of major
conflicts, and if you can make the contracting process succeed for you on a small scale, you will have a much better
chance of resolving large disputes.

7. Monitoring Change

In addition to working out the functional details of the contract, you should *each* keep track of how *both* of you are doing. Each of you should have a sheet of paper with your name and your partner's name on it. On every occasion in which your partner is expected to change the behavior in his or her contract, indicate whether you feel your partner did or did not change appropriately. Also, each time the situation occurs when you are expected to change your behavior as spelled out in the contract, mark down whether you feel you did so or not. Periodically exchange these sheets of paper. This will provide an important source of feedback as well as help increase communication about your mutual progress. Ideally, you should set aside a short period of time each week to discuss how you feel you are doing, how you feel your partner is doing, and any particular difficulties or problems you are having.

After one week of working on the single behavioral change, if you both feel comfortable with it and are easily able to maintain the terms of your contract, you are ready to proceed to the next step. If you are having problems with working out the details of the contract or do not yet feel comfortable and at ease with your newly acquired behavior, do not move ahead just yet. Spend whatever additional time is necessary for both of you to feel that these new behaviors are both comfortable and habitual. If you proceed too quickly, before you are ready, permanent changes are not as likely to occur, and the likelihood that you will give up is greater than if you are patient and systematic. Remember, it took some time for these destructive or objectionable interpersonal habits to develop, and they cannot be expected to disappear overnight. Changing entrenched habits takes a considerable amount of time, and it must be done in small, steady steps.

Next, set up another discussion period during which you talk about your progress and how you feel about yourself and your spouse. As change is occurring, it is most important that you exchange feedback regularly on how both of you feel about the progress you are making. Areas that you both feel positive about can continue with little or no alteration. Areas in which there are still problems or negative feelings may require further discussion, negotiation, and contract modification.

If you both feel comfortable about performing the first set of changes and you're ready to move up to the next set, the second-easiest changes, work out a new contract just as you did before. Based upon your experiences with the first set, you may be able to anticipate specific problems with setting performance standards and deciding whether or not you have each kept your part of the bargain.

As with the first contract, monitor your partner's progress and your own. When you and your partner feel like the second contract is working smoothly, set up a third contract to encourage the next set of desired changes.

Remember, never proceed at a rate faster than one at which you both feel comfortable. As you add more and more changes to your contracts, you will begin to notice that some things are easier than others, that they can be changed more rapidly, and it may become necessary to renegotiate aspects of your agreements.

After you have mastered the eight to ten sets of changes in your original lists, you may construct as many new lists as you want. Now you understand the overall process. The further you progress and the more you continue to talk with one another about change, the more you will notice that the changes from earlier agreements have become automatic elements in your daily interactions with one another.

THE ART OF APPRECIATION

The enemy of satisfaction in long-term relationships is indifference. It is unfortunate but true that human beings are far more intrigued by the deficiencies and inadequacies of their partners than by their good points. It is also true that a long history of unsatisfying and unresolved conflicts over the same problem areas can drive partners into chronic avoidance and withdrawal. Failure to resolve conflicts can lead to an assumed attitude of indifference, a feeling of "what's the use," which is actually a protective mask that we draw over our anger and frustration.

The antidote to these trends is to learn to appreciate one another again actively. You have seen in the preceding pages how we feel problems should be deliberately and methodically discussed and negotiated. Now we'd like to offer you some thoughts on maintaining a high level of interest in one another, which is the ultimate goal of these change techniques and the best way of all to avoid the deterioration of any relationship.

First, during a time of crisis in your relationship, don't make decisions hastily. If things haven't gone too far already, sit down with your spouse, acknowledge the presence and the severity of the conflict, and schedule specific times to work toward identifying and resolving these problems.

Then, agree to set aside all your differences temporarily and to behave toward one another, for a month or so, as if your relationship were a resounding success. Resume all the activities with each other that you enjoyed at the outset of your relationship, acknowledging of course that time will have altered their intensity and focus. This will be hard to do at first. It will seem artificial to you and awkward, but stick to it anyway. Remember, as we explained in the introduction, actions can have a tremendous influence on feelings. Learn to orient yourself more toward all the *pleasant* experiences that your spouse brings to you. Thank one another when you offer each other something positive: a bit of praise, a gesture, a thoughtful action. Remind yourself to consider these experiences as gifts and privileges, not rights, which you earn by offering interest and support to each other. Internally, focus your attention on thinking positive and pleasant thoughts about your spouse. Record these, if you wish, to remind yourself of what you appreciate and enjoy about your relationship. When your partner speaks to you, ask questions to demonstrate your involvement and interest in him or her. *Listen* to one another. Schedule certain times to review the day's activities with each other.

You must begin to take positive action toward one another, even if you don't feel like it. You may think that your spouse doesn't notice the small gestures at first, but in most relationships of any duration, mutual interactions have become much more predictable than we like to think, and even the smallest departures from routine do not go unnoticed. Over time, if you take the initiative and offer positive actions to your spouse, this will generate amicability, and he or she will respond in kind.

Remember, the reactions your partner has toward you are very much—more so than you probably ever thought—under your control. If you act negatively, he or she will do the same. If you act positively, he or she will also reciprocate with the same kind of feeling.

In some cases, it can help to establish new patterns of behavior if you place yourself in new surroundings. Try taking a vacation with each other. Be aware, though, that taking a vacation together isn't a magical answer to marital stress. If you haven't already gotten somewhat accustomed to working on problems together before you go, the new surroundings of a vacation resort won't by any means make the process effortless. In fact, it can be harder to work out problems when you're on vacation, because you're often thrown together for a much greater part of the day than you're probably used to. Another possibility is to set aside one day when one of you agrees to do all he or she can to please the other.

Try hard to reinforce your partner for working to change. When you see him or her making an effort to comply with your agreements, comment on it, tell your partner that you've noticed it and that you appreciate it. More than anything else, this kind of reinforcement will assure improvement in your relationship.

And finally, try not to escalate your expectations constantly, always to expect more. You will only make your partner feel inadequate, and feeling that you can't satisfy someone you care for—no matter what you do or how hard you try—is a very painful experience.

As with all the other procedures in this book, those described in this chapter take time. Don't expect miracles overnight. Sometimes you will bumble it, and your efforts to make your relationship work will go awry. Let these mishaps and failures go by—laugh them off if you can. Stay positive, keep at it, be willing to admit you're wrong once in a while, and you'll be giving your relationship the best chance you possibly can.

ten

Sexual Dysfunction
Learning to
Respond to Pleasure

Civilized people cannot fully satisfy their sexual instinct without love.
—BERTRAND RUSSELL

. . . but lust too is a jewel.
—ADRIENNE RICH

The human sexual response is a blend of powerful, often complex emotions and a relatively simple, two-stage physiological process. Though the underlying sexual drive in humans is generally a strong one, it is also in a sense quite delicate, since it is rather easily disrupted by stress, tension, anxiety, and a host of other environmental and psychobiological factors. Basically, where there is no organic disorder, sexual dysfunction results from psychological sources, many of which are highly susceptible to self-treatment through the procedures we describe. However, if you suffer from one or more of the specific types of dysfunction that we describe in this chapter and, having worked through the appropriate change process recommended here, find that you are still unable to allow your natural sexual responses to take place, consider discussing your dysfunction with a qualified and experienced medical practitioner or therapist. In the last decade or so, notable advances have been made both in our basic understanding of sexual functions and in our ability to apply appropriate and effective remedial steps to their impairment. Your personal physician or a local medical society should be able to refer you to a reputable professional in this area.

There is really nothing exotic or mysterious about any of the self-treatment procedures that we describe in this chapter. Reduced to their basics, they are very much a matter of common sense, helped along with pertinent information from recent sexual research studies. Generally, they are a way of articulating and defining in a programmatic manner the normal erotic impulses that every human being is born with. Most individuals who have ever enjoyed a fulfilling and uninhibited sexual relationship will quickly recognize that these procedures and exercises are those of virtually all loving and mutually gratifying sexual partnerships.

About sexual variance and deviations: we feel that virtually any intimate physical activity between mature, consenting adults that is not physically or psychologically destructive is acceptable. Human sexual expression seems to us to be overwhelmingly of a monogamous, heterosexual nature, but we also feel that it can appear in a multitude of healthy alternate forms, none of which is intrinsically less tolerable than any other. Ideally, sex is a sensitive mutual celebration, not an unconscious reflex or an indifferent chore. And by the same token, active individual choice plays a critical role in optimal sexual functioning.

SEXUAL PHYSIOLOGY

The natural human sexual response is a simple two-stage process that is in most important respects the same for both sexes. The first stage, arousal, consists basically of swelling in the tissues of the external genital organs—the penis in the male and the external vaginal folds in the female. This swelling is caused by a process known as vasocongestion; that is, under a condition of appropriate relaxation and security, parasympathetic dominance in the nervous system triggers increased blood flow to genital capillaries and, at the same time, *decreased* withdrawal of blood along the veins in the genital region. Vasocongestion, the cumulative result of these mechanisms, leads to erection in the male, swelling of vaginal lips in the female, and sensations of warmth and highly enhanced genital sensitivity in both sexes. In addition to this external change, there is also in the female a release of natural lubrication within the vaginal channel and an internal expansion of the vagina, both of which transform it into a warm, receptive sexual organ.

Orgasm, the second stage of sexual response, basically consists of involuntary spasmodic contractions of genital muscles—quite specific in the male, less so in the female—associated with an intense feeling of release and pleasure. In the male, this orgasmic series of muscle contractions can be further divided into two substages—one in which seminal fluid is collected near the base of the penis, and a second, following immediately after the first, in which this fluid is ejaculated.

Orgasms in the female are primarily triggered by physical stimulation of the clitoris, a small, highly sensitive organ located at the uppermost convergence of the vaginal lips. Like the penis, the clitoris becomes enlarged during sexual arousal. The penis and the clitoris have similar anatomical structures, perhaps because of a common evolutionary origin.

In the male, orgasm results from stimulation of the entire penis. However, the most sensitive area of the penis tends to be the zone at and just below its tip.

It is entirely possible for both men and women to become orgasmic through stimulation of other areas of the body than the genitals. Virtually every sensitive body surface has been used at one time or another to induce sexual arousal and orgasm. In truth, the most potent human sexual organ is the mind.

SEXUAL DYSFUNCTION

Sexual dysfunction occurs whenever any stage of the natural response just described is blocked. In other words, either an individual is not able to become aroused at all, which is called impotence in men and frigidity or nonresponsiveness in women, or the individual can become aroused but cannot continue on to effective and satisfying orgasm. This latter condition is known as inorgasmicity in women and retarded ejaculation in men. Some men also suffer from another orgasmic dysfunction, called premature ejaculation, which means that they experience the entire sexual response so rapidly that neither they nor their partners are fully gratified.

These two overall problem areas are customarily divided into four or more specific types of sexual difficulty as follows:

- *Impotence and frigidity*. Impotence and frigidity are externally similar—there is no erection in impotent men and little or no vaginal swelling or lubrication in frigid (or nonresponsive) women—but there may be psychological differences between the sexes for this dysfunction. Impotent men often continue to profess an ardent desire for intercourse; nonresponsive women often profess a disinterest in or even a definite antipathy to the thought of intercourse. The psychological mechanism underlying both attitudes may be essentially one of anxiety, but our culture seems to shape its expression in men and women quite differently.
- *Premature ejaculation*. This is of course a strictly masculine problem, deriving from a loss of sensitivity to the physiological signals that precede orgasm. It is readily corrected in most men.

- *An inability to reach orgasm (inorgasmicity)* is common to both men and women but is more prevalent among women. This disorder results from either a lack of familiarity with the attitudes and physical sensations that successfully culminate in orgasm or from a fear of losing control, of letting go and allowing the sexual response to run its normal course.
- *Vaginismus*, in which the vaginal muscles tighten spasmodically to prevent attempts at penetration of any kind.

Some sexual impairment is caused by accident, disease, surgery, or drug use. Most is not. Perhaps because sex is such a paradoxical drive, so powerful yet so delicate, it seems to serve as a focus for anxiety, much in the same way that sleep does for insomniacs.

The best therapy for sexual dysfunction is to learn to relax and allow your natural responses to take over. Specifically, problems such as frigidity and impotence are caused by the high levels of sympathetic nervous system activity that accompany anxiety. It doesn't matter what the anxiety itself is caused by; as long as it is producing sympathetic dominance, normal sexual responding will be susceptible to disruption. In order to counter excessive sympathetic activity, the parasympathetic division of the autonomic nervous system must be brought forth, or, in other words, the sexually dysfunctional person must learn to relax.

Also, not only can virtually any external anxiety or stress inhibit sexual responding, but the anxieties that are subsequently caused by the inhibited response itself can become self-generating, in a vicious circle known as performance anxiety. A first failure, caused by unrelated tension, can itself become the reason for the development of a chronic pattern of subsequent failures.

Unfortunately, it is far easier said than done for most sexually dysfunctional individuals to learn first to relax and then to apply relaxation skills to sexual problems successfully. But it can be done. The first step is to read through all the practices described in this chapter. Then have your partner read this chapter. Once you both understand the problem and the recommended treatment, begin to follow gradually the appropriate therapeutic steps. Note the word *gradually*. Do not rush ahead or try to push a specific program to a conclusion too rapidly. This will cause tension and anxiety, and as soon as the dysfunctional partner feels anxious, therapeutic progress has by definition stopped. It is far, far better to leave one another wanting more intimate contact than to move ahead too quickly and create countertherapeutic interactions. The goal, throughout all these procedures, is physical arousal that is anxiety free.

Once you're both aware of the dysfunction and the appropriate remedy, begin to follow the exercises recommended in this chapter carefully and systematically. All are based on extensive clinical experience with sexual disorders, and all have been meticulously designed to facilitate gradual, step-by-step reacquisition of normal sexual responsiveness.

TREATING SEXUAL DYSFUNCTION

The treatment procedures for each of the specific difficulties listed earlier differ. We discuss each separately below. First, however, there are three basic steps that anyone experiencing a temporary or chronic sexual disorder should follow.

1. *Obtain a thorough medical checkup.*
2. *Learn to relax, as outlined in the PMR method described in Chapter 2.*
3. *Learn and practice the Masters and Johnson pleasuring technique.*

1. Obtaining a Medical Examination

A relatively small proportion of sexual problems are directly attributable to clear-cut organic conditions. They are the result of physical disorder rather than anxiety. The training and experience of a physician is required to rule out the possibility that a sexual dysfunction is physiogenic before dysfunctional individuals move on to self-treatment measures that focus on mood and attitudinal change. See your doctor, and discuss your sexual problem with him or her, in detail. If you don't feel comfortable with the response you get, see another doctor.

Listed below are just a few of the diseases, drugs, and other conditions that can impair or entirely suppress normal sexual functioning:

- *Protracted and excessive alcohol consumption. (Note, however, that you don't have to be an alcoholic to suffer from alcohol-induced inhibition of sexual responses. Anything over a couple of drinks will be more detrimental than helpful to your performance. Avoid making the common mistake of depending on heavy doses of alcohol to prepare you for sexual interactions.)*
- *Diabetes, even in early stages.*
- *Hypertension medications.*
- *Thyroid disorders.*
- *Pituitary disorders.*
- *Prostate surgery.*
- *Narcotics.*
- *Sedatives.*
- *Certain types of nerve surgery.*

2. Learning to Relax

We now know that both the sympathetic and parasympathetic divisions of the autonomic nervous system can be influenced by systematic, deliberate attempts to regulate them. There are a number of alternative ways to do this, but one of the most widely practiced and clinically accepted is some variant of the progressive muscle relaxation (PMR) procedure that we described in detail in Chapter 2. Go back to Chapter 2, reread the discussion of PMR, and before going on to practice the exercises given in the rest of this chapter, *learn how to relax.*

Once you have learned to bring on a state of deep muscle relaxation quickly and thoroughly in your body, begin applying this skill to stressful situations, such as driving in heavy traffic or at your job. Knowing how to relax in this way gives you greater control over the operation of the parasympathetic division, which, as we already stated, must be in dominance for normal sexual responses to occur. The PMR method will not, in and of itself, cure impotence, frigidity, vaginismus, or any other sexual problem, but it is a powerful and essential basic step in paving the way to effective self-treatment of them.

3. Pleasuring

One of the most effective and widely applied results of recent research by Masters and Johnson into human sexuality is the therapeutic technique of pleasuring, which Masters and Johnson first called "sensate focusing." It can be regarded as an extension of other types of relaxation techniques, and it has the basic purpose of producing a setting and mood that is incompatible with anxiety, but it is comparatively unstructured. Pleasuring is usually divided into two sequential phases—the first excluding genital contact, and the second including genital contact but not orgasm or intercourse.

Simply defined, pleasuring means setting aside a specific interval, ranging from a day or two up to several weeks, in which you and your partner abstain from intercourse. Instead, you concentrate all your attention on relaxing and on experiencing as fully as possible your mutual erotic affection by fondling and caressing one another's bodies in a gentle, loving manner. Agreeing to refrain from intercourse has the desirable effect of removing any pressure to perform, to achieve the "goal" of orgasm that sexually dysfunctional individuals tensely and compulsively struggle to achieve, thus perpetually exacerbating their fears of failure.

Pleasuring is best employed as a prelude for the treatment of impotence and frigidity. It is less effective (or even wholly irrelevant) for treatment of problems with achieving orgasm. However, we include it as a basic, comprehensive treatment step, because—since it is so generally sensual—it predisposes anyone, even couples who are *not* sexually dysfunctional, to realize much greater enjoyment from their erotic interactions.

In the first phase of pleasuring, using your hands, lips, etc., you focus on gentle stimulation of each other's nude bodies with the exception of the genitals and breasts. You will find that this simple exercise, performed while you are appropriately relaxed, can transform your bodies and your entire environment into an erogenous medium. The technique requires that you take turns; first one partner pleasures the other as fully as possible, then the roles are reversed.

As well as expanding the dimensions of your physical interaction with one another, pleasuring can be an occasion to open up better verbal and physical communication about precisely what kinds of touching you most enjoy. Tell your partner, calmly, how his or her pleasuring motions feel. Don't criticize or accuse; just offer as much directive positive feedback as seems appropriate. Bear in mind that changes in sexual interaction are, like changes in any other area of strong emotion, best made gradually and systematically. Don't push one another. Focus your attention on the kinds of sensual contact that give you the most pleasure rather than on those that you don't particularly care for. If he doesn't like the way you stroke his back, or the pressure of your hands at certain moments, he should let you know; but he should also let you know what he prefers instead and how you should offer it.

In the second phase of pleasuring, you include genital stimulation but not of a kind that is directed at causing orgasm. You want to bring each other *gently* to full arousal and to savor fully the pleasure of this stage of sexual excitement, but you do not want to move past this stage for the time being. Remember to continue to include all of the body in this stage, not just one another's genital areas. Ideally, you should find that pleasuring induces a strong sense of mutual physical intimacy and a distinct erotic glow, like a basic change in perception, which will begin to come over you as you both become fully aroused.

The objective of these procedures is to remove temporarily the pressures that most of us feel to acquit ourselves honorably in sex, to perform, to be judged well, to be approved of, and to be reassured. These pressures are the direct causes of most sexual dysfunction—they lead to tension and to exaggerated fears of failure that only exacerbate whatever level of anxiety we may have about sex anyway. Through imposing a paradoxical barrier to actual sexual intercourse and orgasm, pleasuring gives us freedom from this compulsive goal-seeking behavior and lets up recapture the erotic basis of the sexual experience.

TREATING FRIGIDITY
AND IMPOTENCE

The treatment for both these conditions is one of gradual, step-by-step readjustment to the normal sexual response. In both cases, it begins with careful, deliberate experimentation with the two phases of pleasuring just described. There should be absolutely no implicit expectation, no sense of pressure on either partner to produce a genital response during this first stage.

For the nonresponsive woman, the second stage of the treatment process is taken only when genital pleasuring produces no anxiety or irritation. Even though she may not yet be experiencing full arousal during genital pleasuring, as long as she is no longer tense, the next step is slow, careful introduction of her partner's erect penis into her vagina. Lubricating vaginal jelly should be used if she is not yet lubricating naturally. This step requires that the nonresponsive woman's partner is able to respond fully and confidently and to maintain an erection while playing a role secondary to hers in the interaction, and without requiring complete intercourse and orgasm. Most nonresponsive women will find that the superior position—on top of and facing their partner—will allow them the greatest command over stimulation of the clitoris and vaginal area. The partner should assume a passive but alert assisting role, responding as closely as possible to her directions. Both should stay as relaxed as possible. When this stage becomes fatiguing or too anxiety provoking, it should be ended.

This stage should be repeated periodically until the woman can, while remaining as relaxed as possible, reach arousal of orgasmic intensity. At this point, intercourse should be carried to the point of orgasm. If this last step is difficult, refer to our directions below for orgasmic dsyfunctions.

The process of treating impotence is quite similar. Begin with the two stages of pleasuring. Most men, working with a woman they know and trust, will experience spontaneous erections during pleasuring. There are also a number of additional techniques that his partner can employ both to encourage erections and to reassure him that they will spontaneously return if they subside, that the disappearance of an erection is often temporary.

First, to encourage erection, his partner can use a lubricating jelly, which duplicates the gliding sensations of the fully aroused vagina. He should let her know explicitly what kind of penile stimulation he prefers. This varies among men a great deal, but most find that the last third of the penis, the area just below the head, or glans, is most sensitive. At some point, both partners should openly discuss their feelings about oral genital stimulation, which can be an extremely effective method for producing erection. Many men find that they are most responsive early in the morning, when certain hormonal levels are highest, or while clothed, in the shower, etc. These and other especially conducive sexual conditions should be incorporated into pleasuring exercises.

To demonstrate that erection is a natural, spontaneous, and *recurrent* process, his partner should on occasion during pleasuring exercises encircle his penis just below the glans with her thumb and forefinger and squeeze with moderate pressure. Performed properly, this technique will cause an erection to subside by one-third to one-half. However, an erection suppressed in this way will readily return in response to continuation of the genital pleasuring exercises. This experience usually provides the impotent man with adequate reassurance that erection is a resilient natural response, which can be regained even if momentarily lost.

Once the nonresponsive man is able to relax, to experience erections, and to gain reassurance that the diminishment of an erection is a natural, temporary occurrence, the next stage is gradual, gentle insertion of his erect penis into his partner's vagina. If he feels comfortable and free of anxiety, he may then move on to include the typical thrusting motion of normal intercourse. However, this stage should be practiced *without* orgasm. If orgasm becomes inevitable, he should withdraw and ejaculate outside his partner's vagina.

The final step in treatment for the nonresponsive man is complete intercourse with intravaginal ejaculation.

It is essential to understand that progress to each successive stage in treatment for both the nonresponsive man and the nonresponsive woman is made *only* when the dysfunctional individual feels completely comfortable at the current and all previous stages. One should always stop treatment at a stage where one feels one could have moved ahead comfortably, rather than going ahead too rapidly and causing a recurrence of the problematic anxiety.

PREMATURE EJACULATION

This is one of the easiest forms of sexual dysfunction to cure. It really depends more than anything else on the presence of good rapport between sexual partners.

Researchers believe that premature ejaculation results from nothing more complex than inadequate understanding of and sensitivity to the physical sensations that signal imminent ejaculation. The premature ejaculator may have been attaining orgasm for years, but has never really experienced the arousal process in detail and has never learned how to manage it. The treatment exercises logically focus on intensifying the attention paid to these sensations.

The process is quite simple. The couple may begin with pleasuring exercises if they wish or skip them and go directly to intercourse. When the man has attained a firm erection, he withdraws from his partner's vagina, lies back, closes his eyes, and lets her stimulate him to orgasm. His only task is to concentrate as fully as possible on the sensations that precede orgasm, to enhance his ability to anticipate its occurrence.

This entire process should be repeated until the dysfunctional man begins to acquire the ability, first, to identify the sensations that signal orgasm and, second, to anticipate and control it. Control is achieved with the help of his partner, who, at his direction, employs the squeeze technique to suppress erection and thus delay ejaculation. (The squeeze technique, as we already described, involves encirclement of the penis below the glans with thumb and forefinger, plus brief application of moderate pressure.)

During each practice session, the squeeze technique should be employed perhaps half a dozen times before the couple continues on to orgasm. Each time that his erection is suppressed and then reproduced, intercourse should be resumed. Then, as the man senses himself approaching orgasm, he should again withdraw from his partner's vagina and either allow the orgasmic process to subside naturally or direct his partner to use the squeeze technique to block it deliberately. Only after repeating this process a number of times during intercourse should he proceed to orgasm and intravaginal ejaculation.

As a variation, the woman may assume the superior position and manage the stop and start, insertion and withdrawal procedure, aided by indications from her partner as to how close he is to orgasm.

INORGASMICITY

The inability to reach orgasm once aroused stems from anxieties about the sensation of release and the momentary involuntary muscle spasm that it involves. Some dysfunctional individuals fear that abandoning themselves to orgasm may cause unwanted release of other physical processes, such as urination; or the fear may be more directly emotional, entailing expression of suppressed aggressive impulses.

Treatment consists of the carefully graduated introduction into actual intercourse of orgasmic responses acquired through self-stimulation. In general, the process is quite comparable to that of systematic desensitization, which we discussed at some length in Chapter 5. The two-part pleasuring exercises can be a useful adjunct to treatment for inorgasmicity, but they are not usually regarded as a direct component of the treatment process.

For both the inorgasmic man and woman, the first step is masturbation to orgasm in seclusion. For highly inorgasmic individuals, seclusion may mean absolute privacy, even to the point of arranging to have the partner leave the house. The inorgasmic woman may need to start at a somewhat more preliminary stage than the inorgasmic man—with simple visual and tactile exploration of her genitals, using a mirror. Far more inorgasmic women than men are simply not familiar with their own sexual anatomy, and it is essential that they first learn to feel comfortable with the physical conformation of their own sexual organs.

The next step is gentle tactile self-exploration directed simply at determining what areas and types of stimulation feel most pleasurable. Many women report finding that one of the quieter models of vibrator is a useful adjunct at this stage. Again, this step is more often appropriate for inorgasmic women than similarly dysfunctional men. Remember the cardinal rule of all treatment programs discussed in this book: do not move ahead to more advanced stages of any treatment process until you feel entirely comfortable and anxiety free at your present level.

When the inorgasmic individual is able to stimulate him- or herself successfully to orgasm in seclusion, the next step is *gradually* to reintroduce the partner into the self-stimulation scene—first in the imagination, then in fact. It is particularly important at this point in the treatment program to proceed only in stages that can be comfortably tolerated by the inorgasmic person. The partner may at first simply remain inside the home as his or her partner achieves orgasm in an entirely different room. The next step may bring the functional partner into the same room with the self-stimulating individual but without any overt acknowledgment of one another. Then the functional partner may approach closer but again remain relatively detached. Remaining stages may include watching the masturbating partner, touching or holding the masturbating partner, actively helping stimulate the dysfunctional partner, assuming primary responsibility for arousing and bringing the partner to orgasm, and finally initiating engagement in full genital intercourse.

The transfer from manual stimulation to genital intercourse is often facilitated by a maneuver known as *bridging*, which many couples use naturally to enhance their sexual pleasure and responsivity. Simply put, this consists of continuing manual stimulation of one's own or one's partner's genitals during intercourse. If the woman, for example, is having trouble attaining orgasm through genital intercourse but has succeeded in climaxing through oral or manual stimulation by her partner, one or the other of them should continue to stimulate her clitoral area manually during intercourse. This is often most conveniently achieved in a position where her partner enters her from behind, since it leaves the clitoral area more accessible to manual stimulation.

This maneuver is somewhat less successful with men, since the most sensitive area of the penis, at its tip, is not accessible to manual stimulation during intercourse. An alternative, however, is to use a front-to-front intercourse position in which, once his penis is inside his partner's vagina, she brings her legs tightly together and he straddles them with his. This provides a tighter vaginal sheath for him and thus increases the stimulative sensation, more exactly reproducing the pressure of fingers and hands. (Another exercise that is sometimes helpful in increasing vaginal muscle tone, both for her pleasure as well as his, is stopping and starting her stream of urine.)

VAGINISMUS

Vaginismus is a relatively uncommon condition in which the muscles of the external vaginal area tighten spasmodically whenever an attempt at penetration of any kind is made. Nothing of any size—tampons, fingers, or the like—can be comfortably inserted into the vaginal opening, and this of course makes genital sexual intercourse virtually impossible. Most sex therapists consider this condition to be based in a phobic response to sexual intercourse, and they direct treatment at slow, systematic desensitization of the spasmodic muscle response itself.

Women suffering from vaginismus, especially if it has developed only recently, *must* see a gynecologist to be sure that the spasms are not related to disease, injury, or other organic disorder, especially if the vaginismic reaction is associated with genital or pelvic pain.

Assuming the absense of organic pathology, the treatment process is based on gradual self-insertion of increasingly larger artificial devices (usually a graduated series of soft plastic cylinders or tubes) into the vaginal opening until the dysfunctional woman can comfortably tolerate a tampon, or finger-sized object, at which stage her own finger is substituted for the artificial adjuncts. As with any desensitization process, it is essential that the vaginismic woman develop a clear-cut self-insertion hierarchy and that she progress up the steps of the hierarchy only when she is entirely tolerant of insertion of devices at all preceding and current levels.

Once she can tolerate her own finger without discomfort, her partner is introduced into the desensitization process, and a new insertion hierarchy begins, starting with his fingertip, then moving progressively on to his finger, two of his fingers, and finally his erect penis. There should be no pushing ahead to reach the stage of penile insertion and intercourse. She should always feel, at the end of each self-treatment session, that she could comfortably accommodate larger insertions. Both partners should be in agreement on progressions to higher stages in the insertion hierarchy. On the first occasion that she accepts insertion of his erect penis, there should be no continuation to normal sexual thrusting, and after a few moments of insertion, he should withdraw.

The final stage is normal intercourse to orgasm.

FANTASY

What goes on in one's mind is an extremely important part of erotic interactions. Allow and encourage your fantasies, particularly those that arise as you begin to work on self-treatment for a specific dysfunction. They may strike you as being vaguely shocking or abnormal, but they almost certainly are not—nearly everyone has experienced an extensive range of sexual fantasizing—and they serve a very useful purpose in helping to alleviate the anxiety that contributes to your dysfunction by distracting you from it. So let your mind wander wherever it may take you. Once the primary dysfunction has been mastered, if the fantasies then become annoying or the distraction they provide is no longer needed or useful, then you can work on replacing them with more appropriate substitutes. But for the time being, welcome them without hesitation.

eleven

Conclusion

Maintaining Change

Perseverance is more prevailing than violence; and many things which cannot be overcome when they are together, yield themselves up when taken little by little.

—PLUTARCH

The most difficult part of changing is not starting it but keeping it going. Once the novelty of a new pattern of action or thought wears off, you're left with nothing but diligence, perseverance, and commitment to keep your plans intact. Habits that have been built up over years and years, even habits that you know to be self-destructive, depressing, and emotionally bankrupt, are often extremely difficult to alter. No doubt you've heard the line, "It's easy to quit smoking ... I've done it myself, hundreds of times."

Once you've identified what it is that you wish to change, mapped out a plan for altering your life, and started to put it into action, you will find that the excitement of the idea of change begins to wear off as the hard, grinding work of establishing newer, more productive and fulfilling patterns of behavior begins. Once you've found that you can get up at

271

6:30 A.M. and jog four miles in half an hour, the challenge is gone, and you're left with an endless repetition of early morning workouts. You know that the payoff is a healthier, more attractive body and probably a longer, happier life, too, but that reward can seem awfully abstract on a dark, chilly morning when the temptation to stay in bed is nearly irresistible.

Successful change of any kind requires willpower, of course, but it usually needs something more, something that can give you the sense of concrete achievement that will provide the extra measure of self-satisfaction that feeds the willpower that gets you up in the morning that leads to the sense of accomplishment . . . and thus keeps the cycle moving.

The process of maintaining change rests squarely on three essential interlocking activities: setting goals, monitoring your progress, and reinforcing yourself by rewarding your accomplishments and penalizing your failures. In other words, know where you're going, keep track of the process of getting there, and give yourself praise or blame, reward or punishment, for how well you do along the way.

Every time you sit down and make a decision to change some aspect of your life, you're setting a goal for yourself. It may not be very completely defined right at that moment, but as you start working to make it a reality, that goal will become clearer and clearer, as will the exact type and sequence of intermediate steps that are necessary to attain it.

- Set goals.
- Keep close, accurate track of the process of change.
- Reward yourself for initiating change, for expanding your level of change, and for sustaining new levels of change.
- Involve loved ones, colleagues, and friends. Build social support for your new life-style.
- Focus on increasing positive change; let negative behavior simply fade away from lack of attention. Ignore it, and it will lose its hold on you.

First, at every stage of the process, make your goals, your track record, and your reinforcement schemes as explicit as possible. Write them out in detail. Write down what you plan to change. Be specific. Write down the level of your change behavior before you begin your change project. Write down how well you've managed to change as you've moved along. Write out contracts with yourself and with your spouse.

Second, the best kind of support that you can give yourself is the most basic—evidence that change is really taking place. Providing yourself with this evidence means keeping actual paper-and-pencil records of what you've been trying to accomplish. Start keeping the record before you put your plan for change into effect, and compare at regular intervals—daily, weekly, or monthly—how you're actually doing with your original level of behavior, the baseline level. This is what dieters do when they weigh themselves every day. If the scale shows a loss of pounds, the simple evidence of a desired change actually occurring can fill one with an amazing glow of self-satisfaction. Other people keep lists, or charts. Or they use some kind of tokens, like coins or poker chips, to keep track of how many times they do something they want to increase or even a specific behavior that they want to do less often.

Third, an adroit use of rewards is a powerful way to encourage persistence in your program for change. The trick is to build a connection between the way you want to become and the kinds of pleasant, rewarding experiences that are already available to you. One way to do this is to draw up a contract with yourself, much in the same way as we discussed in Chapter 3. In practice, what this amounts to is that you forbid yourself a reward until you've first completed some predetermined level of desired change.

Let's say you want to improve your social life, and you've decided that you need first to practice relaxation before you can feel comfortable with others, particularly with strangers.

You've designed a relaxation schedule, and you've begun to work on it. It's intrinsically rewarding, of course, just to accomplish each set of relaxation exercises, to be able to relax deeply and quickly in less time each day, but it helps to have additional support. Let's also assume that you like to read, that it's one of your most consistent rewards, and that you particularly look forward to reading the newspaper each morning before you leave for work.

So, make a contract. Agree that you won't let yourself read the paper in the morning until you've completed your relaxation exercises.

Write the contract out. It should show, in specific detail, what the rewards are for completing each level of exercise and what the penalties are for not doing it. For rewards, use activities that you like to engage in regularly, like reading the paper, having a cup of coffee, or watching the news at night, and make sure that you deny yourself the reward unless you've first carried out the desired change.

Then stick to it. Don't let yourself read the paper unless you practice first. Or pick a reinforcement that is even stronger and somewhat less likely to occur every day. Maybe you really enjoy dancing, but you don't feel that it suffices as a good exercise program. So make a contract. If you exercise all week, you'll let yourself go to a disco on the weekend. Working out the right contract is an art, but if you manage it, you have a very powerful tool working to help you change.

Change the kind of reinforcement you give yourself now and then, and alter the time intervals at which you reward yourself. Research shows that rewards that come somewhat unpredictably, at different intervals, are more effective than those that come at a regular specific time, like clockwork, or those that fail to come for very long periods of time. Some of the element of surprise won't apply, since you're the one doing the rewarding as well as determining the type of reward, but it helps to prevent reinforcement from becoming completely stale and routine if you vary it now and then.

Once in a while, do something completely unusual: jump in your car and drive to the airport for a test ride in a small plane, for example, or buy yourself a begonia, or dye your hair, or go to the beach and get a tan—whatever you most enjoy.

Fourth, involve your family and friends in your change project. Start by explaining to them what it is that you're trying to do and how you intend to go about accomplishing it. Ask them for their help; then tell them specifically how they can give it to you. Ask them to make comments to you when they observe changes in you, so that you can get feedback on your progress. Ask them to support positive changes only. The best treatment for negative behavior is to have it ignored. Without responses, it will eventually vanish.

Carry this principle of building social support further. Make your surroundings work to assist your change project. For example, it's often easier to develop new patterns of behavior in new physical surroundings, because the old familiar environmental cues are gone. People often find themselves intuitively drawn to taking on a behavior change project, like learning assertiveness, when they get a new job, or move into a new apartment. This is a good basis for change, since the associations evoked by the old surroundings can't continue to exert a negative influence on you. It's also one reason why we occasionally fantasize about moving to an entirely different city or country and starting over. We sense that the familiar environment around us is already powerfully linked in our minds with patterns of behavior that we would like to change but just can't seem to somehow.

One of the fundamental principles of this book is that unrewarded actions, thoughts, and emotions will tend to die away eventually, to extinguish. You can use this knowledge to starve your undesirable patterns of action into nonexistence at the same time that you focus on developing new, preferable behavior. Let's say that you're shy and that you become very obsessive about social gatherings, fearing in an unaccountable way that people will ridicule you. At the same time that you work on your social anxiety by developing more effective powers of assertion and perhaps also by desensitizing yourself to the social setting, you should consciously work to prevent yourself from responding to your obsessive tendencies. Let the obsessive thoughts become dull, boring, routine. Then take it a step further. Actively try to end them the instant they appear by using the thoughtstopping technique that we described in detail in Chapter 4—telling yourself *STOP* firmly and consciously diverting your attention to positive thoughts, memories, or expectations.

Change is a constant process. You never get to a point in life where you've finished becoming what you want to become. On the other hand, you shouldn't deny yourself a sense of personal satisfaction and pride merely because you haven't reached some mythical pinnacle of achievement. The greatest art, and ultimately the most gratifying one, is knowing how to work flexibly with the material of your existence, the medium you were handed at birth. Knowing how to adapt your ceaseless, limitless aspirations to life's boundaries is true wisdom.

FURTHER READING

ANNON, JACK S., *Behavioral Treatment of Sexual Problems: Brief Therapy*. New York: Harper & Row, 1976.

BECK, AARON, *Depression: Causes and Treatment*. Philadelphia: University of Pennsylvania Press, 1972.

BENSON, HERBERT, M.D., *The Relaxation Response*. New York: William Morrow and Company, Inc., 1975.

CAIRD, WILLIAM, and JOHN P. WINCZE, *Sex Therapy: A Behavioral Approach*. New York: Harper & Row, 1977.

Diamond, Seymour, and William B. More, *More Than Two Aspirin: Help for Your Headache Problem.* New York: Avon Books, 1976.

Fensterheim, Herbert, and Jean Baer, *Don't Say Yes When You Want to Say No.* New York: Dell, 1975.

Friedman, Meyer, M.D., and Ray H. Rosenman, M.D., *Type A Behavior and Your Heart.* Greenwich, Conn.: Fawcett Crest, 1974.

Galton, Lawrence, *The Silent Disease: Hypertension.* New York: New American Library, 1974.

Jacobson, Edmund, *You Must Relax.* New York: McGraw-Hill, 1976, 5th ed.

Kline, Nathan, *From Sad to Glad: Kline on Depression.* New York: Ballantine, 1975.

Melville, Joy, *Phobias and Obsessions.* New York: Penguin Books, 1978.

Pomeroy, Claire, *Fight It Out, Work It Out, Love It Out.* New York: Doubleday, 1977.

Seligman, Martin E. P., *Helplessness: On Depression, Development, and Death.* San Francisco: W. H. Freeman and Company, 1975.

Thoresen, Carl E. and Thomas J. Coates, *How to Sleep Better: A Drug-Free Program for Overcoming Incomnia.* Englewood Cliffs, N. J.: Prentice-Hall, 1977.

Index

282 INDEX

To obtain a copy of the relaxation tape prepared by Donald Tasto and Eric Skjei, send your name and address, plus $6.50, to:

Donald L. Tasto, Ph.D.
P.O. Box 5507
Redwood City, CA 94062

Name

Street

City   State   Zip